THE PHARISEES
AND THE TEACHER OF NAZARETH

INSTITUTUM IUDAICUM, TÜBINGEN

OTTO MICHEL

———

ARBEITEN ZUR GESCHICHTE DES SPÄTJUDENTUMS UND URCHRISTENTUMS

BAND IV

THE PHARISEES AND THE TEACHER OF NAZARETH

LEIDEN / KÖLN

E. J. BRILL

1974

THE PHARISEES
AND THE
TEACHER OF NAZARETH

A STUDY OF THEIR BACKGROUND, THEIR HALACHIC
AND MIDRASHIC TEACHINGS,
THE SIMILARITIES AND DIFFERENCES

BY

ASHER FINKEL

LEIDEN / KÖLN
E. J. BRILL
1974

First edition 1964

Reprinted with corrections 1973

Jesus christ –Jewish interpretation

Pharisees

ISBN 90 04 03825 6

PRINTED IN THE NETHERLANDS

*To Gitie
in true companionship*

CONTENTS

ABBREVIATIONS

a) *Old and New Testaments*

Acts	Acts of the Apostles
Am.	Amos
Cant.	Canticles (Song of Songs)
Chr.	Chronicles
Cor.	Corinthians
Dan.	Daniel
Deut.	Deuteronomy
Ecc.	Ecclesiastes
Es.	Esther
Ex.	Exodus
Ez.	Ezekiel
Ezr	Ezra
Gen.	Genesis
Hab.	Habakkuk
Hag.	Haggai
Hos.	Hosea
Is.	Isaiah
Jer.	Jeremiah
John	John, The Gospel acc. to
Jon.	Jonah
Jos.	Joshua
Jud.	Judges
Kin.	Kings
Lam.	Lamentations
Lev.	Leviticus
Luk.	Luke
Mal.	Malachi
Mic.	Micha
Matt.	Matthew
Mk.	Mark
Nah.	Nahum
Neh.	Nehemiah
Num.	Numbers
Pr.	Proverbs
Ps.	Psalms
R.	Ruth
Rom.	Romans
Sam.	Samuel
Zech.	Zechariah

b) *Apocrypha and Pseudepigrapha*

Ap. Ezr.	Ezra Apocalypse
Arist.	Aristeas, The Letter of
E. En.	Ethiopic Enoch
Ezr. Apoc.	Ezra Apocryphon
Gen. Apoc.	Genesis Apocryphon
Jth.	Judith

Jub.	Jubilees
Macc.	Maccabees
Sin. Tob.	Tobit, codex Sinaiticus
Sir.	Wisdom of Sirach (Ecclesiasticus)
Sl. En.	Slavic Enoch
Sus.	Susanna
Test. G.	Testament Gad
Test. L.	Testament Levi
Test. Sh.	Testament Shimeon
Vat. Tob.	Tobit, codex Vaticanus

c) *Philo, Josephus and Eusebius*

Ant.	Josephus, Antiquitates Judaicae
Bell.	Josephus, Bellum Judaicum
Cont. Ap.	Josephus, Contra Apionem
De Op. Mund.	Philo, De Opificio Mundi
De Som.	Philo, De Somniis
De Sp. Leg.	Philo, De Specialibus Legibus
Hist. Eccl.	Eusebius, Historia Ecclesiastica
Leg. Alleg.	Philo, Legum Allegoriae
Praep. Ev.	Eusebius, Praeparatio Evangelica
Q.O.P.L.	Philo, Quod Omnis Probus Liber sit
Vit.	Josephus, Vita

d) *Qumran Texts*

C.D.	Damascus Document from the Cairo Geniza
I.Q.M.	Serekh Hammilchamah from cave I, Qumran
I Q. p. Hab.	Pesher Habakkuk from cave I, Qumran
I Q. p. Ps.	Pesher Psalms from cave I, Qumran
I Q. S.	Serekh Hayachad from cave I, Qumran
I Q. Sa.	Annexes à Serekh Hayachad, Qumran

e) *Mishnah, Tosefta and Talmuds (including the small tractates)*

B.	Babylonian Talmud
J.	Jerusalemian Talmud (Cited acc. to ed. princeps, Venice, 5282)
M.	Mishnah
T.	Tosefta (The numbers in the parenthesis indicate page and line acc. to Zuckermandel's edition)
Ab.	Aboth (Sayings of the Fathers)
A. Z.	Abodah Zarah (Idolatry)
Ara.	Arakhin (Estimations)
B. B.	Baba Bathra (3rd Gate on Torts)
B. K.	Baba Kamma (1st Gate on Torts)
B. M.	Baba Meṣiʿa (Middle Gate on Torts)
Bech.	Bekhoroth (Firstborns)
Ber.	Berakhoth (Benedictions)
Bez.	Beṣah (Egg of the Holiday) or Yom Tob
D. E. R.	Derekh Ereṣ Rabba (The Larger on Manners)
D. E. Z.	Derekh Ereṣ Zutta (The Lesser on Manners)
Dem.	Demai (Doubtful Food)
Ed.	Eduyyoth (Testimonies)
Erub.	Erubin (Blendings)
Git.	Gittin (Bills of Divorce)

Hag.	Ḥagigah (Festival Offerings)
Hal.	Ḥallah (Dough)
Hor.	Horayoth (Decisions)
Hul.	Ḥullin (Unholy Things)
Kal.	Kallah (Bride)
Kel.	Kelim (Vessels), acc. to Tosefta: Kelim B.K. (1st Gate), Kelim B.M. (2nd Gate), Kelim B.B. (3rd Gate)
Ker.	Kerithoth (Excisions)
Ket.	Kethubboth (Nuptial Contracts)
Kid.	Kiddushin (Marriages)
M. K.	Moʿed Katan (Minor Feast)
M. Sh.	Maʿaser Sheni (Tithes of the 2nd year)
Maas.	Maʿasroth (Tithes) or Maʿaser Rishon
Mach.	Makhshirin (Preparations)
Mak.	Makkoth (Flogging)
Meg.	Megillah (The Scroll of Esther)
Men.	Menachoth (Meal Offerings)
Mid.	Middoth (Measurements of the Temple)
Mik.	Mikwaʾoth (Ritual Baths)
Ned.	Nedarim (Vows)
Neg.	Negaʿim (Plagues)
Nez.	Neziruth or Nazir (Nazirite)
Nid.	Niddah (Menstruant)
Ohol.	Oholoth (Overshadowings)
Pea.	Peʾah (Corners of the Field)
Pes.	Pesachim (Paschal Lambs)
R. H.	Rosh Hashanah (New Year)
Sanh.	Sanhedrin (Courts)
Shab.	Shabbath (Sabbath)
Sheb.	Shebiʿith (Seventh Year)
Shebu.	Shebuʿoth (Oaths)
Shek.	Shekalim (Shekels)
Sof.	Soferim (Scribes)
Sot.	Sotah (Adulteress)
Suk.	Sukkah (Booths)
Taan.	Taʿanith (Fast-day)
Tam.	Tamid (Daily Offer)
Tem.	Temurah (Substitutions)
Ter.	Terumoth (Heave Offerings) or Terumah
Toh.	Tohoroth (Purities)
Ukz.	Ukṣin (Stalks)
Yad.	Yadayim (Hands)
Yeb.	Yebamoth (Levirate Marriages)
Yom.	Yoma (Day of Atonement) or Yom Hakkipurim
Zab.	Zabim (Persons with a Flowing Issue)
Zeb.	Zebachim (Sacrifices)

f) *Midrash and other rabbinic works*

A.D.N.	Aboth De Rabbi Nathan (The numbers in parenthesis cite page of Schechter's edition)
Cant. R.	Canticles (Shir Hashirim) Rabbah (Citing page of vol. IX of English translation)

Deut. R.	Deuteronomy (Debarim) Rabbah (Citing page of vol. VII of English translation)
Ecc. R.	Ecclesiastes (Qoheleth) Rabbah (Citing page of vol. VIII of English translation)
Est. R.	Esther Rabbah (Citing page of vol. IX of English translation)
Ex. R.	Exodus (Shemoth) Rabbah (Citing page of vol. III of English translation)
Gen. R.	Genesis (Bereshith) Rabbah (Citing page of Theodor and Albeck edition)
Lam. R.	Lamentations (Ekhah) Rabbah (Citing page of vol. VII of English translation
Lev. R.	Leviticus (Vayiqra) Rabbah (Citing page of vol. IV of English translation)
M. T.	Megillath Taʿanith (Citing page of A. Neubauer's edition)
Mech.	Mechilta on Exodus (Citing page of Weiss' edition)
Mid. Hag.	Midrash Hagadol to Genesis and Exodus (Citing page of Margolioth's edition)
Num. R.	Numbers (Bamidbar) Rabba (Citing page of vol. V, VI of English translation)
Pesiqta	Pesiqta De Rabbi Kahana (Citing page of Buber's edition)
Pirqe	Pirqe De Rabbi Eliezer
R. R.	Ruth Rabbah (Citing page of vol. VIII of English translation)
Rashi	Rabbi Solomon bar Isaac commentary to the Babylonian Talmud
S.E.R.	Seder Eliyahu Rabbah (Citing page of Friedmann's edition)
S.O.R.	Seder Olam Rabbah (Citing page of A. Neubauer's edition)
Sifra	Sifra (the halachic Midrash to Leviticus, citing folio of Weiss' edition)
Sifre	Sifre debe Rab to Numbers and Deuteronomy (Citing page of Friedmann's edition)
Tanh.	Tanḥuma (ed. Buber, unless otherwise specified)
Yad	Maimonides' Yad Hahazaqah (or Mishneh Torah)

g) *Publications*

I. Abrahams, Studies — Studies in Pharisaism and the Gospels, Cambridge, 1917, 1929

W. Bacher, Terminologie — Die exegetische Terminologie der jüdischen Traditionsliteratur II, Leipzig, 1905;

P. Billerbeck, Kommentar — Kommentar zum Neuen Testament aus Talmud und Midrasch, 2 ed. Munich, 1956;

Ad. Buechler, Studies — Studies in Jewish History ed. I. Brodie and J. Rabbinowitz, Oxford University Press, 1956;

R. H. Charles, Apoc. and Pseud. — The Apocrypha and Pseudepigrapha of the Old Testament, Oxford, 1913;

J. W. Doeve, J. Hermeneutics — Jewish Hermeneutics in the Gospels and Acts, Aasen, 1954;

J. N. Epstein, Meb. Les. Hat. — Mebuʾoth Lesaphruth Hatannaʾim, ed. E. Z. Melamed, Jerusalem/Tel-Aviv, 1957;

L. Finkelstein, Pharisees — The Pharisees: The Sociological Background of Their Faith, Philadelphia, 1946;

Z. Frankel, Paläst. Exegese — Über den Einfluß der palästinischen Exegese auf die alexandrinische Hermeneutik, Leipzig, 1851,

A. Geiger, Urschrift — Urschrift und Übersetzungen der Bibel, 2 ed. Frankfurt a.M., 1928;

Ch. D. Ginsburg, Introduction — Introduction to the Masoretico, Critical Edition of the Hebrew Bible, London, 1897;

J. W. Goudoever, Bibl. Cal. — Biblical Calendars, Leiden, 1959

H. Grätz, G. d. J. — Geschichte der Juden von den ältesten Zeiten bis auf die Gegenwart, Leipzig, 1870 ff.;

A. Guilding, The Fourth Gospel — The Fourth Gospel and the Jewish Worship, Oxford, 1960;

H.U.C.A. — Hebrew Union College Annual, Cincinnati, 1924—;

A. M. Haberman, Megilloth — Megilloth Midbar Yehudah, Israel, 1959;

S. B. Hoenig, Gr. Sanh. — The Great Sanhedrin, Philadelphia, 1953;

I.C.C. — International Critical Commentary;

J. Enc. — The Jewish Encyclopaedia, 12 vol. New York, 1901-1906;

J.Q.R. — Jewish Quarterly Review (N.S. denotes New Series), Old Series, London 1888-1906, New Series, Philadelphia, 1909;

J. Klausner, Historia — Historia shel Bayit Sheni, 4 ed. Jerusalem, 1952;

idem, Jesus — Jesus of Nazareth, English translation by H. Danby, New York, 1926;

N. Krochmal, More — More Nebokhe Hazeman, ed. Zunz, Lemberg, 1863;

S. Lieberman, Hellenism — Hellenism in Jewish Palestine, New York, 1950;

M. G. W. J. — Monatsschrift für Geschichte und Wissenschaft des Judentums, 1852-1939;

G. F. Moore, Judaism — Judaism in the first Centuries of the Christian Eıa, Cambridge, Mass. 1927-1930;

R. H. Pfeiffer, Introduction — Introduction to the Old Testament, repr. London, 1953;

E. Schuerer, G. J. V. — Geschichte des jüdischen Volkes im Zeitalter Jesu Christi, 4ed. Leipzig, 1901-1911;

M. Z. Segal, Sir — Sepher Ben-Sira Hashalem, Jerusalem, 1953;

H. L. Strack, Introduction — Introduction to the Talmud and Midrash, Meridian Books Inc. and the Jewish Publication Society of America, 1959;

I. H. Weiss, D. D. Wed. — Dor Dor Wedorshaw, 4 ed. Wilna 1904;

L. Zunz, G. V. d. J. — Gottesdienstliche Vorträge der Juden, historisch entwickelt, 2 ed. Frankfurt a. M., 1892;

INTRODUCTION

PROBLEM AND PURPOSE

During the last two centuries of the Second Jewish Common-wealth (c. 152 B.C.-70 A.D.), there existed a prominent order known as the Pharisees, as it is evident from the testimonies of Josephus [1]), the New Testament [2]), and the rabbinic literature [3]). The Greek term "Pharisaioi", and its equivalents in Aramaic "Perishaya" and in Hebrew "Perushim", is commonly rendered as "the ones who are separated" [4]), which recalls the watchword from the times of the Maccabean contest [5]): separation in contrast to assimilation. It is difficult to state at what precise time the term was first used, but it appears from the sources to have originated from the mouths of the opposition. The followers of this order were pledged to a strict observance of Levitical purity, to the avoidance of closer association with the impure ignorant boors, to the scrupulous payment of tithes and other imposts due to the priest, the Levite and the poor; or as succinctly described by outsiders, such as Nicholas of Damascus (1st cent. B.C.) [6]), "a body of Jews who profess to be more religious than others and to explain the laws more accurately" based on—as

---

[1]) The student should refer to the texts compiled by E. Schürer, G.J.V. II, pp. 449-452.

[2]) The references to the Pharisees in the New Testament are compiled in A Concordance to the Greek Testament, ed. W. F. Moulton and A. S. Geden, p. 597.

[3]) The Mishnaic evidence are listed by E. Schürer, G.J.V. II pp,. 452-455. For the Tosefta see T. Ber. 3.25 (8. 17) = J. Ber. 5a (Pharisees as heretics); T. Hag. 3.35 (238.23) = J. ib. 79d; T. Sot. 15.11 (322.15) and M.ib. 3.4 = b. Sot. 22b, J. Ber. 14b, b. Ket. 62b (Pharisees as ascetics); T. Shab. 1.15 (111.2) = b. ib. 13a; T. Yom. 1.8 (181.1f) = b. ib. 19b, J. ib. 39a; T. Suk. 3.1. (195.19) = b. ib. 43b, J. ib. 54b; T.R.H. 1.15 (210.10) = b. ib. 22b, J. ib. 57d; T. Sanh. 6.6 (424.30) = b. Mak. 5b, J. Hag. 77d and Mech. p. 105b; T. Par. 3.8 (632.18) = M. ib. 3.7, b. Yom. 2a, b. Hag. 23a, b. Zeb. 21a; T. Nid. 5.2,3 (645.23 ff.) = M. Nid. 4.2, b. ib. 33b; T. Yad. 2.20 (684.3) = b.B.B. 115b, b. Hor. 4a = b. Sanh. 33b; M. Men. 6.2 and b. ib. 65a. See further M.T., scholion; A.D.N. 5 (13b), 37 (55a).

[4]) So Klausner, Historia III, p. 118, G. F. Moore, Judaism I, p. 60, K. Kohler, Pharisees in J. Enc.—as rendered in the commentary of Hai Gaon (10th cent. A.D.) on M. Yad. 4.6.

On the other hand, H. Grätz, G.d.J., III. 5, p. 72 ff. and R. Leszynsky, Die Sadduzäer, Berlin, 1912, prefer the translation "exegetes"—as found in Yosippon, ed. Hominer, p. 111.

[5]) II. Macc. XIV. 38 (ἀμιξία = פרישה) Cf. v. 3, refer to L. Baeck, Die Pharisäer, Berlin, 1934, p. 7 ff.

[6]) Bell. I. 5.2 § 110, cf. ib. II. 8.11 § 162.

Josephus states [1]—"regulations handed down by former generations and not recorded in the Laws of Moses". These are exactly the traits that characterize the Pharisees in the Synoptic Gospels and the Acts of the Apostles.

Because of the significance of the Pharisaic order at the beginning of Christianity and the important role the order played in the development of the Jewish religion, the nature of the Pharisees became a matter of investigation and controversy for Jewish and Christian scholars [2]. The majority opinion among the Christian scholars is summed up in the words of M. J. Lagrange [3], "A fraternity boasting a unique acquaintance with the Law of God, both written and oral, and organized for the purpose of imposing it on others". This rigorous line, so long attributed to the Pharisees by the Christian scholars like N. Nicolas [4], E. Renan [5] and A. Réville [6] in France, E. Schürer [7] in Germany, and R. H. Charles [8] in England, is based on materials drawn from a) the New Testament—which is coloured by a strong anti-Pharisaic attitude b) Josephus' works (which J. Wellhausen [9] accepts as the only reliable source of information), works written in the first place for a Roman audience [10], who was not acquainted with Judaism.—For this reason, Josephus compares the Pharisees with the Stoics (Vita 2 § 12); c) the Apocalyptic literature (which W. Bousset [11]) held as writings reflecting authentic Judaism of

---

[1]) Ant. XIII. 10. 6 § 297.

[2]) A list of works and articles written on the subject before 1906 is found in Schürer, G.J.V. II., pp. 447-449; a further complete list is given by L. Finkelstein, The Pharisees, in the Bibliography.

[3]) Le Judaism avant Jésus-Christ, Paris, 1931, 3 rd ed., p. 272.

[4]) Des doctrines religieuse des Juifs pendants les deux siècles antérieurs a l'ère Chrétienne, Paris, 1860. Nicolas also demonstrates that only the praiseworthy Pharisees lived before the time of Jesus.

[5]) In his famous "La vie de Jésus " (German translation 4 ed. Leipzig, 1880) which was criticized by A. Geiger, Das Judentum und seine Geschichte, 2 ed. Breslau, 1865, and H. Grätz, Sinai et Golgatha, Paris, 1867, calls it a "new gospel".

[6]) Jésus de Nazareth, Paris, 1897, Réville also indicates the interpolation found in Josephus (Ant. XVIII. 3.3) on Jesus; see further Schürer, G.J.V., I p. 544 ff.

[7]) In his great and not outdated work, Geschichte des jüdischen Volkes im Zeitalter Jesu Christi, see his Introduction and volume II.

[8]) Apocrypha and Pseudepigrapha, Oxford, 1913, in the Introductions.

[9]) Die Pharisäer und die Sadducäer, 2. ed., Hannover, 1924, p. 33.

[10]) See further A. Shalit's Introduction to Josephus' Antiquities, 2 ed., Jerusalem/Tel-Aviv, 1955.

[11]) Jesu Predigt in ihrem Gegensatz zum Judentum, Göttingen, 1892; and "Religion des Judentums" are strongly criticized by G. F. Moore in "Christian Writers on Judaism", Harvard Theological Review XIV, 1921. See further F. Perles, Bousset's Religion des Judentums kritisch untersucht, Berlin, 1903.

their times) is composed of works whose relation independent from rabbinic influences cannot be clearly defined [1]), and whose origin stems from the popular pietists. As for rabbinic literature, which was employed in the studies of the Christian scholars, F. C. Burkitt [2]) urges a cautious application.

The labours of important Jewish scholars, who have the advantage to be more intimately acquainted with Rabbinica, are devoted to giving a just, critical estimate of the Pharisees based on the Pharisaic followers' literary products [e.g., A. Geiger's "Urschrift und Übersetzungen der Bibel" [3]); H. Grätz in "Geschichte der Juden", Volume Three; L. J. Lauterbach in his article, "The Sadducees and the Pharisees" [4]); J. M. Elbogen's "Einige neuere Theorien über den Ursprung der Pharisäer und der Sadduzäer" [5]), and L. Finkelstein's "The Pharisees: The Sociological Background of their Faith"]. Yet to the study of New Testament accounts, S. Zeitlin [6]) prescribes a critical application of Rabbinica.

Different opinions about the origin of the Pharisees have prevailed among the scholars. S. W. Baron [7]) sees the rise of the Pharisees caused by anti-Hellenistic front; while the priestly Sadducees were still embracing Hellenism. L. Finkelstein [8]) shows that the form of social structure in Judea had resulted in a split; on one side the plebeian teachers, the Pharisees, and on the other side the urban patricians. J. Z. Lauterbach finds the controversies between the Pharisees and the Sadducees in the different approach to oral tradition. This view is accepted and maintained by S. B. Hoenig [9]) saying, "The aristocratic Sadducees generally were conservative; the democratic Pharisees were liberal and progressive". Thus emerged two schools of thought: the former "strict constructionists" and the latter "loose

---

[1]) See J. W. Doeve, J. Hermeneutics, p. 35 n. 1.

[2]) Jesus and the Pharisees, Journal of Theological Studies XXVIII, 1927, pp. 392-397.

[3]) Frankfurt a. M., 1928, 2 ed., and the Hebrew translation המקרא ותרגומיו, Jerusalem, 1949.

[4]) In "Studies in Jewish Literature in Honour of Kaufmann Kohler", Berlin, 1913, p. 177 ff.

[5]) In "Jewish Studies in Memory of I. Abrahams", New York, 1927, p. 135. ff.

[6]) The Halaka in the Gospels and its Relation to the Jewish Law at the Time of Jesus, H.U.C.A.I, 1924.

[7]) A Social and Religious History of the Jews, vol. I, p. 233 ff (New York, 1952, 2 ed.).

[8]) The Pharisees I, p. 73 ff.

[9]) The Great Sanhedrin, p. 44 f.

constructionists" in connection with the interpretation of the Law. This can be concluded that the sum total of the above mentioned reasons, whether social, political or religious, as can be found in almost any other historical situation, has caused the emergence of the two fronts contesting vehemently for the legislative-judicial powers of the state.

As for the identity of the orders, Geiger's close study of the two so-called sects resulted in the following conclusion that the Pharisees are the successors of those who in earlier generations called themselves Hasidim (pious or religious), and the Sadducees are the members of the priestly house of Zadok [1]). The above results are generally accepted among the Christian scholars like E. Meyer [2]), R. T. Herford [3]) and G. F. Moore [4]), and by a majority of Jewish scholars [5]).

As to the question: Do the Pharisaic teachings and decisions represent the products of one school, or is there enough evidence to show that the Pharisaic order did produce opposing schools of its own? L. Ginsberg [6]) and L. Finkelstein [7]) have examined the diverse teachings and practices among the Pharisaic Jews, and S. Zeitlin [8]) has shown that the first major split among the Pharisees themselves was due to the manner of exposition.

At the time of the intense activities of the Pharisaic schools (2 or 4 B.C.-29 or 33 A.D.) [9]) lived a teacher from Nazareth, whose course of life affected the lives and the literary works of millions of men on earth. Since the days of the Reformation great strides were taken to study the life of this man, which led to the analysis of the accounts of his life and teachings [10]), questioning the historical value

---

[1]) Their associates were the Boethusians, members of another priestly house, see Finkelstein, Pharisees II, p. 663 n. 20.

[2]) Ursprung und Anfänge des Christentums, 3 vol., Stuttgart, 1921-1923.

[3]) The Pharisees, London, 1924. German translation by W. Fischel, Leipzig, 1928.

[4]) Judaism I, p. 59.

[5]) See Klausner, Historia III, p. 118 ff. On the other hand B.Z., Katz in "Perushim, Ṣaduqim, Qanaim We-Noṣrim", Tel-Aviv, 1947, claims that the Boethusians are the Essenes; the Zealots, Sadducees and the Hasidim, Pharisees.

[6]) Halachah We-Haggadah, Tel-Aviv, 1960, p. 13 ff., Engl. ed. "On Jewish Law and Lore", Philadelphia, 1955, p. 77 ff.

[7]) The Pharisees I, ch. III.

[8]) The Semikah Controversy between the Zugoth, J.Q.R. VII, 1917.

[9]) For the dates see C. H. Turner's article "Chronology" in Hastings' Dictionary to the Bible I, and R. W. Husband, The Prosecution of Jesus, Princeton, 1916.

[10]) A review on the different accounts and sources for the life and teachings of Jesus is presented by J. Klausner, Jesus, pp. 17-127.

of the Gospels. From the early efforts of H. S. Reimarus and J. J. Griesbach until the end of the nineteenth century, culminating with the work of W. Wrede [1]), a great number of books on the life of Jesus were written, rationalizing the miracles, explaining his consciousness and his role on earth, and discovering the most dependable sources for the historical estimate of his life.

With the beginning of the twentieth century [2]) a noticeable change occurred, not so much in the study of the Gospels [3]) as in the study of the character and the teachings of Jesus, and especially in the study of his Jewish environment in the light of rabbinical Judaism. The spiritual character of Jesus: A. Schweitzer and W. Bousset disagree on the question whether Jesus was a "Weltbejaher" or a "Weltverneiner". On his identity: J. Wellhausen declared, "Jesus was not a Christian; he was a Jew"; whereas E. Häckle, Dr. A. Kaminka and Prof. P. Haupt point to his Aryan origin; and A. Kalthoff and A. Drews claim that the story of Jesus and the existence of Christianity can be explained as a product of later movement and a result of a combination of factors. As for the teachings of Jesus: R. Leszynsky [4]) finds important points of agreement between Jesus and the Sadducees. H. Grätz [5]) called Christianity, "Essenism mixed with foreign elements", and A. Geiger [6]) and J. Klausner [7]) describe Jesus as a Pharisaic rabbi with some divergent opinions and declare that his criticism was actually not an attack but a defense of Pharisaism against hypocrisy.

The study of the New Testament in the light of rabbinic literature began with the great collections of rabbinical data in the middle of the seventeenth century [8]) and culminated with a work that is final in this group, "Kommentar zum Neuen Testament aus Talmud und

---

[1]) See the work of A. Schweitzer, Eine Geschichte der Leben-Jesu-Forschung, 6 ed., Tübingen, 1951.

[2]) For an evaluation of the works mentioned refer to Klausner, Jesus, p. 92 ff.

[3]) A recent valuable book on the study of the Gospels is F. C. Grant's "The Gospels: Their Origin and their Growth", London, 1957.

[4]) Die Sadduzäer, Berlin, 1912. Criticized by H. Revel in J.Q.R.N.S. VII, p. 429-438.

[5]) In Sinai et Golgatha, p. 376 and as found in the "romances" of K. F. Bahrdt, Ausführung des Plans und Zwecks Jesu" 12 vol., 1784-93, and K. H. Venturini, Natürliche Geschichte des großen Propheten von Nazareth, 4 vol. 1800-02. See also J. Parkes, Jesus, Paul and the Jews, London, 1936.

[6]) Das Judentum und seine Geschichte, 2 ed. Breslau, 1865.

[7]) Jesus, p. 215 and p. 361 ff.

[8]) J. W. Doeve, J. Hermeneutics, ch. 1, presents a review of works on the study of the New Testament in the light of rabbinic literature.

Midrasch" by H. L. Strack and, mainly, P. Billerbeck. This commentary fails to give a just picture in understanding the New Testament
times, since it is a copious collection of rabbinical material grouped
around texts, which necessitates the sifting of subjects in accordance
with the time of origin. With the beginning of the twentieth century
many studies, articles and excursuses were written on special topics
in relation with the time of Jesus. [Among the most important are:
The excursuses of H. L. Strack and P. Billerbeck [1]); P. Fiebig's
studies: "Die Gleichnisreden Jesu", Tübingen, 1912, "Jesu Bergpredigt", Göttingen, 1924, and "Das Vaterunser", Gütersloh, 1924;
I. Abrahams' "Studies in Pharisaism and the Gospels", Cambridge I,
1917, II, 1924; J. Mann's article, "Rabbinic Studies in the Synoptic
Gospels", H.U.C.A., 1924; J. Jeremias' "Jerusalem zur Zeit Jesu",
2ed., Göttingen, 1958; C. G. Montefiore, "Rabbinic Literature and
the Gospels' Teachings", London 1930, and his commentary, "The
Synoptic Gospels", 2ed., London, 1927; H. Schoeps' "Die Jüdischen
Prophetenmorde" in "Aus frühchristlicher Zeit", Tübingen, 1950;
J. Klausner's "The Messianic Idea in Israel", English Translation,
London, 1956-; S. Mowinckel's "He that Cometh", Eng. translation,
Oxford, 1956; J. W. Doeve, "Jewish Hermeneutics" and A. Guilding's
"The Fourth Gospel"]. Another topic for study was the linguistic
problem of the Gospels. One trend led to the translation of certain
parts of the New Testament from the Aramaic [2]), and a second trend
discovered the Aramaic and Hebrew equivalents of the Greek used in
the New Testament, which was named by J. W. Doeve [3]) the semasio-
logical school.

   This work is a study of the Pharisaic order, its teaching and differences which are presented in the oral tradition. The work follows
with an analysis of the message of Jesus as expounded in a
Pharisaic atmosphere [4]), where Jesus' declaration [5]), "Repent for

---

[1]) Found in the fourth volume of Kommentar; part 1 contains 23 excursuses,
and part 2, 10 excursuses.

[2]) A pioneer in this field of study was J. Wellhausen in "Einleitung in die
drei ersten Evangelien", Berlin, 1905.
Refer to the works of C. F. Burney, Ch. C. Torrey and M. Black.

[3]) J. Hermeneutics, p. 21, e.g. the works of G. Dalman: Die Worte Jesu,
Leipzig, 1898, Jesus-Jeschua, Leipzig, 1922, and Orte und Wege Jesu, Gütersloh,
1924.

[4]) Relying in the main on the accounts of the Synoptics with related parts in
other sources.

[5]) Matt. 4.17 = Mk. 1.15, so spoke his forerunner, John the Baptist (Matt. 3.2),
and it was declared by Jesus to his disciples (Matt. 10.7 = Luk. 10.9).

the Kingdom of Heaven is at hand", must have been understood; and where also his other teachings, expounded in the various parts of the country, are presented to Jews of his time.

This study is based on the thesis that the Mosaic Laws, and the consequent interpretations, with decrees, customs and ordinances found alongside, since the days of Ezra and Nehemiah, played a most important role in the daily lives of the teachers and the people of Judea. As of this phenomenon, already the contemporary non-Jewish writers speak with awe [1]), and the literary products of the time declare with no doubt.

In order to have a clear understanding of the era of the Second Jewish Commonwealth, as in regard to the development of the Jewish religion along the lines of oral and written tradition, I must refer back to the generation of Ezra, the crucial period for the development of the Judaic religion. This requires a description of the important religious body, the Great Synagogue, attributed to the period prior to the Hasmonaean revolt by rabbinic tradition, and the works of the Scribes. This will be presented in Part A. Part B of the dissertation describes the religious practices and legal decisions emanating from the Pharisaic schools during the Hasmonaean and Herodian times. The existing accounts of the Pharisaic teachings can at best be grouped under four headings: a) Laws of Separation and Purity; b) Judicature, c) The Festivals, and d) Education. Part C attempts to discover the form of oral and written tradition, which guided the authors and teachers of the Hasmonaean and Herodian period. This study will include an evaluation of the Gospels, a source for the teachings of Jesus. Part D is designated for the understanding of the message of Jesus in the light of the Pharisaic practices and teachings. An evaluation of the teachings of Jesus is presented, in connection with two fields of study, the opposition to the Pharisees, and the similarities with the Pharisaic teachings and manner of presentation.

EVALUATION OF THE SOURCES

The study in Part A depends on the following sources: a) The latter works of the Old Testament, which embrace the writings of the prophets of the Babylonian exile and of the return to Judea, the diaries

---

[1]) For example Hecataeus of Abdera (4-3 cent. B.C.), see Cont. Ap. I. 22.6; Clearachus, a disciple of Aristoteles, ib. I. 22.5 and Agatharchides of Cnidos (2 cent. B.C.), ib. I. 22.7; see further Th. Reinach, Textes d'auteurs grecs et romains relatifs au Judaisme, Paris, 1895.

of Ezra and Nehemiah, the Chronicles, parts of the Psalms, the Five
Scrolls, Proverbs and the apocalyptic Daniel, written at the close of the
period; b) The Apocrypha which include the work of Ben-Sira, the
prolific thinker at the close of the era and other, yet later, works which
do refer and shed light on this period; c) The Samaritan version of
the Pentateuch, and the translations of the Pentateuch such as the
Septuagint, the Aramaic renditions, and the terse interpretations found
in the early Tannaitic literature; d) The historical description found
in Josephus' works which requires a cautious application, and the
meager, yet valuable, information in rabbinical literature which does
refer to the times of Ezra and recalls hoary customs, to which evidence
from the Maccabean period show that these practices were already
commonly accepted, e.g., the strict observance of the Sabbath and
the lectionary readings in the synagogue; and e) Information gathered
from the archaeological findings, such as Elephantine papyri. The
study in Parts B, C and D depends mainly on five sources of information: a) The rabbinic literature; b) The New Testament; c) Josephus'
and Philo's works; d) The Apocrypha and Pseudepigrapha; and e)
The Dead Sea Scrolls.

In order to obtain a serviceable use of the rabbinical literature, at
first one must resort to critical texts [1]). Secondly, one must examine
the account, the source from which it is derived, the time and school
of the teacher to whom the statement is attributed [2]), and the particular
archaic phrases found in some anonymous accounts [3]). Thirdly,
much Talmudic information stems from the days of collecting
materials at Jamnia and the subsequent schools (from c. 70-500 A.D.);
but the early Rabbis did collect valuable information, as attested by
the members of earlier Pharisaic schools [4]). These reports, about
which the works of Jewish scholars [5]) have contributed a critical
estimate, should only be examined.

---

[1]) A list of texts will be found in the Bibliography, the rabbinic texts.

[2]) It was obligatory to report precisely the words of the teacher (as in the case
of Hillel, M. Ed. 1.3) and to relate the name of the teacher responsible for the
statement, see Tanh. Bamidbar § 27 (p. 11).

[3]) See Ch. Albeck, Introduction to the Mishnah, Tel-Aviv 1959; L. Ginzberg, Halachah We—Haggadah, p. 41 ff, and Eliezer ben Yehuda, Introduction to the Hebrew
Dictionary. (Refer to M. H. Segal, A Grammar of Mishnaic Hebrew, Oxford, 1927).

[4]) See T. Ed. 1.1 (454.22), on collecting early halachah of the two schools at
Jamnia, and T. Zab. 1.5 (676.33) indicates that Rabbi Aqiba's school processed
the early halachah. See further J. N. Epstein, Meb. Les. Hat., p. 15 ff.

[5]) Among the most important are W. Bacher, Die Agada der Tannaiten (Straß-

As for the application of New Testament's materials, the Synoptic Gospels represent the earliest accounts (from c. 64-90 A.D.) [1]) based on two original sources, Q (Logia) and Mark—as formulated by the majority of scholars—with other additions, such as special material found in Luke and Matthew and different infancy and passion narratives. Whereas the Gospel according to John (c. 90-100 A.D.) is a dramatic presentation of the life, ministry, death and glorification of Jesus for purpose of both instruction and worship within the church; the Gospel of Ephesian or perhaps Alexandrian tradition.

As for the works of Philo [2]), Josephus [3]), Apocrypha and Pseudepigrapha [4]) a critical application of the materials is necessary; since the first two are written in a Hellenistic atmosphere and the last two are, in most cases, based on Greek translation of the original in Hebrew, with some presented in different versions.

---

burg, 1903). Die Agada der palästinensischen Amoräer (Straßburg, 1892-99), Die Agada der babylonischen Amoräer (Straßburg, 1878) and Tradition und Tradenten in den Schulen Palästinas und Babyloniens (Leipzig, 1914). The Introductions to the different critical texts. I. H. Weiss, Dor Dor Wedorshaw (Zur Geschichte der jüdischen Tradition), vol. I-III, 4 ed., Wilna, 1904. L. Zunz, Gottesdienstliche Vorträge der Juden, Frankfurt a. M., 1892 2 ed., Ch. Tchernowitz, Toledoth Halachah, 3 vol., 1934-43, S. Krauß, Talmudische Archäologie, 3 vol. Leipzig, 1910. A. Hyman, Toledoth Tannaim We-Amoraim, London, 1910. A. Schwartz, Die Controversen der Schammaiten und der Hilleliten, Vienna, 1893, and his other works on hermeneutics (listed in the bibliography). For aids to the study of Rabbinica refer to the Bibliography. On rabbinic literature, On Mishnah: D. Hoffmann, Die erste Mishna und die Controversen der Tannaim, Berlin, 1882. Ch. Albeck, Redaktion der Mishna, Berlin, 1923 and idem, Introduction to the Mishnah (Hebr.), Tel-Aviv, 1959. Z. Frankel, Darkey Hamishnah (Hodegetica in Mishnam), Leipzig, 1859 and J. N. Epstein, Meb. Les. Hat. (Introduction to Tannaitic Literature). On Tosefta: A. Guttman, Mischna und Tosefta, Breslau, 1828, S. Lieberman, Tosefta Kifshutah, New York, 1956. On Talmud: Z. H. Chajes, The Student's Guide through the Talmud, Engl. translation, London, 1952. A. Weiss, Lecheqer Hatalmud, New York, 1956. M. Mielziner, Introduction to the Talmud 2 ed., New York, 1952. H. L. Strack, Introduction to the Talmud and Midrash, English translation, New York/Philadelphia, 1959 (which also lists many other important works). On the Jerusalemian Talmud: Z. Frankel, Mabo Hayerushalmi (Introductio in Talmud Hieresolymitanum), Breslau, 1870 and L. Ginzberg, Perushim Wechidushim Beyerushalmi, vol. I (the Introduction), New York, 1941.

[1]) As shown by F. C. Grant, op. cit. He reconstructs the sources and discusses the different structures of the Gospels.

[2]) For the influence of Palestinian teaching on the Alexandrian writings see the work of Z. Frankel, Über den Einfluß der palästinischen Exegese auf die alexandrinische Hermeneutik, Leipzig, 1851.

[3]) The notes of A. Shalit on Josephus' Antiquities and J. N. Simchoni on the Jewish War include rabbinic parallels.

[4]) The commentaries of A Kahana's "Sepharim Hisonim," Tel-Aviv, 1955. present rabbinic parallels.

The information gathered from the discoveries in the Judean desert must follow the critical texts issued by different scholars [1]) with an awareness of the annotations and insertions in the texts.

With the said approach I propose to reexamine the sources and to present the results on the Pharisaic activities in the area of Halachah [2]) (signifying guidance, a rule of practice, a legal decision; and the term extends also to the usages, customs, ordinances and decrees), and to analyse the teachings of Jesus in the light of these findings, and particularly the form of homilies attributed to Jesus.

---

[1]) A general good text is A. M. Haberman, Megilloth Midbar Yehudah (the Scrolls of the Judean Desert) with a concordance, Israel, 1959, and much material and information can be gathered from "Discoveries in the Judean Desert" I, by D. Barthélemy and J. T. Milik, Oxford, 1955 II, by P. Benoit, J. T. Milik and R. de Vaux, 1961 (on the findings at MURABBA'AT).

[2]) See S. Schechter's definition in "Studies in Judaism", 3. series, Philadelphia, 1945, p. 195.

PART A

THE COMMON BACKGROUND

The return of exiles to Judea, induced by Cyrus' proclamation [1]), unfolds a new era which encompasses six centuries, and is known as the Second Jewish Commonwealth. This era can be studied historically [2]) according to three basic periods; the Persian period, the Greek period and the Roman period. For a better assessment of the religious activities present in the era, and for a better understanding of important changes that evolutionised in the era [that finally brought about the growing pains of a new daughter religion known as Christianity] another division can be introduced as follows: a) the period of Zadokite ministry (536-165 B.C.) [3]), b) the period of Hasmonaean part or complete rule (165-37 B.C.) [4]), c) the period of Hero-

[1]) As recorded in II Chr. 36.23 (cf. Ezr. 1.1-3) and as substantiated by the manner Cyrus treated his subjects. Cf. the inscription of Cyrus' cylinder in Pritchard's Ancient Near-Eastern Texts Relating to the Old Testament (Princeton, 1955), p. 315.

[2]) A division adopted by most eminent scholars writing about this era, as H. Grätz in G.d.J., Vols. II, III; E. Schürer in G.J.V., 3 vols; W. O. E Oesterley, A History of Israel, vol. II (Oxford, rep. 1957) and J. Klausner, Historia, 5 vols.

[3]) The chain of high priesthood from the Zadokite stem begins with the restoration of Joshua, the son of Jehozadak (who was exiled by Nebuchadnezzar, I Chr. 5.41) at the time of the erection of the altar (536 B.C. see Ezr. 3.2)—a descendant of Zadok (I Chr. 5.38-40). The following are the high priests in succession during the Persian period: Jeshua (above), Jehoiakim his son, Eliashib his son, Joiada his son, Jonathan or Jehochanan mentioned in Elephantine papyrus c. 404 B.C. and Jaddua (see Neh. 12.10, 11, Ant. XI. 7.1 § 297, ib. XI. 7. 2 § 302). During the Greek period until ten years before the Maccabean revolt (Josephus, Ant. XII. 5. 1 § 238, maintains that Menelaus in the days of Judas Maccabaeus is to be identified with Onias, a brother of Jason, of the Zadokite line) the following high priests served: Onias I, son of Jaddua, his son Simon I the Just, his brother Eleazer (see Ant. XI. 8. 7. § 347 and ib. XII. 2. 5. §§ 43, 44)—the high priest mentioned in Arist. § 35—followed by Menasses, his uncle and Onias II, son of Simon I (Ant. XII. 4. 1. § 157), his son Simon II the Just—praised by Ben Sira, see Sir. 50. 1—and his sons, Onias III (Ant. XII. 4. 10 § 224) and Jason (Jeshua), see Ant. XII. 5. 1. § 237 and II Macc. 4. 7.

[4]) In the year 165 B.C., after military gains over the forces of Antiochus IV, the Temple was cleansed and rededicated (I. Macc. 4. 52). Three sons of Mattathiah the Hasmonaean, of the priestly Watch Jehoiarib, served as leaders and high priests: Judas Maccabaeus, d. 160 B.C., (according to Klausner, Historia III, p. 39), Jonathan, d. 143 B.C., and Simon, d. 135 B.C. John Hyrcanus I, d. 104

dian-procurators administration until the fall of the Second Temple
(37 B.C.-70 A.D.) [1]).

The period of Zadokite ministry is designated by an unbroken
chain of high priesthood in the hands of Zadok's descendants, which
came to an end several years before the rise of the Hasmonaean
family [2]). In the days of King Solomon, Zadok served as high priest
and of whose descendants Ezekiel, the prophet of Babylonian exile [3]),
spoke as the true heirs to the priesthood. In the days of restoration of
the Second Temple, Zechariah, the prophet of return, is told in a
vision of the installation of Jeshua, a direct descendant of Zadok,
with a crown made of gold and silver [4]).

The exiles did not ask for a restoration of a monarchy remembering
the closing incidents [5]) leading to the destruction of the former state,

---

B.C., son of the latter, extended his domain and according to Oesterley, op. cit.,
pp. 285, 286, assumed the kingship. Judas Aristoblus I, d. 103 B.C., succeeded
his father as king and high priest, and was followed by his brother Alexander
(Yehonathan) Jannaeus, d. 76 B.C. Their wife, Salome (Salom Zion) Alexandra,
d. 67 B.C., became the queen after the death of the latter, and her son, Hyrcanus II
(Jehochanan), served as high priest, d. 30 B.C. Later he was appointed by Caesar
as ethnarch, 63-40 B.C. His brother, Aristobulus II, d. 49 B.C., and son, Alexander
II, d. 49 B.C., contested for the Judaic throne. Finally Mattathias Antigonus,
d. 37 B.C., the brother of the latter, was in power in the years 40-37 B.C. until
he was overthrown by Herod the Great, an Idumean by birth.

[1]) Herod the Great ruled from 37-4 B.C. His sons were appointed by Augustus:
Archelaus as ethnarch over Judaea, Samaria and Idumaea (4 B.C.-6 A.D.). Antipas
as tetrach over Galilee and Peraea with districts in East of Jordan (4 B.C.-39 A.D.),
and Philip as tetrach over Batanaea, Trachonitis and Auranitis (4 B.C.-34 A.D.).
The grandsons of Herod the Great and Mariamne I, a granddaughter of Hyrcanus
II the Hasmonaean, ruled over parts of Palestine: Agrippa I (37-41 A.D.) over
north of Samaria and from 41-44 A.D. as king over the whole country. Herod
of Chalkis ruled there in 41-48 A.D. and from 44-48 A.D. appointed high priests.
The son of Agrippa I, Agrippa II, who ruled in Chalkis 50-53 A.D., was given
added districts 53-100 A.D. and appointed high priests 50-66 A.D. For a list of
procurators refer to Klausner's charts in Historia, vols. IV, V, and Schürer,
G.J.V. I, § 19.

[2]) Two high priests served in the years following the Zadokite period and
during Judas Maccabeaus' lifetime: Menelaus, of Miniamin descent (Klausner,
Historia II, p. 174) or of Bilgah descent (so in Latin version of II Macc. 3.4)—both
are priestly watches (I Chr. 24.9 ff) and Jakim (Alkimus) from another priestly
Watch (I Macc. 7.57). Schürer, G.J.V. I. 4, p. 215 n. 16, places Onias IV, son of
Onias III (cf. Ant. XIII 3.1 § 64 f), who later had built a temple in Alexandria,
as a high priest in the span of years left vacant as described by Josephus, Ant.
20.10 and 12.11, 12. See Klausner's argument, Historia III, pp. 38, 39.

[3]) Ez. 44.15.

[4]) Zech. 6. 11; see I.C.C., Zecharia, p. 183 ff, on this difficult text. J. Wellhausen, Israelitische und Jüdische Geschichte (1904), p. 163 ff, explains that in the
years that follow, the high priest became the head of state.

[5]) Especially the death of Gedaliah in the hands of Davidic descendant which

and did not wish to awaken the anger of the benevolent Persian kings, as it is reflected in the fears of Nehemiah invoked by Sanbellat's statesments [1]); instead they welcomed and accepted a theocratic rule under the guidance of the high priest [2]).

The crystallization of a theocratic state began with the activities of Ezra, the scribe and Nehemiah, the statesman [3]). Ezra introduced the Mosaic law as the state's constitution and shaped the form of Jewish religion that radiated throughout the coming era. The religious writers after the close of the era saw in the personality of Ezra the greatness of Moses, the lawgiver, and more precisely a new epoch for the Jewish religion. Rabbi Jose (c. 150 A.D.), responsible for the collection of rabbinic interpretation of history, states [4]): "Ezra was worthy of being the vehicle of the Law had it not been already given through Moses". The author of the Apocalyptic Ezra (c. 66-96 A.D.)[5]) assumes the identity of Ezra and is instructed by a voice from the bush, as it is recorded of Moses, to preserve in writing the teachings. With the aid of five scribes he issues twenty-four books, which are identified with the general recognised books of the Old Testament, and seventy books containing the fountain of wisdom, the unrecorded teachings [6]). Thus, the author wishes the reader to believe that Ezra is responsible for both the reproduction of the written law and for the publication of the unrecorded law. A similar view is expressed by a contemporary Rabbi [7]), "As he was a scribe for the words of the Torah, so he was a scribe for the words of the Wise".

---

caused the complete destruction of the state (II Kin. 25. 25, 26; Jer. 41. 1, 2). The date of his death was declared a fast day on the seventh month (Zech. 8. 19 according to b.R.H. 18b).

[1]) Neh. 6.6.

[2]) Cf. Cont. Ap. II 16 § 165, Josephus coined the word theocracy to describe a system under which the Jews lived in Judea (refer to Hoenig, G. Sanh., exc. XIII).

[3]) W. O. E. Oesterley, op. cit., ch. X, is in the opinion that Nehemiah's activities began at 444 B.C. and Ezra's in 397 B.C. A contrasting view is held by Klausner, Historia I, lectures 16-19, that Ezra arrived in Judea in the year 457 B.C. and Nehemiah followed in 444 B.C.—whose opinion I follow in this work.

[4]) The statement is recorded in b. Sanh. 21b, T. ib. 4. 7 (421.23), on the work of R. Jose, see Z. Frankel, Darkey Hamishnah, p. 164 ff.

[5]) Ap. Ezr. ch. 12, refer to the Introductions in A. Kahana's "Sepharim Ḥisonim" I, p. 427 ff. and Charles, Apoc. and Pseud. II.

[6]) On the type of teachings recorded in the books: G. H. Box in Charles, Apoc. and Pseud. II, p. 624, comments that they were of apocalyptic nature, while J. N. Epstein, Meb. Les. Hat., pp. 15, 16, maintains they were of halachic and midrashic nature.

[7]) J. Shek. 48 c. (In the name of R. Eliezer, c. 100 A.D.).

THE GREAT SYNAGOGUE

It is recorded (Neh. chs. 8-10, cf. Ezr. Apoc. 9.37-55) that in the days of Ezra and Nehemiah a general gathering of the people took place in Jerusalem, which resulted in the promulgation of the Mosaic law and the observance of the Feast of Tabernacles. At the end of three and a half weeks of religious undertakings, a body of eighty-five members [1]), representing the heads of priestly and Levitical families and of the laity, affixed their signatures to the covenant, attesting to the rule of Mosaic law and adopting a theocratic state. This group is known later in rabbinic writings as "the Men of the Great Synagogue" [2]) and these men are also identified in parallel sources [3]) as "Ezra and his associates". Since the Rabbis also maintained that there existed a similar body during the Zadokite period, A. Kuenen [4]) and E. Bickermann [5]) argue that the Rabbis assigned a legendary body to this period to explain the gap in the chain of tradition between the last of the prophets and the Pairs of the Hasmonaean period. S. Zeitlin [6]), on the other hand, cites four such Great Assemblies during the era, and L. Finkelstein [7]) declares that this body is to be identified

---

[1]) A body of 85 elders, with 30 prophets present were responsible for the acceptance of Esther in the canon, see J. Meg. 70 d and R.R. on 2. 4 (pp. 53, 54). N. Krochmal, More, p. 97, identifies them with the signatories (Neh. 10. 2-28, which lists 22 priests with Nehemiah at the head of the list. Ezra is identified (Klausner, Historia I, p. 253) with Azaria, unless he is the one mentioned in Neh. 12. 33-18 Levites and 44 heads of state. See further Klausner's comment, Historia II, pp. 36,37 and H. Grätz, Die Große Versammlung, ihre Geschichtlichkeit, Zahl, Bedeutung, Zeit und Leistung, M.G.W.J., 6 (1857).

[2]) See Gen. R. on 17.5 (p. 394), compare J. Ber. 4a referring to Neh. 9. 7, also Ex. R. on 38.21 (p. 564) refers to Neh. 1.7, and Ex. R. on 31.18 refers to Neh. 9. 18 (p. 469). Since Nehemiah and the Levites mentioned in the above texts were represented in the body, the Rabbis maintained that they were the men of the Great Synagogue and were, therefore, responsible for the statement. See further M. Englander, The Men of the Great Synagogue, H.U.C. Jub. vol., p. 145 ff.

[3]) See Lev. R. on 1. 5 (p. 31), on the exposition of Cant. 7. 14, where it is stated: "The associates of Ezra". The same exposition is found in Cant. R. on 7. 14 (p. 302) with the variant "the men of the Great Synagogue".

[4]) In "Gesammelte Abhandlungen zur biblischen Wissenschaft", 1894, pp. 125-160, and H. L. Strack article "Große Synagoge" in Protestantische Real-encyclopädie XIX, 3 ed.

[5]) "Viri Magnae Congegationis", Revue Biblique, vol. 55, (1948). See the comments of Hoenig, G. Sanh. exc. XIV.

[6]) שמעון הצדיק וכנסת הגדולה, Ner Maʿaravi, New York, 1924; See further G. Allon, Toledoth Hayehudim Beʾereṣ Israel, vol. 2, p. 223, 224.

[7]) הפרושים ואנשי כנסת הגדולה, New York, 1950. For a review of the opinions mentioned, see G. F. Moore, Judaism III, pp. 7-11.

with the judiciary body of the Hasideans, the forerunners of the Pharisees.

Yet, from the days of the return of exiles, the sources do mention the gathering of assemblies (ἐκκλησία or συναγωγή) to decide important religious and national questions. Josephus [1]) uses the term "synagoge" in reference to a gathering by the high priest Jeshua and the governor Zerubabel of the people at Jerusalem to build the altar. In the days of Ezra [2]) a gathering (ἐκκλησία) is called to declare actions against intermarriage with foreigners. Nehemiah [3]) also convokes an ἐκκλησία μεγάλη to rebuke the oppressors. Similarly, Judah Maccabaeus and his brothers call [4]) an ἐκκλησία μεγάλη to decide on military operations at a time of national crisis, and in the presence of ἐκκλησία 'Ισραήλ [5]) they declare the days of rededication of the temple a national holiday. A further mention of a Great Synagogue [6]) (συναγωγῇ μεγάλη), composed of priests, elders and heads of state, is associated with the appointment of Simon Hasmonaean as a high priest and the prince of the people of God [7]) (Σαραμέλ).

The men of the Great Synagogue mentioned in the early rabbinic chain of tradition [8]), "Moses received the Law from Sinai and delivered it to Joshua, and Joshua to the Elders, and the Elders to the Prophets, and the Prophets delivered it to the Men of the Great Synagogue", are identified [9]) as the carriers of the oral tradition from the latter prophets Haggai, Zechariah and Malachi, who lived a half century before the days of Ezra and Nehemiah. In all probability, they were considered as the latter associates, the signatories of the

---

[1]) Ant. 11. 4. 1 § 75 compare Ezr. 3. 1. (אסף).

[2]) Ezr. 10. 1, the word קָהָל is rendered in Ezr. LXX., ad loc., ἐκκλησία.

[3]) Neh. 5. 7 and see the LXX rendition.

[4]) I Macc. 5. 16.

[5]) I Macc. 4. 59. Thus, in a letter sent to Aristobulus, the scribe, asking the Alexandrian Jewry to adopt the festival by the Great Assembly, Judas and the Gerousia are mentioned, II Macc. I. 10.

[6]) I Macc. 14. 28, see I Macc. 14. 19 where ἐκκλησία is mentioned.

[7]) I Macc. 14. 27. The reading in Greek is Σίμωνος τοῦ ἀρχιερέως ἐν Σαραμέλ should be rendered in Hebrew שִׁמְעוֹן הַכֹּהֵן הַגָּדוֹל וְשַׂר עַם־אֵל. See Charles, Apoc, and Pseud., I Macc. XIV n. 28, Compare the Hebraic title of the books of Maccabees rendered by Eusebius (Hist. Eccl. VI. 25. 2) as "Σαρβήθ Σαβαναιέλ" to denote סִפְרֵי בֵּית שָׂרֵי עַם־אֵל See the opinions of H. L. Strack, Introduction, p. 16; and S. Zeitlin, The First Book of Maccabees, Dropsie Edition, 1950, Appendix A.

[8]) Ab. I. 1, cf. p. 14 n. 3 on chain of tradition.

[9]) I.A.D.N. 1 (p. 2).

covenant mentioned above. Such men [1]) are later known as scribes
(γραμματεῖς), members of the ekklesia [2]) or the synagoge [3]), or as
elders (πρεσβύτεροι) of the gerousia [4]).

In the above rabbinic chain of tradition, three fields of activity
are designated to the men of the Great Synagogue. This is recorded
in a saying attributed to them [5]): "Be deliberate in judgement, and
raise up many disciples; and make a fence for the Torah". As for the
establishment of a judiciary system, Ezra was authorized to appoint
judges [6]) and judges are present in his days [7]). Ben-Sira [8]) (c. 200 B.C.)
also speaks of civil questions under the jurisdiction of the courts.
As for spreading the Judaic teachings among the people, Ezra with
the aid of Mebinim (teachers) [9]) explains and reads the Law, and the
Chronicler [10]) (c. 300 B.C.) describes the existing education system.
Ben-Sira also is pictured as the head of a school[11]). As for the enactments of measures to preserve the Mosaic law, since the days of
Ezra measures are taken against the children of intermarriage [12]),
and Nehemiah appoints[13]) a body of Levites to shut the gates of
Jerusalem in order to discourage transactions on the Sabbath.

The closing phase of the Great Synagogue is also mentioned in the

---

[1]) In Tannaitic literature the names of these men are not mentioned but in all
probability they were prominent teachers and members of the community. In
later periods "X the man of X", e.g., Jose ben Jochanan, the man of Jerusalem
connoted a prominent teacher. So Ἰσκαριώτης, a learned individual from Keriyoth
(Matt. 10. 4).

[2]) Sir. 38. 24, 33; 39. 10. The Hebrew Sir. renders סוֹפֵר and קָהָל; see Segal,
Sir., pp. 251, 252.

[3]) I. Macc. 7. 12.

[4]) See above n. 5 and refer to Hoenig, G. Sanh. exc. VII and VIII—presbyteroi, a synonym of geron, and compare L. Finkelstein, Pharisees II, p. 576 ff.

[5]) Ab. I. 1, see Z. Frankel, "Über den Lapidarstyl der talmudischen Historik,
M.G.W.J., 1851-52, p. 209.

[6]) Ezr. 7. 25.

[7]) Ib. 10. 14 (elders and judges).

[8]) Sir. 38. 33 (a scribe as a judge), 42.4b-5a (compare M.B.B. 5. 10) and ch. 18. 20

[9]) Neh. 8. 3, 7, compare I Chr. 25. 8 (mebin with a talmid).

[10]) II Chr. 17. 7-9; see further p. 81.

[11]) Sir. 51, 23 in Segal, Sir., p. 358, בְּבֵית מִדְרָשִׁי and in Greek ἐν οἴκῳ παιδείας,
an equivalent of musar (instruction); see Sir. 39. 8 (ib. v. 13 speaks of students)
and on limmud see Sir. 51. 28.

[12]) Ezr. 10. 3, where the children of a foreign woman are also expelled from the
Jewish community. Compare the halachic interpretation in b. Kid. 68 b and
J. Kid. 64 d.

[13]) Neh. 13. 22 on the prohibition of transferring goods on the Sabbath in the
days of Nehemiah, which is interpreted as a norm, see b. Shab. 123 b, J. ib. 16a.

above rabbinic tradition [1]), "Simon the Just was a prince [2]) of the Great Synagogue; he used to say: On three things does the world rest —on the study of the Law, on the [Temple] services and upon acts of kindness." In rabbinic sources [3]) there are four high priests serving at different times who are surnamed "Simon the Just". Therefore, the identity of the above-mentioned Simon is disputed among scholars [4]). Yet a non-rabbinic source, the first book of Maccabees [5]), does mention a Simon as a prince in connection with a Great Synagogue, and in that instance Simon is identified as Simon the Hasmonaean. The same author, in the Praise dedicated to Simon the Hasmonaean, describes his major activities which are identical with the above teaching attributed to Simon the Just. He writes (I Macc. 14.14, 15), "He strengthened all that were brought low of his people (an act of Kindness). He sought out the Law and put away the lawless and the wicked (the study of the Law). He glorified the sanctuary and multiplied the vessels of the Temple (the services)".

Thus, the rabbinic tradition supported by outside sources demonstrates that the vehicle of tradition (i.e., the process of religious affairs), in the period of Zadokite ministry and in the former years of the Hasmonaean period, was regulated by the consent of a general assembly convoked on important occasions [6]). The scholarly

---

[1]) Ab. I. 2 as translated by Hoenig, G. Sanh., p. 176 and see n. 4.

[2]) For the reading שָׂרֵי instead of שִׁירֵי see Hoenig G. Sanh., p. 33, Exc. 14

Simon captured Bet Sur and it was named after him מגדל שר. See Lichtenstein, H.U.C.A. 8-9, pp. 281, 282.

[3]) The following Simons are surnamed "the Just" in rabbinic literature: Simon I the son of Onias I (c. 280 B.C.) see Lev. R. on 11.5 (p. 176); M.T. 9 (pp. 14, 15) and Ant. XII. 2.5 § 43 renders Σίμων ὁ δίκαιος. Simon II, son of Onias II (c. 220 B.C.), see J. Yom. 43 c, d. Whereas Ant. XII § 387, cf. Bell. VII § 423, speaks of Onias III, son of Onias II, and not of Simon II, who was the latter father. This is explained since in Hebrew "son" denotes also "grandson" see b. Yeb. 62 b. Simon the Hasmonaean (c. 135 B.C.), see b. Meg. 11a (cf. Hoenig, G. Sanh., pp. 33, 34, 175) and Simon Kantharus, see b. Sot. 33 a and T. ib. 13. 6 (319. 9), and refer to Klausner, Historia IV, pp. 285, 286.

[4]) See G. F. Moore, "Simon the Righteous", Israel Abrahams Memorial Volume, 1927 and idem, Judaism, III, p. 8 ff.

[5]) I Macc. 14. 27, 28, so maintain L. Loew in "Gesammelte Schriften", Szegedin, 1881 and S. Hoenig, G. Sanh., p. 31 ff.

[6]) The mention of synagogue (Kenishtha or Qahal), convoked on important occasions in the years following the Zadokite period, see M.T. ch. 10 (p. 16). On "Kenishtha" see H. Lichtenstein, Die Fastenrolle, H.U.C.A. 8-9, pp. 297, 298 and for "Qahal" compare the practice mentioned in I Q.Sa I. 25, as referred to me by Dr. O. Betz.

men responsible for the religious activities were the Scribes, the teachers and the scriveners, who were under the leadership of the high priest.

THE SCRIBE

According to rabbinic tradition [1]) the period of the Zadokite ministry at the time of the appearance of Alexander the Great witnessed "the termination of prophecy"; prophets who were responsible for the propagation of the belief in Yahweh, the rights of men and the teachings of ethics and morals. The historic order of Hebrew prophecy begins with Moses (c. 1200 B.C.). The Rabbis [2]) consider him "the father and greatest of prophets", and this concept is founded upon the fact that through him the Law was given to Israel [3]). All later true prophets kept Israel in the same course outlined by Moses and along the lines of religious and moral development. Prophets appear throughout the period of Judges [4]). Samuel, at the outset of the First Jewish Commonwealth, was associated with the guild of prophets [5]), and great divined orators were present both in the Kingdom of Judea and that of Israel [6]). With the destruction of the First Temple, the prophetic activity continues in Babylon [7]), and with the restoration of the second house of Yahweh, the prophets reappear in Judea [8]). Traces of prophetic activities appear as late as the period of Nehemiah [9]).

The prophet [in Greek προφήτης (forthspeaker) and the Hebrew equivalent Nabi (mouthpiece, Ex. VII. 1)] is the orator of Yahweh's messages [10]). He is inspired with the holy-spirit (Ruah-Haqodesh) [11]),

---

[1]) See S.O.R. 30 (p. 65).

[2]) b. Meg. 13a, b. Yeb. 49 b.

[3]) Mal. 3. 22 (compare Deut. 33. 4) and Sir. 24. 23.

[4]) See Jud. 2. 1 ff and 4. 4.

[5]) The guild of Prophets at Newayoth see I Sam. 19. 18 ff. See "Prophets and Prophecy" by J. F. Mc Curdy in J. Enc.

[6]) As Elijah (in the days of Ahab), Elisha and their school of prophets, (II Kin. 2. 1 ff.) Amos, Hosea, Isaiah and Jeremiah.

[7]) As Ezekiel and Deutero-Isaiah.

[8]) As Haggai, Zechariah and Malachi.

[9]) As Deutero-Zechariah see Pfeiffer, Introduction, p. 611 and the false-prophets mentioned in Neh. 6. 14.

[10]) The prophet usually introduces his oracle or words with the statement "Thus saith Yahweh" (I Sam. 2. 27, 10. 18, II Sam. 7. 5, Is. 22. 15, Jer. 2. 5, Ez. 14. 21 and elsewhere).

[11]) Ruah Haqodesh (for the expression see Is. 63. 10) departs with the termination of prophecy T. Sot. 13. 2 (318.22). The "Spirit of Yahweh" speaks through the mouth of David (II Sam. 23. 2) and stirs Balaam (Num. 24. 2), Saul (I Sam. 10. 6) and others.

and the words uttered are considered divinely transmitted. It follows that the works achieved [1]) in his presence are also regarded divinely guided and inspired, and consequently in the days when prophets are lacking, a decision cannot be reached in case of important religious questions "until a prophet will come" [2]), who can render a true divine instruction. Thus, institutions or decisions formulated in the years prior to the Hasmonaean period [3]), which also witnessed "the termination of prophecy", are attributed to the prophets. The institution of reading the Scriptures periodically on the Sabbath, the national rest-day, and on Monday and Thursday, the marketdays, which was developed in the period of Ezra [4]), is also considered to have been directed under prophetic inspiration [5]). Psalms and especially forms of early liturgy, which are attributed to this era, are said to have been achieved under prophetic participation [6]). The Esther scroll, and consequently the Purim festival introduced in the Persian period [7]), are attributed to the prophets [8]). Therefore, literary works that found their origin later were excluded, and later authors, who wished to present their works as inspired writings had to cloak themselves with the mantle of great personalities of the past. It stands to reason why a work such as Ecclesiasticus (c. 200 B.C.) originating in the period of Zadokite ministry was later excluded from the canon; since the author was known to have lived after the termination of prophecy [9]). Yet a

---

[1]) For example, the erection of the Second Temple (Ezr. 6. 14) and the wall partitioning the temple yard are considered the work of the prophets, see I Macc. 9. 54.

[2]) See I Macc. 4. 46, compare M. Mid. I. 6, in connection with the concealment of the stones of the altar. I Macc. 14. 41 is in reference to the appointment of Simon the Hasmonaean as the high priest and not of the traditional Zadokite family. In Mishnaic literature: a decision awaits the arrival of Elijah the prophet, see M. Ed. 8. 7, M.B.M. 3.4, 5 and compare I Q.S. 9. 11.

[3]) During the Hasmonaean period the oral tradition was transmitted by the "Pairs". A decision (in this case concerning the law of corners of the field) was considered authoritative since it was transmitted by the prophets and the pairs, see M. Pea. 2.6. On T. Yad. 2. 16 (683. 24) see further Part C, p. 122.

[4]) See b. B.K. 82 a, compare J. Meg. 75a.

[5]) Compare above with the statement in Mech. on 15. 22 (p. 52 b).

[6]) J. Ber. 4d and b. Meg. 17b.

[7]) The festival is mentioned as a "Day of Mordechai", II Macc. 15. 36. For the historical background see J. Hoschander, The Book of Esther in the Light of History, Philadelphia, 1923.

[8]) J. Meg. 70d, R.R. on 2. 4 (p. 53).

[9]) Segal. Sir. pp. 45, 46 writes: "It is apparent ... that the sages deprived canonicity from the book of Ben-Sira not because they have counted it with the books of the Sadducees and the Minim, but because they were aware that the book was composed later than 'termination of vision and prophecy', after the Holy Spirit had departed from Israel".

later work, the Book of Daniel (c. 165 B.C.) produced at the close of the period, was included; the anonymous author assumed the ancient revered personality of Daniel [1]).

The early phase of the Zadokite period is linked with the latter activities of the prophets. It also served as a background for the formation of a new school—possibly initiated byEzra [2])—the school of Scribes, the scrivener-teacher. As early as in the days of the First Jewish Commonwealth, the Sofer (Scribe) [3]) occupies an important position in the king's court. As in the other countries of the Levant [4]), the Sofer was not merely an amanuensis but rather a clerk or a secretary whose duties were to read, to write and to interpret the different documents and correspondence. Yet in the days of prophetic activity the scribe was not consulted in matters concerning national policies nor religious questions. Inquiries on such matters of importance needed divine approval, and thus the Nabi was consulted—as was the case with the "Urim and Thummim" [5]) (objects connected with the breastplate of the high priest, and used as a medium for divine oracle for "revelation and truth"). A gloss in I Sam. 9.9 states: "Beforetime in Israel, when a man went to inquire of God [לִדְרוֹשׁ אֱלֹהִים] thus he spoke, come and let us go to the seer: for he that is now called a prophet was beforetime called a seer." Thus, in the days of Judean kings [6]) and later during the period of Babylonian exile [7]) and the years prior to the generation of Ezra [8]), the prophet is consulted and asked to relate the words of God. The scribe merely records the words of the orator-prophet as they are dictated to him [9]).

In the days following the restoration of the Second Temple inquiries

---

[1]) See Ez. 14. 20 (Daniel is included with the ancient saints, Job and Noah). Daniel is mentioned in a Ras-Shamra poem.

[2]) See b. B.B. 21b, "Ezra enacted for Israel that they should sit a scrivener next to another scrivener". This text is lacking in most manuscripts; yet compare the statement in b. Pes. 50b concerning the copyists. This refers mainly to the activities of the teachers which were common in the days of Ben-Sira (see p. 16 n. 11).

[3]) See Jer. 36. 12.

[4]) See G. R. Driver, Aramaic Documents of the 5th Century B.C., Oxford, 1957, pp. 18, 19.

[5]) See J. Enc. W. Muss-Arnolt article "Urim and Thummim"; See Josephus, Ant. III. 8. 9 (ἐσσήν λόγιον).

[6]) See for example, I Kin. 22. 7 (in the days of Jehoshaphat), II Kin. 19. 2 (in the days of Hezekiah), II Kin. 22. 13, 14 (in the days of Josiah).

[7]) See Ez. 20. 1.

[8]) Zech. 7. 1 ff.

[9]) Jer. 36. 4; 45. 1; 52. 59.

cannot be made directly of God; since the "Urim and Thummim" were missing [1]), and prophecy had departed from Israel. With the arrival of Ezra, the scribe replaces the prophet. Ezra is not only a proficient scrivener who records dutifully "the Law of Moses which Yahweh, God of Israel had given" [2]), but he is also endowed with a wisdom which enables him to make inquiries into the words of God (לִדְרוֹשׁ אֶת־תּוֹרַת יהוה). The Sofer is not like his forerunner, the Nabi, who can communicate directly with God; rather he can resort to explanations and interpretations of God's law in order "to fulfil it and to teach in Israel statutes and judgements" [3]). Since the scribe replaced the prophet, Ezra who is a scribe admonishes and calls for repentance as did his predecessors, the prophets. Only in early times the Nabi had declared the admonitions in oracles, whereas in the days of the Second Temple the scribe resorts to declarations and prayers of confessions [4]).

Along these lines Ben-Sira, a scribe living during the Zadokite period, describes the wisdom of the Sofer [5]): a) "He concentrates his thought on the Law of the Most High (i.e. the Law which Moses commanded) [6]). He will seek out (יִדְרֹשׁ) the wisdom of all the ancients (denoting the commandments [7])), and occupy himself with the study of prophecies, and pay attention to expositions of the famous men"—i.e., the scribe studies and expounds the written Law of Moses and the words of the prophets, and he also transmits the oral tradition. b) "He will resolve to rise early to the services of his Creator, and will make his petition to the Most High; he will open his mouth in prayer and beseech forgiveness for his sins"—i.e., the scribe resorts to prayers and petitions, thereby he can exhort the community and at the same time he can glorify the works of God [8]).

---

[1]) See Ezr. 2. 63 and refer to T. Sot. 13. 2 (318. 19); cf. Ant. III. 8, 9. § 218.

[2]) Ezr. 7. 6, compare ib. 7. 11.

[3]) Ib. 7. 10.

[4]) For example, Ezr. 9. 5 ff (compare Ezekiel's admonition in the form of an oracle, Ez. 14. 1 ff).

[5]) Sir. 38. 24, 39. 1-6 (compare Segal, Sir. pp. 251, 252 and notes) also quoted by Moore, Judaism I, pp. 40, 41.

[6]) Sir. 24.23

[7]) The Hebrew reads חָכְמַת כָּל הָרִאשׁוֹנִים and the Greek σοφία πάντων ἀρχαίων compare Matt. 5. 21 ἐρρέθη τοῖς ἀρχαίοις quoting from the Decalogue—not as Segal (Sir. p. 258 n. 2) assumes that it refers to apocalypses.

[8]) As it is found in the book of Ben-Sira (Sir. 39. 6 ff, 51.1 ff and elsewhere).

The scholarly man of the Zadokite period, the Sofer, was not only a γραφεύς [1]), a copyist who dutifully preserved and recorded the Sacred Scriptures, but he was also a γραμματεύς [2])—a scribe who can be compared with the Alexandrian grammarians in their methods applied to the Greek bible [3]). He was a teacher, of whom Ben-Sira says [4]): "He himself directeth counsel and knowledge, and setteth his mind on their secrets. He himself declareth wise instruction, and glorieth in the Law of God . . . His wisdom doth the congregation (ἐκκλησία = קָהָל) publisheth".

Our main concern is with the two areas of activity effected by the Soferim, a) collecting and preserving the Holy Scriptures, b) the transmission of oral interpretations and teachings.

THE ERA OF COLLECTING AND PRESERVING THE HOLY SCRIPTURES

The era of collecting and editing the Holy Scriptures is related in rabbinic tradition to the period of the "Men of the Great Synagogue" [5])—which we have designated in the days of the Zadokite ministry and the early years of the Hasmonaean period. The gathering and editing of older sources and the introduction of newer material is confined by two distinct times [6]). Its beginning is determined by the activities of Ezra and Nehemiah (the middle of the 5th cent. B.C.) and its close by the early works of the Hasmonaean family (the middle of the 2nd cent. B.C.) [7]). With the promulgation of the Mosaic law in the days of Ezra and Nehemiah, the first steps were taken to preserve the material of the earliest division of the Holy Scriptures. The date of the Samaritan schism is uncertain, but must fall within

---

[1]) As Symmachus renders the translation of Ps. 44.2.

[2]) As it is rendered by the LXX (see Concordance of the Septuagint I, Oxford, 1897, p. 275), and as found in the New Testament (see Theologisches Wörterbuch zum Neuen Testament I, p. 740 ff.).

[3]) See S. Lieberman, Hellenism, p. 20.

[4]) Sir. 39. 7-10.

[5]) See b. B. B. 15a, which indicates that Ezra was responsible for editing his own book and the Chronicles, whereas the Men of the Great Synagogue were responsible for Ezekiel, the Minor Prophets, Daniel and Esther (for the latter refer to p. 14 n. 1) . This implies that the Men of the Great Synagogue were responsible for the conclusion of the last two divisions—since the Minor Prophets close the second division and Daniel was the last written work of the Hagiographa.

[6]) See II Macc. II. 13, 14.

[7]) For a further discussion of the Jewish canon see L. Blau, Bible Canon in J. Enc., J. Fürst, Der Kanon des Alten Testaments nach den Überlieferungen in Talmud und Midrasch, Leipzig, 1868 and R. H. Pfeiffer, Introduction, ch. IV

the century 432-322 B.C. We may infer, therefore, that the Samaritan community adopted the Pentateuch as its bible soon after its canonization about 400 B.C. Ezra, in his diary, records passages from Leviticus and Deuteronomy [1]). In the covenant signed by the Great Assembly [2]) and in the declaration pronounced by the Levites [3]) references are made to the five books of Moses as if they were a published work. As for collecting and editing prophetic works, the statements made by Ben-Sira in his "Praise to the Fathers" and his description of a Sofer [4]) show that prior to his days (c. 200 B. C.) the second division of the Bible—namely the Former and Latter Prophets—was defined. A number of different sources mentioned by the Chronicler [5]) (c. 300 B.C.) were probably used in editing the historical books and the works of the prophets. In order to designate the close of the second division, the editors attached a canonical ending [6]) to the last book of the division, Malachi.

Other works not included in the above divisions and yet were in existence prior to the days of Ben-Sira [7]); or works which originated before the close of the Zadokite era, including compilations of different sources [8]), and works which received a religious stamp [9]), were designated in later times as [Holy] Writings [10]). Josephus

---

[1]) Ezr. 9. 11, 12 quotes with slight modifications Lev. 18. 27, Deut. 7. 3; 23. 7,
[2]) See Neh. 10. 31-40, which refers to Deut. 7. 3, Ex. 23. 12, 10, Lev. 25. 4; 6. 5, Ex. 23. 19 and Num. 18. 11 ff.
[3]) See Neh. 9. 6-37, with references to Gen. 1. 1; 11. 31; 17. 5; 15.6, 18, Ex. 2. 25; 14. 11; 9. 16; 14. 22; 15. 5; 13. 21; 19. 20; 16. 4; 17. 6; 32. 8, Deut. 1. 8; 29. 4; 5, 6.
[4]) Sir. 46-49. 10; 39. 2 and compare the introduction to the book by his grandson.
[5]) As for historical works mentioned, see II Chr. 16. 11; 24. 27; 25. 26; 27, 7; 28. 26 and for Prophetical works, see I Chr. 29. 29, II Chr. 9. 29; 12. 15; 32. 32.
[6]) The prophecy of Malachi is composed of oracles ending with the phrase "Saith Yahweh, Lord of Hosts". Therefore, the book should rightfully close with ch. 3. 21. The implication is that the last verses are additional and therefore a canonical ending, see L. Blau, Bible Canon, J. Enc. and Weiss, D. D. Wed. I, p. 32 n. 1 and p. 85.
[7]) Sir. 39. 2, 3 alludes to works such as Proverbs and Ecclesiastes with which the author seems to be acquainted, see Segal, Sir., p. 259 n. 3. While in his "Praise to the Fathers" references are made to Job. [49. 9], Psalms [47. 8], Proverbs [47. 17] and to Zerubabel and Nehemiah [49. 11-13] (i.e., the book Ezra-Nehemia, composed of diaries).
[8]) For example, Psalms, as attested in rabbinic tradition see b. B.B. 14b, 15a and compare Cant. R. on 4.4 (p. 180), and Proverbs, already referred to in the book, see Pr. 10. 1; 22. 17; 24. 23; 25. 1; 30. 1, 31. 1.
[9]) Such as the Book of Job and the Esther Scroll.
[10]) See b. B.B. 14 b and b. Sanh. 90 b; L. Blau, Bible Canon, J. Enc., and Bacher's Terminologie, כתובים.

(c. 38-95 A.D.) enumerates twenty-two books [1]) which he divides as follows: five books of Moses; thirteen histories containing the history of Israel from Moses' death down to Artaxerxes I written by the prophets (probably (1) Joshua, (2) Judges and Ruth [2]), (3) two books of Samuel, (4) two books of Kings, (5) the Chronicles, (6) Ezra and Nehemiah [3]), (7) Esther [4]), (8) Job [5]), (9) Isaiah, (10) Jeremiah and Lamentations [6]), (11) Ezekiel, (12) the twelve Minor Prophets [7]), (13) Daniel [8])) and four remaining books consisting of hymns and admonitions (probably (1) Psalms, (2) Song of Songs, (3) Proverbs, (4) Ecclesiastes). In regard to these books, he states [9]): "How firmly we have given credit to these books of our own nation is evident by what we do, for during so many ages as have already passed, no one hath been bold as either to add anything to them, to take anything from them, or to make any change in them". The testimony given by Josephus implies that the books of the Old Testament, containing the Pentateuch, the Prophets and Hagiographa, were already in the days prior to his generation (i.e., the Hasmonaean period) considered authoritative. Further evidence seems to support Josephus' testimony since in the days of the Hasmonaeans the books of the Old Testament (Pentateuch, the Historical and Prophetic Works and the Hagiographa) were copied and commented on even among the sectarians as the Qumran findings suggest. (See M. Burrows, More Light on the Dead Sea Scrolls, part 3, London, 1958). J. Finkel in "Essays on the Dead Sea Scrolls in Memory of E. L. Sukenik", p. 163 ff. (Jerusalem, 1961) shows that the story of Esther, the only scroll not found at Qumran (see M. Burrows, op. cit., p. 175), was known to the Qumran community. The Qumran community, like Paul later

---

[1]) Cont. Ap. I. 8, see Thackeray notes, ad loc., and H. L. Strack, Kanon des Alten Testaments, in Real-encyklopädie für protestantische Theologie und Kirche IX, 3 ed., Leipzig, 1901.

[2]) In b. B.B. 14b they are both considered to be written by Samuel, the prophet, and R. 1. 1 refers to the time of the Judges.

[3]) In b. B. B. 15 b they are considered as one, see Pfeiffer, Introduction, p. 813.

[4]) Since Josephus' histories contained the history of Israel until the days of Artaxerxes I, therefore the story of Esther according to Josephus took place in the days of said king, see Ant. XI. 6.

[5]) In b. B.B. 14 b, Job was considered an ancient work written in the days of Moses.

[6]) In b. B.B. 15a, Jeremiah wrote his book and also the Lamentations.

[7]) In Sir. 49. 10, the twelve Minor Prophets are considered as one unit.

[8]) Josephus places Daniel's activities during the reign of Nebuchadnezzar and the Persian kings as in the Old Testament, see Ant. X. 10.

[9]) Cont. Ap. I. 8 § 42;

(see O. Michel, Paulus u. seine Bibel, ch. 1, Gütersloh, 1929), had regarded highly the Deuteronomic scroll, the Book of Isaiah and the Minor Prophets, and the Psalms; thus lending equal authority to works from the Pentateuch, the Prophets and the Hagiographa. Barthélemy (see M. Burrows, ad loc.) remarked that the Book of Daniel apart from the rest of the Scriptures was not regarded sacred in the Qumran community. Yet sources attributed to the centuries 100 B.C.-100 A.D. such as the Book of Maccabees [1]), the Gospel according to Matthew [2]), the Book of Enoch preserved in the Ethiopic recension [3]), the Testament of Levi [4]) (of the latter two fragments were found at Qumran) and the decision of Shammai's academy [5]) make references to the Book of Daniel, which most scholars agree is the last edited work of the Hagiographa (c. 160 B.C.) [6]), and thereby confirming its authority. In the controversy which prevailed during the Herodian period in the seminaries of Shammai and Hillel [7]), over which books of the Hagiographa are considered sacred, reference is only made to Ecclesiastes, a work originating in the Zadokite period.

From the above evidence and from the fact that the work of Ben-Sira was considered as late as Amoraic times [8]) to be as authoritative as the other Holy Writings, we can assume that the establishment of the Hasmonaean dynasty (with fruitful literary activity during the period rejected by the seminaries as authoritative works) served as a terminus ad quem for the consideration of works as Holy Writings by the rabbinical academies. Thus, credit is due to the Scribes for collecting, editing and preserving a set of books—24 in number (so Ap. Ezr. 12.45) in addition to the Book of Ecclesiasticus—which were wholly transmitted to succeeding generations. It is also true that these men, by issuing and preserving the set of books, had in the same time discriminated against other works which are referred to by the Chronicler. Their motive can only be surmised and explained as follows: Books which were attributed to the prophets and had,

---

[1]) I Macc. 1. 54 compare Dan. 9. 27, I Macc. 2. 59, 60 compare Dan. 3, 6.
[2]) Matt. 24. 30, 31 refers to Dan. 7. 13, 14.
[3]) The vision in E. En. 85-91 is influenced by Dan. 8 and E. En. 46. 1, 4 refers to Dan. 7. 9, 14.
[4]) Test. L. 17. 1 refers to Dan. 9. 24.
[5]) See T. Sanh. 13. 3, the statement of Shammai's academy refers to Dan. 12. 2.
[6]) See Pfeiffer, Introduction, p. 23 and p. 764 ff.
[7]) See M. Ed. 5. 3.
[8]) See Segal, Sir., in the introduction, pp. 37-40.

thus, embodied in writing the revelation of God, or those which were used for the Temple liturgy were considered worthy. This was the case with the Pentateuch (referred by Ezra (Ezr. 9.11 ff.) as Words of the Prophets), the Former and Latter Prophets including Ruth and Lamentations, the Psalms, the Books of Job and Daniel (assumed to be the work of an ancient revered personality) [1]), the scroll of Esther (considered a prophetic work) [2]) and the works of Ezra, Nehemiah and the Chronicler which contained informations of the early days of the Temple. Works on wisdom and collection of songs which contain proverbs, love poems and gnomic sayings were, fortunately after much deliberation, included and not discarded or "put-away" (גנז) [3])—as was the case with similar works mentioned by the Chronicler. This was the case with the books of Ecclesiastes, Proverbs and Song of Songs.

Even in later generations objections were made against the inclusion of above mentioned books, and not until the days of Jamnia's council (c. 90 A.D.) were they declared sacred [4]). About the same time, the Rabbis declared that certain other books were not canonical [5]): "The Gospel and the books of the heretics do not contaminate the hands (i.e., they are not considered holy, since the restriction of defilement was levied in order to secure holy objects from mishandling [6])). The book of Ben-Sira [7]) and whatever books have been written since his time do not contaminate the hands."

As the Scribes were responsible for the transmission of Holy Scriptures, they were also responsible for the introduction of certain innovations in order to establish genuine texts [8]). They introduced

---

[1]) See p. 20 n. 1

[2]) Refer to p. 19 n. 8.

[3]) See A.D.N. (both recensions) ch. 1 and compare b. Shab. 30 b, where in later times the Rabbis declare Ecclesiastes and Proverbs worthy and not to be "put-away". The same was even applied to Ezekiel, see b. Shab. 13 b (refer to Moore, Judaism I, p. 247).

[4]) See for a fuller discussion Moore, Judaism I, part I, ch. II.

[5]) T. Yad. 2. 12, 13 (683.9 ff).

[6]) As the reason given by R. Jochanan ben Zakkai, (T. Yad. 2. 19 (684. 2), compare b. Shab. 14a and J. Sot. 18 a).

[7]) The Book of Ben-Sira was declared apocryphal along with the books of heretics, see b. Sanh. 100 b, whereas the books of Ecclesiastes, Proverbs and Canticles are attributed to Solomon, see Cant. R., the beginning (pp. 2,7). Thus, Ben-Sira was discriminated against, since the author did not disguise himself and had lived after the termination of prophecy. Other books, mentioned above, were penned anonymously and were, therefore, attributed to an early personage. See further p. 19 n. 9 and Moore, Judaism I p. 243.

[8]) See the work of Ch. Ginsburg, Introduction, ch. XI.

an Aramaic square script to facilitate writing [1]). While the Jews
have adopted the international script for preserving their books, the
Samaritans adhered to the original form in order to present themselves
as the veritable heirs of the ancient Hebraic tradition [2]). Other important innovations in the script are attributed to this era: the final
letters of M'N'Ṣ'P'Ḳ'[3]); the ornamentation of letters to indicate
differences between similar letters [4]); the division of consonants into
words [5]), and words into sentences [6]) (since letters were written
uninterrupted in a line), and the introduction of variants through the
medium of Qeri (to be read) and Ketib (to be written) [7]). The great
works of the Scribes in fixing the Biblical texts and especially that of
the five books of Moses (as attested by the Qumran findings) — of
which carefully annotated texts were kept in the Temple court as stand-
ards for further copying [8])—paved the road for the future school of

---

[1]) See T. Sanh. 4. 7 (421. 29).

[2]) See also b. Sanh. 21b (in the name of Mar Uqeba, c. 230 A.D.): "In the
beginning the Tora was given in a Hebrew-Canaanite script and the Holy Tongue,
then it was reissued in the days of Ezra in the Assyrian script and the Aramaic
tongue. The Israelites selected the Assyrian script and the Holy Tongue and have
left for the commoners the Hebrew Canaanite script (as attested by the coins found
from that period) and the Aramaic tongue. Who are the commoners? the Samaritans". See further the introduction of E. Ben-Yehuda to his dictionary, p. 95 ff
and see b. Zeb. 62a—the introduction of Assyrian script is considered the work
of the Prophets.

[3]) b. Meg. 2b: "M'N'Ṣ'P'Ḳ' (final letters) the prophets have declared",
compare J. Meg. 71d "M'N'Ṣ'P'Ḳ'(the final letters written in the scroll) due to
Halacha from Moses on Sinai" indicating an early dating for the innovation.
Compare the writings of the Qumran texts.

[4]) Known as Taggin (crowns). There is a book on Taggin (of medieval times),
see Eisenstadt, Oṣar Hammidrashim (New York, 1915), p. 564, which ascribes
ornamentations to hoary times. Yet the employment of ornamentations to indicate
a distinction between similar square letters (e.g., Resh and Dalet, Ḥet and He,
Bet and Kaf, see Tan. printed, Gen. I. 1) is noted in Qumran scrolls. Matt. 5. 18
mentions ϰεραία (Tagga), see Billerbeck, Kommentar I, p. 248.

[5]) Division of words can be noted from a comparative study of the Septuagint
e.g., Am. 6. 12 Massora renders בַּבְּקָרִים (with oxen) while LXX בְּבָקָר־יָם (with

the oxen of the sea) for further analysis see W.O.E. Oesterley, Introduction to
the Old Testament, London, 1934, p. 18 ff.

[6]) b. Ned. 37 b on "to understand the reading" (Neh. 8. 8) explains "division
of sentences" (compare b. Hag. 6 b). See also b. Kid. 30 a and Moore, Judaism
I, p. 303 ff.

[7]) See b. Ned. 37 b: "To be read and not to be written etc. is Halacha of Moses
on Sinai", indicating an early dating. As noted in the omission of the name of God
in the Qumran texts, see Isaiah roll ed. Burrows, plate XXXIII. See further A.
Sperber, H.U.C.A. XVII, p. 293-390.

[8]) See T. Sanh. 4. 7 (421. 17) compare Sifre Deut. § 160 (105b) n. 6. On ib.
§ 365 (148b) see Lieberman, Hellenism, p. 21 ff.

Masoretes in later centuries, as noted in the works of Rabbi Aqiba (c. 130 A.D.) and those of Jamnia's academy [1]).

The Oral Tradition

The generations of Scribes were instrumental in the issuance of written books, which were accepted as revealed and sacred works in their times and in successive generations. The Scribes also acted as teachers who interpreted and explained the contents of the texts with their archaic phraseology, idioms and terminology which was un-familiar to the common people who spoke a language different from the ancient Hebrew [2]). Thus, the efforts of the teachers-scribes resulted in translations of the texts and in the introduction of dots and possibly other signs in their copies which served as an aid in instruct-ing the people.

A rendering of the Law in the spoken language is recorded in the narrative describing the epoch-making day during Ezra's time. It relates [3]): "So they read in the book, the Law of God, rendering it [in the vernacular] [4]) and gave it sense and they were given to under-stand the reading". Expounding the Holy Scriptures in the vernacular in the public places and the synagogues [5]) made the Pentateuch the living heritage of the new colony. No wonder Josephus says at the close of the era [6]): "For although such long ages have now passed, no one ventured either to add, or to remove or to alter a syllable (so Matt. 5.17-19) and it is an instinct with every Jew, from the day of his birth, to regard them as the decrees of God to abide by them and if need be, cheerfully to die for them (so in the early days of the Macca-bees)".

The early exegesis and interpretation of the former Scribes can be noticed in the translations of the Pentateuch. Two such works have their origin before the close of the period of the Scribes. A Greek rendition, attributed to seventy-two Palestinian scholars and known as the Septuagint, is said to have been commissioned under Ptolemy

---

[1]) See Ch. Ginsburg, Introduction, Pfeiffer, Introduction, p. 73 ff and P. Kahle, The Cairo Geniza, London, 1947, and his other monumental works on the Maso-retes in "Masoreten des Westens" und "Masoreten des Ostens".

[2]) See Neh. 13. 24 and refer to Klausner, Historia I, p. 311.

[3]) Neh. 8. 8.

[4]) See Klausner, Historia I, p. 293 and compare b. Meg. 3a and the rendering in LXX (Ezr. 18. 8 and Ezr. Apoc. 9.48).

[5]) See further pp. 143, 148.

[6]) Cont. Ap. I. 8 § 42.

Philadelphus (285-247 B.C.) [1]), more probably it was issued by Alexandrian scribes for the Greek-speaking Jews [2]). An Aramaic translation (Targum) [3]) that was perfected by the post-Destruction schools for Palestinian and Babylonian Jewries (of which two such works are extant now; the Targum of Onkelos [4]), a Babylonian edition and Targum Pseudo-Jonathan, a Palestinian edition [5])) contains early interpretations transmitted orally by the translators (meturgeman)—teachers of the past.

The main feature of the method of interpretation introduced by the Scribes is noted in the brevity and direct rendering of the difficult verses, which also employs known terms to illuminate the forgotten meaning. The latter application is adopted by the Chronicler when introducing difficult verses from older sources [6]). The following examples introduced in the two translations of the Pentateuch reflect the above methodology: a) In case one deposits his valuables in a friend's house and they are stolen, Ex. 22.7 states: וְנִקְרַב בַּעַל־הַבַּיִת אֶל־הָאֱלֹהִים (which according to parallel law of Hammurabi § 37 should be rendered "then the master of the house shall come near unto the gods"). The Scribes interpreted the text according to present-day practices. Thus, the Septuagint renders (LXX ib. 22.8) καὶ ὀμεῖται for וְנִקְרַב. Its parallel is found in a Tannaitic source (Mech., p. 97b) based on oral tradition [7]): לִשְׁבוּעָה (by declaring an oath). The word אֱלֹהִים (gods) is defined in Onkelos לְקֳדָם דַּיָּנַיָּא (before the judges) [8]); as indicated by the same Tannaitic source: בְּבֵית־דִּין (in the

---

[1]) See Arist. §§ 41-50, b. Meg. 9a.

[2]) See H. B. Swete, Introduction to the Old Testament in Greek, 2 ed., Cambridge, 1914 and Pfeiffer, Introduction, p. 104 ff.

[3]) Targum denotes any translation including Greek see J. Kid. 59 a referring to Aquila's.

[4]) See P. Kahle, The Cairo Geniza, A. Geiger, Urschrift, pp. 162-167 and on the dependancy of the Syriac translation (Peshitto) on Onkelos see J. M. Schönfelder, Onkelos und Peshitto, München, 1869.

[5]) See S. Baer, Über den Geist des Jeruschalmi (Pseudo Jonathan) M.G.W.J., 1 (1851-1852); L. Zunz G.V.d.J., pp. 65-86 and P. Kahle, Cairo Geniza.

[6]) for example, I Chr. 15. 29 מְפַזֵּז וּמְכַרְכֵּר for II Sam. 6. 16 מְרַקֵּד וּמְשַׂחֵק, I Chr. 13. 8 וּבִמְנַעְנְעִים וּבְצֶלְצְלִים for II Sam. 6.5 וּבִמְצִלְתַּיִם וּבַחֲצֹצְרוֹת, II Chr. 9.17 טָהוֹר for I Kin. 10. 18 מוּפָז Note also the paraphrasing in the Chronicles.

[7]) As it is apparent from the second case cited Ex. 22. 10.

[8]) Compare Onkelos on Ex. 21. 6 and see Mech. on 21. 6 (83b).

court-house). b) Ex. 22.17 declares: מְכַשֵּׁפָה לֹא תְחַיֶּה ("Thou shall not suffer a sorceress to live", since in ancient times women practiced witchcraft[1])). The Scribes explain the law relevant to all who deal with sorcery. Thus, the Septuagint renders (LXX ib. 22.18) Φαρμακοὺς οὐ περιποιήσετε as does the Jerusalemian Targum: כָּל עֲבִיד חַרְשִׁיוּתָא לָא תְקַיְימוּן which concurs with the Tannaitic source (Mech., p. 100b) אִשָּׁה אֶחָד אִישׁ וְאֶחָד (either man or woman). c) Lev. 23.15 states that the reckoning of the Pentecost should follow מִמָּחֳרַת הַשַּׁבָּת (lit. "from the morrow after the Sabbath"[2])), a date which also permits the eating of new bread (ib. 23.11). The scribes inserted in the text describing the event of eating the new bread in the days of Joshua (Jos. 5.11) the reading מִמָּחֳרַת הַפֶּסַח [3]) (from the morrow after the day of slaughtering the Paschal lamb), which confirms the later Pharisaic opinion (Sifra, p. 100d, b. Men. 65a) מִמָּחֳרַת יוֹם־טוֹב, i.e., the count should follow the day after the holiday (the first day of Passover). In the same manner, the Septuagint (ib. 23.11) renders τῇ ἐπαύριον τῆς πρώτης and the Targum מִבָּתַר יוֹמָא טָבָא [4]). d) Deut. 6.8 [5]) states: "And thou shalt bind them for a sign upon thy hand, and they shall be טֹטָפֹת (head-dress [6])) בֵּין (lit. between) thine eyes". The type of signs or bands referred to in the law was explained by the Scribes as prayer-capsules containing Biblical texts [7]) which were placed firmly on the head and upon the hand. Thus, the Septuagint renders ἀσάλευτον, immovable. These objects became known among the Aramaic-speaking Jews as תְּפִילִין (so Targum, ad loc.), prayer-objects or among the Greek-speaking

---

[1]) See I Sam. 28. 7 and see Ab. 2. 7 and J. Hag. 77 d, 78 a.

[2]) The later view of the Sadducees, whereas the LXX, ad loc., renders the literal translation in contrast to 23. 11.

[3]) The reading is lacking in LXX (codices Alexandrinus and Vaticanus).

[4]) Whereas the Peshitta (the Syriac Christian tradition) and the Falashas (see Tarbiz, VII, pp. 129, 378, 387) explain it as the last day of Passover which is also a holiday (Lev. 23. 8).

[5]) See also Ex. 13. 16 and Deut. 11. 18. Refer to Frankel, Palästinische Exegese, p. 89.

[6]) See M. Shab. 6. 1 and Targum on II Sam. 1. 10 for אֶצְעָדָה. Compare Nachmanides' commentary on Ex. 13. 16.

[7]) Samples of prayer-capsules were discovered at the Dead Sea area. See Discoveries in the Judean Desert II ed. Benoit, J. T. Milik and De Vaux, p. 80, containing texts from Ex. 13. 1-10, 11-16, Deut. 6. 4-9, 11.13-21, compare b. Men. 34b, see further K. G. Kuhn, Phylacterien aus Höhle 4 von Qumran, Heidelberg, 1957.

Jews as φυλακτήρια (so Matt. 23.5). The rendering πρὸ in the Septuagint for the Hebrew word בֵּין also denotes the halachic ruling (Mech., p. 26a, Sifre Deut. § 35 (75a)) בְּגוֹבָה שֶׁל רֹאשׁ (at the crown of the head) and not directly between the eyes; so, too, is it rendered in the Palestinian Targum [1]).

The above examples demonstrate the employment of existing customs and traditions in the translations effected by the Scribes. These explanations were later inserted in the Oral Law (i.e., the Tannaitic literature). They can be recognised by the brief form of the statements and in the discussions of early schools based on the statements [2]). Thus, the Palestinian Amoraim (interpreter-teacher) [3]) attributed to the Men of the Great Synagogue (i.e. the scribe) the systematization of the Midrash (the exegesis), Halachoth (the formulated rules) and Aggadoth (expositions) [4]).

The type of Midrash employed by the Scribes can be noticed in the work of the Chronicler [5]) (c. 300 B.C.). He describes present institutions and practices and attributes them to an early personage, thereby placing their origin in early times to lend them authority. In his endeavour the Chronicler raises the prestige of the Levites, from whose rank came the Temple singers and gatekeepers [6]). This form of Midrash is adopted also by later writers and teachers, such as the author of Jubilees who ascribes customs and institutions to generations prior to the days of Moses to demonstrate their antiquity. In the same manner, the Chronicler places the judicial reorganization during the reign of Jehoshaphat (II. Chr. 19.5-11), a play on the king's name meaning "Jeho had judged". He also interjects moral explanations [7])

---

[1]) On Deut. 6. 8: וִיהַוֹון לִתְפִילִין עַל מוֹקְדָךְ כְּלוֹ קָבֵיל עַל עֵינָךְ.

[2]) The rule in M.B.M. 3. 1, to take an oath in court in case the deposited valuable is stolen, is based on early decision; see M. Shebu. 5. 1, on which the disciples of R. Aqiba comment. The Rabbis at Jamnia comment on the death penalty meted out to a man practicing witchcraft, see M. Sanh. 7. 11. The date of Pentecost was debated in the days of the Pharisees and Sadducees, see M.T. 1 (pp. 3, 4). The findings at the Dead Sea area point to an early application of the prayer-capsules.

[3]) J. Shek. 48 c.

[4]) On definition of Halachah Aggadah and Mishnah, see S. Schechter, Studies in Judaism III on Talmud, W. Bacher, Terminologie אגדה, הלכה, מדרש and H. L, Strack, Introduction, part I, ch. 1.

[5]) See Pfeiffer, Introduction, p. 785 ff and A. C. Welch, The Work of the Chronicler: Its Purpose and its Date, London, 1939.

[6]) for example, I Chr. 25, 26.

[7]) for example, I Chr. 10. 13 (on Saul), II Chr. 21. 12-20 (lacking in II Kin. 8). No

for the collapse and defeat of the king's rule, and attributes the plague in the days of David to the work of God's adversary [1]). In his work, the Chronicler discredits the claim of the Jewish antagonists, the Samaritans, that Mount Gerizim is the abode of Yahweh by showing that the Temple in Jerusalem in all its glory was the appointed place of Yahweh [2]). In later years the author of Judith writes with the same purpose [3]).

The type of halachoth transmitted orally by the Scribes can be traced in the translations of the Pentateuch—as demonstrated above— and also in the different signs inserted in the copies of the Pentateuch. An exhibition of an early result in textual criticism on the part of the scribes is noted by the ten extraordinary points found in the Penta- teuch [4]). The insertion of points above a given text was employed by ancient scribes to denote the erasure of the word [5]). Yet the presence of these critical marks does point to an existing explana- tion that can be only surmised [6]). Three such notes do prevail on halachic conclusions that were probably orally transmitted. a) The law requires the observance of a second Paschal ceremony if, and only if, the person is defiled or is unable to observe the prescribed ceremony in the month of Nisan since he dwells in a far-away place (בְדֶרֶךְ

רְחוֹקָה); Num. 9.10. The critical mark on the "He" (which is grammati-

---

mention is made of Solomon's intermarriage, see II Chr. 9, compare I Kin. 11 and Neh. 13. 26, For he was responsible for the erection of the first Temple and thus, according to the Chronicler, no misdeeds can be attributed to Solomon. He also refrains from designating David's sons as priests (I Chr. 18. 17, Cf. II Sam. 8. 18).

[1]) I Chr. 21. 1. The Satan is only mentioned in later works, see the prologue to Job (1. 6) and Zech. 3. 1.

[2]) See Pfeiffer, Introduction, p. 808 ff.

[3]) See A. Büchler, Studies, part 2, p. 73 ff.

[4]) See I A.D.N. 34. 4 (p. 51a), compare Num. R. on 3. 39 (p. 91, 92) and Sifre Num. § 69 (18 a); refer to Lieberman, Hellenism, p. 43 ff.

[5]) As noted in the Isaiah scroll found at Qumran, ed. Burrows, pl. XXXIII. This explanation is rendered by the Rabbis, see I A.D.N. 34. 4, "So intended Ezra (who according to rabbinic tradition established the school of scribes): If Elijah (who according to tradition will decide the correct readings of the Pentateuch) will come and say: why have you written so? I shall say unto him: I have already placed points above the text—denoting an error in the text, If he will say: you have written correctly, I shall remove the points above the text".

[6]) The interpretation by the early school, the disciples of R. Aqiba, see b. Sanh. 43 b, b. Men. 87 b and M. Pes. 9. 2. The rule was employed by R. Shimeon ben Elazer (c. 200 A.D.). Gen. R. 78 (p. 927): "Where one finds the written letters are in excess to the points, you can employ exegesis for the written letters; if the points are in excess to the letters, than you can employ exegesis for the points"; whose opinion is further discussed at the school of R. Judah (c. 200 A.D.), J. Pes. 36 b.

cally correct [1]) widens the rule; even a person who lives in the proximity of the Temple but is unable to reach the threshold of the temple-court and one who is defiled, they can be excused from the ceremony and can participate, instead, in the ceremony of the Second-Passover [2]). b) It is related (Num. 3.39) that Moses and Aaron took a count of the number of male Levites in order to bestow upon them the Temple duties by releasing the first-born in exchange. The name "Aaron" in the verse is marked which can be explained as an error since the declaration was made only to Moses. The Rabbis explain this extraordinary note to imply that Aaron was not included in the exchange. This explanation in turn can result in a halachic consequence that, in as much as the rest of the Levites are exempted from the priestly rule which requires the redemption of the first-born with a payment to the priest [3]),Aaron's children (i.e. the priest's), on the other hand, fall under this rule [4]). c) For judging the contents of a given Meal-offering a measure cup of "Issaron" was used. In cases where the contents exceeded the limit of one measure it was unlawful to measure it in any other manner. The implication of this rule is connoted by the critical point above the "waw" of Issaron in Num. 29.15 [5]).

Another type of critical marks found in the Pentateuch is the inverted Nuns—which is referred to by the Rabbis as σημεῖα = סִימָנִיּוֹת [6]). These marks are explained either as signs designating a dislocation of the verses or as an indication that the enclosed section is a separate book [7]). Following the latter implication the Rabbis employed the rule: "A Torah-scroll that contains eighty-five errors as the portion of ···וַיְהִי בִּנְסֹעַ הָאָרֹן (Num. 10.35, 36 where these marks are found) should be emended and then used for reading" [8]). Another

---

[1]) Since דֶּרֶךְ is also of a feminine gender see b. Kid. 2b.

[2]) Mentioned in Num. 9 and see M. Pes. 9. 3.

[3]) See Num. 18. 16 and M. Bech. 8. 7.

[4]) The formulated halachah, on the other hand, excludes the priests from redeeming the first-born, see M. Bech. 2.1. Based on the argument that they are also considered Levites (Ez. 44. 15), see b. ib. 4a.

[5]) See M. Men. 9. 1 and b. ib. 87 b.

[6]) See b. Shab. 115 b, 116 a and I A.D.N. 34 (50a), refer to Lieberman, Hellenism, p. 38 ff. Compare the "nun" signs in I.Q.S. ed. Burrows, pl. IV.

[7]) See Sifre Num. § 84 (22 a) the opinions of R. Judah and R. Shimeon (c. 200 A.D.).

[8]) J. Meg. 71 c.

similar ruling was that a scroll which contains eighty-five letters is considered holy [1]).

The Scribes, as copyists of the Law, employed in their work helpful signs or critical notes connoting for the early schools of Rabbis halachic conclusions. These marks were examined in the same way the Alexandrian grammarians treated the critical signs in the classical texts [2]). In Talmudic times verbal-marks on given Mishnaic texts were used to remember orally a whole given lecture [3]).

The type of Halachic collections transmitted by the Scribes to later generations were remembered orally by their quantitative structure of which some are still found in our present Mishnah-text and are based on Pentateuchal rulings, e.g., "Four principal categories of damages" (M.B.K.I.1) [4]); "Five species (of cereal) are subject to the priest share of the dough" (M. Hal. I. 1) [5]); and "Thirty-six [transgressions which are punishable with] excision" (M. Ker. I. 1) [6]). Thus Epiphanius [7]) speaks of the collection of the tradition of the elders as παραδόσεις τῶν πρεσβυτέρων δευτερώσεις (Heb. מִשְׁנָיוֹת) [8]) and attributes one such collection to the Hasmonaeans [τῶν υἱῶν Ἀσαμωναίου] (cf. Schürer, G.J.V. I, p. 113 n. 1.; p. 122 n. 24). As the Hasmonaeans were responsible for collecting the Holy Scriptures [9]) edited by the Scribes, so it can be assumed they were also instrumental in gathering the different collections of oral tradition, i.e.,

---

[1]) See Sifre Num. § 84 (22 a), referring to T. Yad. 2. 10 (683. 2), and see also b. Shab. 116a which permits the Holy Scriptures to be retreated in case of fire on the Sabbath—a definition of their sacredness.

[2]) See Lieberman, Hellenism, p. 41 ff.

[3]) See Bacher, Terminologie סִימָן. e. g. the mnemonic sign given by Nachman ben Isaac (c. 350 A.D.), b. Ket. 6a and other signs found in Talmud, b. Meg. 31a, ib. 27 b and b. B.M. 21 b denoting lectures beginning with the letters. See further b. Erub. 54b and B. Gerhardsson, Memory and Manuscript, ch. 11, part D.

[4]) Referring to Ex. 21. 28-32 (the goaring ox), ib. 21. 33, 34 (the pit), ib. 22. 4 (for the expression מַבְעֶה see the Samaritan recension cited in Frankel, Palästinische Exegese, p. 108), ib. 22. 5 (the fire). Thus, the Scribes classified the categories according to the order of the Scriptures, see Rashi, M.B.K. 1. 1.

[5]) Based on the Biblical expression לֶחֶם (leavened bread) in Num. 15. 19. The five sorts of cereal are mentioned according to J. Hal. 57 b in Is. 28. 25.

[6]) The expression כָּרֵת (excision) is mentioned in the Pentateuch in these 36 cases, see Rashi on the Mishnah.

[7]) Haereses 33. 9 (ed. Holl I. 459) see H. L. Strack, Introduction, p. 249, n. 25. Epiphanius erroneously defines Mishnah as Second Book, whereas it denotes Oral Teachings, compare Arabic "Sunna".

[8]) See J. N. Epstein, Meb. Les. Hat., p. 17.

[9]) See above p. 22 n. 6

the halachoth originating with the Scribes. Ben-Sira, too, speaks [1]) of
dusting scales and balances and cleaning measures and weights. So
does the Mishnah prescribe the brief rule [2]): "A shopkeeper must wipe
his measures twice a week and wipe off his weights once a week and
wipe his scales every time he uses them."

Other types of halachic formulations consist of decrees (Gezeroth)
and enactments (Taqqanoth); the former designates prohibitions and
the latter ordinances of a positive nature [3]). The Gezeroth and Taqqanoth are known to have been issued in the days of Ezra and Nehemiah.
In the covenant signed by the Great Assembly two enactments
(Miswoth) and two decrees are mentioned: a) An ordinance which
requires the payment of a third a shekel—a reduction in value was
necessary to comply with the economic situation of their times [4]).
b) An ordinance to deliver a wood-offering at appointed times by
selected families. These occasions became important days of celebration during the Second Temple era [5]). c) A decree against intermarriage
was extended in the days of the Hasmonaeans [6]) to cohabitation with
foreign woman. d) A decree against transactions on the Sabbath was
enforced by closing the gates of Jerusalem [7]).

The interpretations found in the translations of the Pentateuch
also shed light on the correct vocalisation of the words. This is known
as "Miqra Soferim" [8]) (the reading prescribed by the scribes), from
which the noted rule: "there is a basis for the reading" [9]) was applied
since the days of Shammai. The correct reading of a given text entailed
halachic consequences as illustrated: a) Lev. 12.5 reads: "If she gave
birth to a maidchild, then she shall be unclean שבעים". The vocalisation
of the word can read either שְׁבָעִים (seventy days) or שְׁבֻעַיִם (two weeks).
The "Translations" confirm the accepted scribal reading of "two

---

[1]) See Sir. 42. 4. Ben-Sira also mentions in ch. 42 the law of inheritance (compare M.B.B. 8.1) and a transaction was made by a written document (cf. T.B.B.
10. 12 (412. 25)).

[2]) M.B.B. 5. 10.

[3]) See Bacher, Terminologie, תקנה, גזרה.

[4]) See M. Shek. 2.4 (didrachmon). Refer to Krauss, Talmudische Archäologie
II, p. 405, and Matt. 17. 24.

[5]) See M. Taan. 4.5 and compare Bell. 2. 17. 6. § 425

[6]) See b. A.Z. 36 b.

[7]) Neh. 13. 22.

[8]) See b. Ned. 37 b which cites the examples: ארץ in pausa, and מצרים, שמים
read with a consonantal "Yod". See Oṣar Hageonim, Nedarim, p. 35.

[9]) For the school of Tannaim who adopt the rule see b. Sanh. 4 a.—from the
days of Shammai until Juda the Prince (c. 1-200 A.D.).

weeks" [1]). b) Ex. 23.19 reads: "Thou shalt not seethe a kid in his mother's חלב", it can be rendered either as חֵלֶב (fat) or חָלָב (milk). The "Translations" in this case are in accord with the later halachic view [2]), i.e., in the milk [3]).

The emendations of the scribes (Tiḳḳuney Soferim) [4]) can at best demonstrate the early application of Aggadah (a religious and moral instruction and edification which reflects also the theological concepts of the teachers), the form of interpretation introduced by the Scribes. In the "Translations" [5]) and the work of the Chronicler [6]) the Scribes removed phrases denoting anthropomorphism. They also employed euphemism for indelicate expressions [7]); a form of rendition that can be traced in the Chronicles, the qeri-readings introduced by the Scribes [8]) and in the suspended letters as the "'ayin" in מִיַּעַר (Ps. 80.14) [9]) and the "nun" in מְנַשֶּׁה (Jud. 18.30) [10]).

This can be summarized: the Scribes, in the period of collecting the

---

[1]) See b. Sanh. 4 a (b. Zeb. 38 a). Onkelos reads מְסָאֲבָה אַרְבְּעָה עֲסַר. Peshitta:

ܡܣܒ̈ܐ ܢܫܘܐ ܐܪܒ̈ܥܐܠܒ̈ܐ ܗܘܐ ܐ and LXX: καὶ ἀκάθαρτος ἔσται δὶς ἑπτὰ ἡμέρας. Compare Jub. 3. 11.

[2]) See Mech. on 23. 20 (p. 109a) compare b. Sanh. 4b and the Halachah in M. Hul. 8. 1. Onkelos reads: לָא תֵיכְלוּן בְּשַׂר בַּחֲלָב, Peshitta: "ܠܐ ܬܐܟܠ ܗܓ̈ܪܐ

ܟܠܒ̈ܐ ܘܐܪܡܗ and Septuagint: οὐχ ἑψήσεις ἄρνα ἐν γάλακτι μητρός αὐτοῦ.

[3]) Probably as a negation of the Canaanite practices. See U. Cassuto, The Godess Anath (Jerusalem, 1951), p. 40. Cf. Maimonides, Moreh, part 3 ch. 48.

[4]) Tanh. (regular ed.) Beshalach § 16 states "It is the correction of the scribes, the Men of the Great Synagogue" and refers to the emendation of Zech. 2. 12 עֵינִי עֵינוֹ for עֵינִי (God's eye). See Ex. R. on 10. 1 (p. 151) and on 21. 1 (p. 363) and refer

to Lieberman, Hellenism, p. 28 ff, Ginsburg, Introduction, chs. IX, XI, and Geiger, Urschrift, p. 30 ff.

[5]) See Frankel, Palästinische Exegese, p. 30 ff. For the employment of מֵימְרָא

in Targums see Billerbeck, Kommentar II, pp. 302-333.

[6]) For example, II Chr. 7.7 for I Kin. 8. 64 and p. 32 n. 1. In the same way the Chronicler omits all expressions for idolatry see II Chr. 32. 14 and compare II Kin. 18. 33, 34, 35. Refer also to Pfeiffer, Introduction, p. 87.

[7]) See Ginsburg, Introduction, chs. VIII, XI. The Chronicler employs delicate expressions for the narrative in I Chr. 10. 12 גּוּפַת for גְּוִיַּת (I Sam. 31. 12), I Chr.

10.9, 12 deletes וַיִּכְרְתוּ and וַיִּשְׂרְפוּ (I Sam. 31. 9) and I Chr. 10. 12 וַיִּשְׂאוּ for

וַיִּקְחוּ (I Sam. 31. 12) and I Chr. 15. 29 omits the derogatory statement made by

Michal, compare II. Sam. 6. 20.

[8]) T. Meg. 4. 39, 40 (228, 20); see Geiger, Urschrift, p. 385 ff.

[9]) I A.D. N. 34 (p. 50b), compare T. Sanh. 14. 7, 8, 9 (437. 9-16).

[10]) See b. B.B. 109b.

Holy Scriptures, were dutifully preserving the text in its exact written form and were transmitting along side the tradition governing the explanation of the given texts with instructions touching different religious and civil questions, enactments and ordinances. The greater application of hermeneutic rules and analytical study of the Biblical sources is manifested only after the era of the Scribes. The Scribes and teachers in the generations following the Zadokite period were active in two main areas: a) in preserving, interpreting and imitating the set of books edited by the former scribes which was authoritative in their times (see further Part C), b) in furthering and broadening the scope of oral tradition which resulted in the issuance of new rules and decrees to guide the Jewish people (see further Part C).

In the years prior to the Hasmonaean period, the Zadokite priests and members of the aristocratic classes embraced Hellenism, for which they were rejected by a great number of the people. On the other hand the pious religious teachers (Ḥasidim) [1], from among the common folk, and the members of the Hasmonaean family adhered to the true teachings of Judaism as formulated by the Scribes of old. The followers of the Hasidim are recognised by modern scholars [J. Klausner, Historia III, lecture 8; L. Finkelstein, The Pharisees, ch. 21; G. F. Moore, Judaism I, ch. 5, and K. Kohler's article, "Pharisees", in J. Enc.] to be the Essenes and the Pharisees; whereas the descendants of the Zadokite family are identified with the Sadducees. The Hasmonaean revolt caused the removal of the Zadokite heirs from the high priesthood and in their stead installed the descendants of the Hasmonaean family as high priests and leaders of the state. This change gave rise to the internal strife in Jerusalem between the sympathizers of the old class of priests, the Sadducees and the Pharisaic scribes; at the same time it was responsible for the appearance of Essene teachers [2].

---

[1] See Finkelstein, Pharisees II, ch. XXI and Klausner, Historia III, p. 118 ff.

[2] As remarked in I Q p. Hab. 8.9, 11. 8 and pesher Nahum (ed. A. M. Haberman, Megilloth, p. 153, lines 3-9). See furher Y. Yadin, Hamegilloth Hagenuzoth, p. 195 ff. An opinion is expressed by S. Zeitlin that the Pharisaic-Sadducean split occurred at the beginning of the Second Temple era and that the Hasidim are to be identified only with the Essenes. This view is not verified in Josephus' works (mentioning the orders at the time of Jonathan the Hasmonaean) and Tannaitic source. See next page.

THE PHARISEES AND THEIR CONTROVERSIAL HALACHIC TEACHINGS

The Judaic Orders

The emergence of three profound orders in the early Hasmonaean period formed a distinct background for the growth of Christianity and the later development of rabbinic Judaism [1]. The appearance of three branches in Judaism—the Pharisaic order, the Sadducean-Boethusian houses and the Essene communities—is associated, in later sources, with the centralization of the free Judean state achieved in the days of Jonathan and his brother Simon, the Hasmonaeans (153-135 B.C.). Josephus, a Jewish historian of two centuries later, mentions [2] the three αἱρέσεις (philosophical schools or sects) at the closing stages of Jonathan's activities. A rabbinic tradition, too, places [3] the Sadducean-Boethusian split with the Pharisees in the days of Simon the Just—of the Hasmonaean house as shown above —and Antigonus of Sokho [4].

Upon the removal of the foreign Greek yoke the reins of power were vested in the hands of a priestly family other than the old established Zadokite house, with the approval of the common people

---

[1] For special studies on Christianity in the light of a Jewish background refer to Ch. Guignebert, The Jewish World in the Time of Jesus (New York, 1959) with an extensive bibliography; J. Klausner, Jesus of Nazareth, his Life, Times and Teaching (English translation, New York, 1926) with a review of the different works written on the subject; W. Bousset, Die Religion des Judentums im neutestamentlichen Zeitalter (Berlin, 1906); Judaism and Christianity, vol. I edited by W. O. E. Oesterley, vol. II edited by H. Loewe (London, 1937) and vol. III edited by E. I. J. Rosenthal (London, 1938). For special studies on the background of rabbinic Judaism see L. Finkelstein, The Pharisees, 2 vol., with an extensive bibliography and G. F. Moore, Judaism, 3 vol. with extensive notes. A good introduction to the "Intertestamental Period" was written by R. H. Pfeiffer, History of New Testament Times with an Introduction to the Apocrypha (New York, 1949).

[2] Ant. XIII. 5. 9 § 171; compare Ant. XVIII. 1. 2 § 11.; φιλοσοφίαι.

[3] I A.D.N. ch. 5 and II A.D.N. ch. 10 (p. 26).

[4] According to Ab. 1.4 the chain of tradition was continued by Simon the Just and Antigonus of Sokho, who are considered contemporaries, see Hoenig, G. Sanh., p. 36.

and presbyteroi [1]). The former ruling classes, composed of aristocrats[2]) and the Zadokite family, established an opposing front known later by the name Sadducees, i.e., the adherents of the house of Zadok [3]). This group insisted on the preservation of the former doctrines concerning priestly matters and the sanctuary which, in effect, also directed the policies affecting the common folk. Their teachings were based on the written word of the priestly Mosaic law and the oral tradition formulated by the priests during the Zadokite period, which later were also introduced in writing [4]). In this manner the Sadducees insisted that legislators, interpreters of the law, can not change the written word; thereby, in their circles they have caused the religion to stagnate. The law and the religion need teachers to further their study and interpretation, in order to comply with changes of times and conditions and to introduce new doctrines, legislations and instruction. The heirs to the Scribes-teachers of old came from the lower priestly classes, Levitical families and the plebeians. These teachers introduced new regulations and explained minutely the laws as recorded in the Books of Moses. Because these teachers insisted on a strict code of separation and cleanliness and formed closed circles composed of strict observers, the opposition nicknamed them "The Pharisees", i.e., the ones who are separated [5]). These Pharisees stressed the continuity of the oral tradition along with the written word and declared the former authoritative [6]). On the one hand, they created a stricter code of laws governing the daily life of their adherents; on the other hand, they introduced changes, in the spirit of their times, affecting

---

[1]) I Macc. 14. 28.

[2]) See Ant. XIII. 10. 6 § 298 and cf. the statement in I A.D.N. ch. 5 (p. 26), refer to Finkelstein, Pharisees I, p. 80.

[3]) The opinion expressed by A. Geiger in "Urschrift" and in "Judentum und seine Geschichte" (Breslau, 1865) p. 77 ff., and see the article "Sadducees" by K. Kohler in J. Enc.

[4]) For example, "The Book of Ordinances" mentioned in M.T. 4 (p. 8). Refer to H. Lichtenstein, Die Fastenrolle, H.U.C.A. VIII-IX, pp. 297, 298. The judges of ordinances are in debate with the priests (M. Ket. 13.1, 2) and are paid from Temple funds (b. Ket. 105a).

[5]) J. Klausner, Historia III, p. 118, cites the parallel in Ezr. 6. 21, 9. 1, 10. 11 and Neh. 10. 29. Compare L. Baeck, Die Pharisäer (Schocken Verlag, 6), p. 9ff. Moore, Judaism I, p. 61, R. T. Herford, Die Pharisäer (1928), p. 34 n. 1, and J. Elbogen, Religionsanschauungen der Pharisäer (Berlin, 1904) ch. 1.

[6]) So Ant. XIII. 10. 6 § 297. The Pharisees described two laws, a written and an oral, b. Shab. 31a and ascribed them to Moses, J. Pea. 17a, see further H. L. Strack, Introduction, part 1, ch. II.

the Temple services, the ceremonies and the juridical and educational systems—thereby bringing the religion closer to the common people. The inevitable·clash between the two fronts, the Pharisees and the Sadducees, which resulted from the different approach to the religion and its law, can be compared to the split with the Samaritans in the early days of the Zadokite period. Whereas the followers of Ezra, the Scribe, widened the scope of the law and formed a new path for the Jewish religion, the Samaritans, on the other hand, claimed to be the true heirs of the ancient Hebraic lore, and consequently preserved only the written works of the past and the archaic tradition.

The teachers of the law who were bold enough to introduce changes in various religious areas, claiming that they possess the true knowledge in explaining the hidden words of the prophets [1]), were persecuted by the members of the ruling priestly families [2]). They, therefore, divorced themselves completely from the seat of learning, the city of Jerusalem, and dwelled instead among the villagers or in remote hills and caves [3]). There they sought and preached a new covenant [5]), an ascetic communal life [4]) devoted to prayer and study [6]) and in their seclusion contemplated a better future, setting down their conclusions in writing [7]). These men were known in the Qumran writings as Teachers of Righteousness [C. D. 1.11, I Qp. Hab. 1. 13] or in the Aramaic vernacular Essenes, i.e., the pious ones [8]). They were

---

[1]) I Q. p. Hab. 7. 4, 5, 2. 8, 9. In this work I accept the opinion of Y. Yadin in Megilloth Hagenuzoth, 1958, p. 205 ff. that the inhabitants of Qumran are to be identified with the Essenes. For other views: A. M. Haberman's introduction, Megilloth, identifies them with the Sadducees, C. Roth in The Historical Background of the Dead Sea Scrolls (Oxford, 1958) and J. Klausner, Historia V, appendix, maintain that they were the Zealots. On the other hand, S. Zeitlin, J.Q.R.N.S., 1955, ascribes the scrolls to Middle Ages. The view of Y. Yadin, which follows his father's opinion, is generally accepted.

[2]) I Q. p. Hab. 11. 4, 5. The Hasmonaean priests, as history shows, were at first accepted by the Jews and then despised for their eagerness to obtain riches and power, cf. I Q. p. Hab. 8. 8-13 and I Q. p. Ps. 37. line 40.

[3]) Josephus in Bell. II. 8. 4 § 124, Philo in Q.O.P.L. § 76 and in the lost treatise entitled "Apology for the Jews" quoted by Ch. D. Ginsburg, The Essenes (London, 1956), p. 36 ff.

[4]) I Q p. Hab. 2. 3, C.D. 8. 21 and the covenant is described in IQ.S. 1.11-2.18

[5]) Described in the sources cited in n. 3, above.

[6]) Bell. II 8. 5 §§ 128-133, cf. I Q. S. 6.2-8.

[7]) As found in the Pesher literature, the scrolls of Thanksgivings and the War of Sons of Light with the Sons of Darkness and Manual for the Brotherhood.

[8]) Klausner, Historia III, p. 111, refers to Philo's explanation. Yosippon ed. Hominer, p. 112, calls the Essenes Hasidim. A list of possible explanations of the name is given in Ch. D. Ginsburg, Essenes, pp. 27-30; In Qumran writings "Ḥesed" and "Ṣedeq" are related; e.g., I Q.S. II. 24.

responsible for the creation of a society of "Yaḥad" (brotherhood) [1]).

From the days of old Jerusalem, the city which the house of David designated as its capital and the dwelling place of Yahweh [2]), was the recognised seat of learning. Isaiah proclaims [3]): "From out of Zion (another name for Jerusalem) [4]) shall go forth the Law and the word of Yahweh from Jerusalem". The Psalmist chants [5]): "Let us go to the house of Yahweh ... Jerusalem ... whither the tribes went up to the sanctuary in Israel ... For there were set seats for judgement". During the Hasmonaean-Herodian period, the city of the Temple was also the city of the supreme-court, the Great Sanhedrin [6])—a haven for teachers-scribes and their academies [7]), a center for learning. Thus, Jerusalem was to witness the heated controversies between the teachers and followers of the two major fronts, the Sadducees and Pharisees. Jesus of Galilee (2-4 B.C.-29 or 33 A.D.) [8]) also arrived in Jerusalem, and at the Temple [9]) he expounded his doctrines and proclaimed the arrival of "the Kingdom of Heaven". There, Jesus was confronted with the representatives of the two parties, and by refuting the Sadducean teachers he was released from the hands of the Pharisaic scribes [10]). Paul, advocating the new Christian teachings, was also attacked by the members of the two orders, and realizing the dilemma he sided with the Pharisaic view [11]).

The noted differences emanating from the two bodies touch various topics in the Jewish religion. These differences bear on important halachic questions —i.e., the laws governing the Temple-services,

---

[1]) As identified in I Q.Sa I. 27 (עֲצַת הַיַּחַד, the council) II. 21 (עֲדַת הַיַּחַד, the community) I Q.S. V. 2-3 (אַנְשֵׁי הַיַּחַד הַמַּחֲזִקִים בַּבְּרִית, the men of the Brotherhood who uphold the covenant).

[2]) David was instructed by the prophet, Nathan, that his son should erect the temple, II Sam. 7. 4 ff, and the parallel, I Chr. 17. 3 ff.

[3]) Is. 2. 3c, recited by Jews in the synagogues before the Holy Ark, see S. Baer, Abodath Israel, p. 122.

[4]) See the list of names for Jerusalem in Z. Wilnai, Jerusalem, 1960, p. 27 ff.

[5]) Ps. 122. 1-5—one of the Psalms, according to rabbinic tradition, recited by the Levites in the Temple at the steps leading to the second court.

[6]) M. Mid. 5. 4, Sifre Deut. § 152 (104b) and cf. M. Sanh. 11. 2.

[7]) J. Meg. 73d and b. Ket. 105a.

[8]) Matt. 16. 21 ff (note v. 28 predicting that the "Son of Man" will arrive with the Kingdom).

[9]) ib. 21. 10, 12, 23 and parallels.

[10]) Luk. 20. 39, 40 and parallels.

[11]) Acts 23. 6.

the practices and customs, civil and judicial matters—which can illustrate the daily life of the community. In order to demonstrate the two principal paths of development in the written and oral tradition, the two lines of approach adopted by the Pharisees are presented: a) Their emphasis on strict observance of the Mosaic precepts, which govern the laws of separation and purity, resulted in the closed units [1]) of the Pharisaic teachers and, indirectly, in their separation from the common boorish folk. b) Their liberal approach to the interpretation of the law with the emphasis on creating closer ties between the Jewish religion and the people—in the areas of judicature, legislation for festival observance and education. This study will trace the halachic questions to the early sources and show the later development during the years of the Hasmonaean, Herodian and procurators rule, the period of Pharisaic activities.

THE LAWS OF SEPARATION AND PURITY [2])

The book of Leviticus, a composition of a Priestly Code (chapters 1-16) and the Laws of Holiness (chapters 17-26) [3]), outlines the rules of separation in regard to the consumption of clean and sacrificial animals [4]), purification and pollution [5]), unlawful marriages and chastity laws [6]), rules on the observance of festivals [7]) and on the various duties levied on the farmer [8]). The principle of separation is stated in a concluding statement [9]): "Ye shall therefore put a difference ... and ye shall be holy unto Me, for I, Yahweh, am holy and I have severed you from the nations, that ye should be Mine". It is addressed to the Judaic society as a whole, a society that is to become according to the priestly dogma "a kingdom of priests and a holy nation" [10]). A nation seeking a status of holiness (i.e. the adoption of a theocratic

---

[1]) חבורות, for example, T. Meg. 4.15 (226.14).

[2]) See Allon, Mechqarim betoledoth Israel, I, p. 148 ff.

[3]) See R. H. Pfeiffer, Introduction, ch. VI.

[4]) A list of clean and unclean food is found in Lev. 11. 2-24 (cf. Deut. 14. 1-21), of sacrificial clean animals see Lev. 1. 2, 14. A reason is given in Arist. §§ 130-171.

[5]) On pollution see Lev. 11. 24-43, on purification see ib. chs. 12-16.

[6]) Lev. chs. 18, 20. Cf. Ant. 3. 12. 1.

[7]) Lev. ch. 23 (cf. Deut. ch. 16). Cf. Ant. 3. 10. 1-6.

[8]) Num. 18. 8-24 and Lev. 19. 9-10.

[9]) Lev. 20. 25, 26—stated after listing the unlawful marriages and the clean animals.

[10]) Ex. 19. 6 compare v. 5 with Deut. 14. 2, an introductory note to the list of unclean animals.

rule) must accept, according to the Priestly Code prescription, restrictions on the habits of food, apparel, cohabitation and the upkeep of the household. In the Pharisaic schools [1] "holiness", the key-word of the Priestly Codes, is identified with the word "separation": Separation from the heathens and foreigners in order to preserve the identity of the Jewish people [2]; separation or classification among its own members, segregating the priests and the strict observers of the Code from the non-observers, the boorish and the common folk [3]. Also among the Essene societies created by the Teacher of Righteousness—as the Qumran writings suggest—to achieve a status of holiness, the community must stress the rules of separation and purity as prescribed in the "Order of the Brotherhood" [4] (Serekh Hayachad). The words of Rabbi Pinḥas ben Jair [5], a known Jewish saint of the early part of the third century A.D., reviews the important steps to be taken by the individual or the society in order to achieve a status of holiness or piety. He enumerates the steps as follows: "Heedfulness leads to diligence [6], diligence to cleanliness, cleanliness to separation and separation to holiness [7] (a name for the Pharisaic order) or as the variant reads piety [8] (a term for the Essene community)".

In the days of the first Jewish Commonwealth, the Judaean society was centralized about the Temple and its services, and thus the spiritual leaders were sought from among the priestly classes. The occupation of the land of Canaan and the establishment of a monarchy caused the ancient Mosaic Code to be neglected, since it came into direct opposition with the natives among whom the settlers had

---

[1] See Mech. on above verse (71a) and Sifra on 19. 2 (86 c), see L. Baeck, Die Pharisäer, p. 10 ff and Moore, Judaism I, p. 61.

[2] Sifra on 20. 7 (91d): קְדוּשַׁת פְּרִישׁוּת עוֹבְדֵי־כּוֹכָבִים. Compare Arist. § 242

[3] According to M. Hag. 2. 7: בִּגְדֵי עַם הָאָרֶץ מִדְרָס לַפְּרוּשִׁים.

[4] Cf. Bell. II. 8. 10 §150. The grades of purity for the Essene community is similar to the four degrees of purity of the Pharisees, see p. 59, and Rabin, Qumran studies, Ch. I.

[5] I follow the recension in b. A.Z. 20b (compare M. Sot 9. 15—an addition, J. Shab. 3c and J. Shek. 47c). Compare the chain-formation in Rom. 5. 3-5.

[6] Ch. D. Ginsburg, Essenes., p. 13, interprets the statement in reference to the Essene grades of cleanliness and renders "apron" for זָרִין (περίζωμα).

[7] So the variants in J. Shab. 3c and J. Shek. 47c: טָהֳרָה מְבִיאָה לִידֵי קְדוּשָׁה.

[8] So in b. A.Z. 20b. Z. Frankel, Die Essäer nach talmudischen Quellen, M.G.W.J., 2 (1853), identifies חֲסִידִים הָרִאשׁוֹנִים with the Essenes, see further the article of L. Jacobs, "The Concept of Ḥasid in the Biblical and Rabbinic Literatures" in Journal of Jewish Studies, vol. VIII (1957).

mingled physically and culturally. Only the sporadic efforts of the fanatic priests [1]—of whom some were also prophets [2]—kept the Mosaic laws alive. The main body of the priests had failed to lead the people in the path of the Mosaic teaching, therefore, they were publicly reprimanded by the early prophets [3]. With the complete devastation of the Judaean state and the growing pangs of the Babylonian exile the Judaeans were willing to adopt a theocratic rule under the leadership of the priests and the elders. At this time—as maintained by a majority of present day scholars [4]—the Priestly Code was edited based on early material with the purpose of guarding the identity of the nation among the heathens, and theoretically establishing a kingdom of priests on a foreign soil. Ezekiel, a priest and a spokesman of the Babylonian exile, envisions [5] the restoration of Israel and the re-establishment of a utopian state based only on the Priestly Code. He speaks symbolically of the purification of Israel through the purifying waters in the hand of Yahweh [6] and directs the Zadokite family to accept the role of the hegemonic class in the re-established Judaean state because of their observance of the code [7]. Jeshua [8], a Zadokite descendant, does accept the leadership of a restored society in Jerusalem.

A colony replanted in the Judaean hills was centralized by the Temple activities. The priests and their associates, the Levites, were responsible to the Temple, and naturally they became the vehicle for the preservation of the religious conduct and the Priestly Code. A contemporary prophet declares [9]: "For the priest's lips should keep knowledge and they (the people) should seek the law at his mouth, for he (the priest) is the messenger of Yahweh, the Lord of Hosts". Yet the priests, at the dawn of the Zadokite period, in their ambition for complete control of the Temple had neglected their co-workers, the Levites and

---

[1] II Kin. ch. 12.

[2] For example, Elijah (according to rabbinic tradition, b. B.M. 114 b), Jeremiah (Jer. 1.1) and Ezekiel (Ez. 1. 3).

[3] E.g. I Sam. 2. 27 ff.

[4] See R. H. Pfeiffer, Introduction, p. 256 ff.

[5] Ez. chs. 34-48.

[6] Ib. 36. 25.

[7] Ib. 44. 15.

[8] Jeshua, the high priest, in association with Zerubabel, a non-priest, are at the head. So does the Chronicler describe a pair of leaders, and duumvirates are described as heads of the community in rabbinic sources. See further pp. 58, 59.

[9] Mal. 2. 7 was later interpreted by the Rabbis to denote the scholar, b. M.K. 17a.

were later bitterly denounced by Nehemiah [1]). The priests in their zeal for power had failed in their mission as teachers and were, hence, reprimanded by the contemporary prophets [2]). The task of restoring a theocratic rule, according to the Priestly Code, was undertaken by a zealous Babylonian priest and scribe, Ezra.

Ezra, who possibly heard of the neglect of the Mosaic law in the Holy City, initiated a religious drive for resettling Jerusalem with the full support of the Persian king. His major act of preparation on route was the classification of different families [3]) and the inclusion of Levites and Temple-keepers (netinim) [4]) as part of the caravan. This preparatory act of Ezra alone manifests his zeal for preserving the structural identity of the Jewish classes according to the Priestly Code. To prevent future assimilation of the colonists greater measures were introduced by Ezra upon his arrival in Jerusalem. This priestly Scribe, imbued with the spirit of the prophetic teachings, saw in assimilation the absorption of alien, heathen ideas [5]) that, in turn, could result in the complete eradication of Judaean identity and in the elimination of Judea as a cradle for the cultivation of the Jewish religion [6]). At a public meeting, with complete approval from heads of state, he formed a committee which spread in every town in a network of elders and judges whose duties were to enforce the strict measures [7]). As in the case of all religious reform the passage of time was necessary to crystallize these new ideas. The ground work laid by Ezra became the rule for the measures taken by later reformers—in the latter days of Nehemiah [8]), the period of the Hasmonaeans [9]) and that of the Zealots during the Herodian rule [10]).

The spirit of Ezra's age is reflected, particularly, in the establishment of a theocratic state. The acceptance of the Priestly Code was

---

[1]) Neh. 13. 10-13.
[2]) Hag. 2. 11 ff., as interpreted in b. Pes. 17a, and the prophecy of Malachi.
[3]) See Ezra's diary, Ezr. 8. 1-14.
[4]) Ezr. 8. 15-20.
[5]) As stated in Ezra's petition, Ezr. 9. 10-14. The references to the teachings of the prophets are recorded in Lev. 18. 27 and Deut. 6. 8, 7. 3, 23. 7.
[6]) Compare the teachings recorded in the Prophets: Jos. 23. 5-7a, Jud. 2. 1, 2; I. Sam. 12. 10, 20. Ez. ch. 20. Ezra's opposition to the heathens did not include, however, the ones who accepted the Jewish faith (Neh. 10. 29b), the first known proselytes in Jewish history. On proselytes see Schürer, G.J.V. III § 31. 5.
[7]) Ezr. 10. 8, 14, 15 and cf. b. B.K. 82a (days of courts in session).
[8]) Neh. 13. 25.
[9]) See b. A.Z. 36b, b. Sanh. 82a and refer to I. H. Weiss, D. D. Wed. I., p. 103.
[10]) M. Sanh. 9. 6.

affirmed by the articles of the covenant signed by the eighty-five heads of the colony [1]). In the succeeding generations, the high priest and his associates who remained loyal to the Mosaic principles were regarded as the leaders and esteemed as teachers of the law [2]). Their decisions concerning religious affairs reached diasporean Jewry[3]). Jerusalem became the seat of learning and has produced prolific writers of law, liturgy and books on wisdom [4]). The presence of the Temple with its conscientious priests assured the strict observance of the Priestly Code among the inhabitants [5]).

With the incoming Seleucidian rulers and the influence of Greek culture in the higher strata of society, the aristocratic families-members of the Zadokite wealthy priests—were rejected as teachers by the people. Hellenism, the introduction of an alien culture [6]), was the complete antithesis of Judaic ideals and the spirit of the Priestly Code. The Temple was desecrated [7]); the priesthood received a pricetag [8]); the laws of purification were neglected [9]); and the Mosaic law was observed only in secrecy [10]). The religious plebeians, the fanatic priests of the different Watchgroups and the Scribes of Levitical and Israelite origin remained the only true observers of the Mosaic law. Their fanaticism and martyrdom—the first recorded in history—are portrayed in tales describing the heroic deeds [11]). These men were known as Hasideans (the pietists) who contested

---

[1]) The articles enumerated in Neh. 10. 31-40 (cf. Klausner, Historia I, p. 299 f) can be classified as follows: a) rules regarding the sanctity of the nation, vs. 31, 32; b) rules regarding the sanctity of the Temple vs. 33-40.

[2]) See above p. 44.

[3]) The Elephantine Jewry address Yehochanan the High Priest and he is ranked with Baguai, the satrap, see Klausner, Historia II, lecture 7, and A. Cowley, Aramaic Papyri of the 5th Century B.C. (1923), pap. 30.

[4]) The Letter of Aristeas speaks of 72 teachers of the Law (cf. b. Meg. 9a). Ben-Sira and the Chronicler are examples of Scribes and teachers. The authors of Psalms, as well as Ben-Sira (Sir. 51. 21-35), wrote liturgy for the Temple.

[5]) The seventy-two men sent to Egypt to translate the Pentateuch adhere to the laws of purification, Arist. §§ 305, 282. Tobit, the elder, adheres to the laws of purification, Sin. Tob. 2. 9, and to the laws of tithes, ib. 1.6-8.

[6]) I Macc. I. 41-54, II Macc. 4. 7-17 and Dan. 11. 31, 32. In rabbinic literature Hellenists are described as "those who declare that we have no part with God of Israel", J. Hag. 77 d.

[7]) I Macc. I. 36, 37, 54 cf. Dan. 9. 27, 11. 31, 12. 11.

[8]) II Macc. 4. 7-10, 23-25.

[9]) The decree of Antiochus IV, I Macc. 1. 45-48 and compare the activities of Judas, I Macc. 3. 49.

[10]) The decree of Antiochus IV, I Macc. 1. 49.

[11]) See I Macc. 2. 37, II Macc. 7, compare b. Git. 57b, and the moral teachings in IV Macc.

and opposed "those who act wickedly against the covenant" [1]), the Hellenists—who were also identified as evil-doers and impure [2]). The Hasideans rose under the banner of Mattathias, a zealous priest of a lesser watch group. The result of their successful revolt was the restoration of the spirit of the Priestly Code. The Temple was cleansed, purified and rededicated. The abominations placed in the Temple by the Greeks were removed and the Mosaic rule was reinstated [3]). The leaders and teachers of the new movement were not, as in the days of old, the members of the Zadokite priestly class; they were the religious plebeians and the priests of the lesser family-Watches. These teachers are responsible in the succeeding generations for the enforcement of the laws of separation and purity—the introduction of priestly laws even for the non priests.

In the Hasmonaean period and the subsequent Herodian-procurators period the teachers who were responsible "for passing on to the people certain regulations handed down by former generations", and who "have the reputation as the most accurate interpreters of the laws" are identified by Josephus [4]) as the Pharisees. The Pharisees adopted the principle of "Holiness" as prescribed in the Priestly Code, and regarded themselves the heirs to Ezra's teachings. They ascribed to their community the title "the Holy Community of Jerusalem"—as shown by L. Baeck in his book, "Die Pharisäer" [5]). The members of the Pharisaic community were simply addressed as Ḥaberim (members) [6]) and the teachers as Ḥakhamim [7]) (men of wisdom) or Zeqenim (elders) [8]). The name Pharisees, as mentioned above, originated from the mouth of their antagonists, [9]) the Saddu-

---

[1]) Dan. 11. 32: מַרְשִׁיעֵי בְרִית and 11. 30: עֹזְבֵי בְּרִית קֹדֶשׁ.

[2]) I Macc. II. 44 and I. 15.

[3]) I Macc. 4. 36 ff.

[4]) Ant. XIII. 10. 6 § 297, Bell. II. 8. 14 § 162.

[5]) Schocken Verlag 16 (Berlin, 1934), p. 15. Yet Rapoport, mentioned in Z. Frankel's article, M.G.W.J., 1853, Die Essäer, identifies them with the Essenes, so in a later period: עֵדָה קְדוֹשָׁה, Ecc. R. on 9. 9 (p. 237). See further Ch. Rabin, Qumran Studies, ch. 3 and J. Jeremias, Jerusalem zur Zeit Jesu, II p. 116 ff.

[6]) See the list in E. Schüer, G.J.V. II, p. 454; So C.D. XII 8.

[7]) For example, b. Sot. 15a Hakhamim are identified with Soferim. So Josephus refers to Judas and Matthias, two experts of the Law as σοφισταί (Bell. I. 32. 2 § 648). M.T. scholion 12 (p.20) identifies the Soferim with the Hakhamim, the Pharisees persecuted in the days of Jannai.

[8]) So Sifre Zutta 19. 2. "The Elders (Zeqenim) of Jerusalem". Members of Hillel's and Shammai's academy, were called Zeqenim, see b. Men. 41b.

[9]) Compare M. Yad. 4. 6, 7. Matt. 23. 13 writes Φαρισαῖοι for Luk. 11. 52, νομικοῖς = Ḥakhamim.

cees and Boethusians [1]), and denoted "those who are separated". This name which even among the Pharisaic teachers was regarded with scorn [2]), denoting ascetics [3]), became the literary and historical identification of the party—as in our own times the rivals of Hasidism received the name Mitnagdim (opponents).

The Pharisees, as in the days of Ezra, have regarded the selection of priestly and Levitical descent and that of other Jewish classes a necessary step in preserving the sanctity and identity of the Jewish people. The Great Sanhedrin according to the Pharisaic sources sat in judgement to render decisions on the qualifications of the priests [4]) and, thus, the Pharisaic teachers exercised control over the pure lineage of the Temple ministry. The Pharisees, too, demanded that the head of state belong to a family of pure Jewish blood [5]). This demand resulted in their expulsion from the seat of the supreme-court in the later years of Hyrcanus I reign [6]) and also caused them to become bitter enemies of Herod the Great, an Idumaean [7]). As in former days the authors of the Priestly Code [8]) and the Chronicles [9]) recorded the existing family lineages, so in the Hasmonaean-Herodian period archives were designated for the keeping of genealogical records [10]). Such records are preserved in the works of the Gospel writers [11]), and those of Josephus [12]) and the Talmudists [13]). In the days following the destruction of the Temple,

---

[1]) The Talmud records the two families, Sadducees and Boethusians, in some cases separately: T. R. H. 1.15 (210. 10) Boethus, M. Yad. 4. 6, 7 Sadducees; and in other cases jointly: I A.D. N. ch. 5 (p. 136) or interchangeably: T. Yad. 2. 20, Boethus = b. B.B. 115b, Sadducee. The statement in I A.D. N. ch. 5 defines Sadducees as Zadokites and Boethusians as the family of Boethus, see further Finkelstein, Pharisees II, p. 663 n. 20.

[2]) See b. Sot. 22b cf. J. Ber. 14b, the list of seven types of Pharisees. In Jerushalmi R. Elazer and R. Juda the Prince (c. 180 A.D.) refer to a hypocrite as a Pharisaic plague.

[3]) M. Sot. 3. 4, the statement of R. Jehushua (c. 120 A.D.) and see b. B.B. 60b; See S. Zeitlin, Who Crucified Jesus, 2ed., 1947, p. 12.

[4]) M. Mid. 5.4, T. Hag. 2. 9 (235. 18, 19) see Hoenig, G. Sanh., p. 103.

[5]) See T. Sanh. 4. 10 (422. 17).

[6]) See b. Kid. 66a, cf. Ant. XIII. 10. 5.

[7]) See b. B.B. 3b at the end. Cf. Ant. XIV § 491, XV § 388, XVII § 176.

[8]) See the list in Pfeiffer, Introduction, ch. VI.

[9]) As found in the first ten chapters of I Chronicles.

[10]) See Cont. Ap. I. 7 and compare M. Kid. 4. 4.

[11]) Matt. 1. 1-17 and Luk. 3. 23-38.

[12]) For example Ant. 20. 10; for other sources used by Josephus see F. J. Foakes Jackson, Josephus and the Jews, London, 1930.

[13]) J. Taan. 68a, R. Levi declared that a genealogical roll was found in Jerusalem, see J. Z. Lauterbach on "Three Books found in the Temple" J.Q.R.N.S., 8. p. 401 ff.,

a reputable family lineage was considered an important factor in the appointment to the presidency of the academy [1]).

Steps were taken by the Pharisaic teachers to preserve the matrimonial laws enumerated in the Priestly Code. A list of ten genealogical classes—based on the classification issued by Ezra and attributed to Hillel [2])—was instrumental in regulating marital ties among different family groups. Further restrictions were introduced by the Pharisaic scribes against nuptial ties with one generation removed from the relations outlined in the forbidden marriages of the Priestly Code [3]). The Pharisees also insisted that levirate marriages were considered valid only if the deceased brother left no offsprings of either sex. They interpreted the rule in Deut. 25. 5: "In case brothers dwell together and one of them dies and to him is no son (וּבֵן אֵין־לֹו)" to denote any offspring besides a son. An interpretation based on the additional reading of the words אֵין־לֹו in the form עַיֵּין־לֹו [4]) (hold an inquiry concerning him); namely, if the deceased brother had been survived by any offspring, then the levirate marriage is not in accordance with the law. The Septuagint also renders σπέρμα δὲ μὴ ἦν αὐτῷ, σπέρμα for בֵּן, instead of the usual translation παῖς (or υἱός). In this manner the Pharisees sought to restrict the improper application of the primitive law of levirate marriage which purpose originally was to secure the position of the oldest son in the clan and thus in later generations the Pharisees discouraged such marriages [5]). The acceptance of the Pharisaic rule among the people resulted in bitter opposition to the marriage of Antipas and Herodias, the wife of Herod II, after the death of her husband [6]) who was a stepbrother of Antipas [7]). This marriage provoked John the

See also b. Yeb. 49b, possibly referring to Jesus, see Klausner, Jesus, pp. 35, 36.

[1]) See b. Ber. 27b, R. Elazer ben Azariah was appointed to the presidency of Jamnia's academy because he was considered a tenth generation descendant from Ezra.

[2]) M. Kid. 4. 1, for its early dating see Epstein, Meb. Les. Hat., p. 54. For the classification by the Essenes, see C.D. 14. 3-6.

[3]) T. Yeb, 3. 1 (243. 14-16) lists the שְׁנִיּוֹת (nuptial ties of a generation removed from the forbidden marriages listed in Lev. 18), and the decree is attributed to the "acts of the Scribes".

[4]) The interpretation is recorded in b. Yeb. 22b to include an illegitimate son, see also Maimonides, Yad, Hilkhoth Yibum, 1. 3.

[5]) M. Bech. 1. 7.

[6]) So in the Slavic translation of Josephus' Bellum Judaicum, see Klausner, Jesus, p. 242 and the edition of A. Bernedts and K. Grass (Dorpat, 1924), p. 265.

[7]) On the prohibition see Sifra on 20. 21 (93b).

Baptist's reproof saying [1]): "It is not permitted (ἔξεστιν = שָׁרֵי) for
thee (Antipas) to have thy brother's wife".

The Pharisees also took steps to define and preserve the Priestly
Code relating to the laws governing purity and pollution. The
Priestly Code prescribes rules about legal uncleanliness arising
from certain conditions in women. Lev. 15. 19-24 (20.18) defines the
period of menstruation as seven days of uncleanliness, in which
the woman upon contact with objects causes their contamination;
the woman must also abstain from marital relations. The Pharisaic
teachers determined which blood of a menstruant is considered
impure [2]), and thus women had to show their discharge to them. The
Sadducees, on the other hand, did not accept the Pharisaic conclusions,
since they were not recorded in the law of Moses. Yet their wives sub-
mitted to the Pharisaic rulings [3]), based on investigations of the latter,
so that their sons will not be regarded by the people as "children
of impurity" [4]). Lev. 15.25-28 declares: "And if a woman have an
issue of her blood [Zabah] many days not in the time of menstruation
. . . she is unclean . . . But if she be cleansed of her issue, then she
shall number to herself seven days and after she shall be clean". Since
the law does not specify the number of days in which the discharge
appears, the Pharisees designated the eleven days following the period
of menstruation as the period of "zabah" [5]). If during this time
blood appeared three days in succession the woman was then considered
"zabah" [6]), and had to follow the prescribed law as outlined in Lev.
15.28-30. A woman who witnessed blood in one of the eleven
days had to await an additional clean day [7]) [שׁוֹמֶרֶת יוֹם כְּנֶגֶד יוֹם] and
during this time the husband had to abstain from marital relations.
The Sadducees, as well as the Samaritans [8]), did not accept the above

---

[1]) Mk. 6. 18, cf. Matt. 14. 4.

[2]) M. Nid. 2. 6 enumerates the five types of blood considered impure, a list
dating back to the days prior to the period of the Academies. The authority of the
Pharisaic court to examine the blood of a menstruant was inferred from Deut. 17.
8. See b. Nid. 19a and Sifre Deut. § 152 (104b).

[3]) B. Nid. 33b.

[4]) Kall. 1: "the children of a menstruant" are equated with "the illegitimate
children".

[5]) b. Nid. 72b, 73c. The eleven days are referred to as "Halachah of Moses
from Sinai", designating a rule of pre-Destruction period.

[6]) See the interpretation in Sifra on 15. 25 (79a).

[7]) See Sifra on 15. 25 (79a).

[8]) See M. Nid. 4. 1, 2 and b. Hor. 4a. The Sadducees did not accept the
oral tradition as stated in Ant. XIII. 10. 6 § 297.

Pharisaic ruling since it was based on oral tradition and not on the written law.

The imposition of a "rule of defilement" on objects served a strong weapon in the hands of the Pharisaic teachers in order to secure strict observance of the laws of purity and pollution on the one hand, and, on the other hand, to introduce decrees for the general welfare. The Priestly Code points to eleven principal categories of pollution. Defilement can be caused by a contact with the following: a) a swarm (Lev. 11. 29-38), b) a carcass (ib. 11. 39-40), c) a human corpse (Num. 19. 11-22), d) semen (Lev. 15. 16-18), e) water of purification (Num. 19. 21), f) red heifer (ib. 19. 7-10), g) a man with a flow (Lev. 15. 2-15), h) a woman with a flow (ib. 15. 25-30), i) a menstruant (ib. 15. 19-24), j) a woman in the event of birth (ib. 12. 2-8), and k) the leper and the afflicted (ib. chs. 13, 14).

On pollution caused by a human corpse, the Pharisaic teachers defined the minimum size of the corpse's parts which can cause defilement upon contact, e. g., a bone as large as barley-corn, a member of a corpse or a quarter of a "log" of blood [1]). An olive-sized portion of the flesh of a corpse or a quarter of a "kab" of bones comprising the structural majority of the corpse [2]), when is overshadowed by a tent, causes defilement of the objects therein. An opinion expressed by an early Pharisaic teacher that only direct contact with a corpse causes defilement (as directed in Num. 19. 16) was considered by the later schools as too lenient. They maintained that defilement can be caused also by the corpse's garments, even, his sword [3]).

Jose ben Joezer and Jose ben Johanan, two Pharisaic leaders who lived in the early days of the Hasmonaean period, issued two decrees [4]): Lands outside the Holy Land are ritually impure, and that glassware—objects not listed in Lev. 11.32, ff and Num. 31. 22, 23—are capable of becoming ritually impure. I. H. Weiss [5]) and

---

[1]) M. Ohal. 2. 2, 3—note the discussion by the members of Shammai's and Hillel's academy.

[2]) M. Ohal. 2. 1, cf. M. Ed. 1. 7, a disputation of the members of the Academies.

[3]) M. Ed. 8. 4 and as explained in b. A.Z. 37b, cf. Sifre Num. § 127 (45b). Jewish scholars disagree about the halachic significance of the statement, "He that approaches a dead body is contaminated". I. H. Weiss, D. D. Wed. I., p. 100, explains the law to say only "he that approaches", i.e., in case of certainty. Z. Frankel in Darkey Hamishnah, p. 32, stresses the word "is contaminated", a derivative of the source of impurity causes defilement.

[4]) b. Shab. 14b, J. Ket. 32c.

[5]) D. D. Wed. I, pp. 99, 100.

L. Ginzberg [1]) have noted that these decrees were issued to restrict the emigration of Jews to foreign lands and to impose a ban on foreign goods. An emigration from the Holy Land began as a result of the persecutions by Antiochus Epiphanes. In the days of Hasmonaean rulers efforts were also made to secure the economic position of the country. To limit the competition of foreign products the Pharisaic leader of the following generation, Joshua ben Peraḥyah, issued a decree against the import of wheat from Alexandria [2]). He explained that it was customary in Egypt to bring water from the river by means of ἀντλία (a pumping wheel); therefore, there was reason to fear that water had fallen on the wheat, thus conditioning it to receive ritual impurity as prescribed in Lev. 11. 38. While the intention of Joshua ben Peraḥya was for the benefit of the Judaean farmer, his colleagues disagreed for they preferred, for the sake of the general good, to encourage competition in foodstuffs and to secure wheat in time of famine.Their reply was succinctly stated: "Let the wheat be impure for Joshua ben Peraḥyah and pure for all Israel".

The Pharisees desisted from imposing restrictions on goods when they were to cause hardship on the general public, but they still maintained that decrees should be imposed on objects imported by the wealthier families. As shown above, in the early days of the Hasmonaean period, a decree was issued against glassware, and also during the reign of Salom Zion (c. 76-67 B.C.) Shimeon ben Shetach issued a decree against metallic instruments [3]). Num. 31. 22, 23 states: "Only the gold and the silver, the brass, the iron, the tin and the lead, every thing that may abide by the fire ye shall make go through the fire and it shall be clean". Shimeon ben Shetach declared that even defiled metallic utensils which were destroyed and then recasted were still considered in a state of impurity, unless they were immersed in water [4]). The Talmud (b. Shab. 16b) relates that Salom Zion, who befriended the Pharisaic teachers, [5]) while preparing a feast for her son, the metallic utensils had become impure. Abiding by the Mosaic law, she had the utensils destroyed and remolded. The Pharisaic scholars insisted that the newly fashioned utensils contained the former state of impurity and thus her action was invalid.

---

[1]) On Jewish Law and Lore, Philadelphia, 1955, pp. 79, 80, 81.
[2]) T. Mach. 3. 4 (675. 21-23).
[3]) b. Shab. 14b and J. Ket. 32c.
[4]) See Maimonides, Introduction to the Commentary on Toharoth.
[5]) Compare Ant. XIII. 16. 2 § 408.

A preliminary step by the Pharisaic teachers was introduced in cases of pollution. In order to achieve cleanliness—in addition to the prescribed rules in the Priestly Code: sprinkling with "water and ashes of purification", awaiting the sunset or bringing of sacrifices—the defiled person or object must be immersed in a river or a pool of forty Se'ah of rainwater [1]). This rule applied even to the acceptance of proselytes [2]), since they were regarded in their former state unclean as a man with a flow [3]). This rule was accepted also by the Teacher of Righteousness [4]) and preached by John the Baptist [5]). Thus, in above incident, Shimeon ben Shetach declared that defiled metallic utensils even though cleansed according to the Mosaic prescription must be immersed. In the same manner, the Pharisees required the ablution of the Temple's metallic instruments after the days of great festivity [6]), fearing that the instruments might have been defiled by one of the visitors. The Pharisaic insistence on ablution of instruments caused nothing but abuse and comments among their contemporary rivals, the priestly Sadducees. On one occasion [7]) when the Pharisees applied the rule to the Temple's candelabrum, the Sadducees watching the procedure mockingly said: "Come and see how the Pharisees are about to bathe the orb of the sun".

The Pharisees were persistent in enforcing the rule of ablution on the Temple priests since they had to be always in a state of purity according to the Mosaic law. No one was permitted to enter the temple court, although he was clean, unless he bathed first [8]). The High Priest or any other priest, who had bathed upon entering the Temple at the outset of the day, were required to purify their hands and feet from the Temple's laver; in case they had neglected to do so they were under a death penalty [9]). In the event the High Priest

---

[1]) Maimonides, Yad; Hilkhoth Miqwaoth, 1. 1-4, see M. Hag. 3. 2, M.A.Z. 5. 12, b. ib. 75b and on utensils M. Mik. 1; 5. 6.

[2]) b. Yeb. 47a, b and see b. Ker. 9a, the accepted rule among the post-Destruction Rabbis, see further H. Rowley, Jewish Proselyte Baptism, H.U.C.A., 15 (1940), and I. Abrahams, Studies in Pharisaism, I chs. III, IV.

[3]) Sifra on 15. 2 (74 d), cf. b. Nid. 34a and the rule in T. Zab. 2. 1 (677. 25); See Allon, Mechqarim betoledoth Israel, I, p. 121 ff.

[4]) I Q.S. 3. 4, 5 lists the methods of purification.

[5]) Matt. 3. 6 and parallels—the ablution of sinners is required as of the proselytes, since both must enter the holy community.

[6]) M. Hag. 3. 7, 8.

[7]) T. Hag. 3. 35 (238. 23), cf. J. ib. 79 d.

[8]) b. Yom. 30a.

[9]) T. Men. 1. 11, 12 (513. 14 ff.).

was compelled to withdraw from the Temple upon his return he had to bathe again [1]). The High Priest administering the service of the Day of Atonement had to go through a ritual of five bathes and ten applications of water upon his hands and feet [2]). This strict regulation even among the adherents of the Pharisaic school was subjected to comments [3]).

The Pharisaic teachers, who were prohibited by the Mosaic law from administering the Temple services, still imposed their rules on the preparatory stage of the Day of Atonement and that of the preparation of the red heifer. They isolated the High Priest for a week of instruction and purification on both occasions [4]). In one recorded incident [5]) the High Priest, Ismael the son of Piabi (61-59 B.C.), prescribed that the red heifer could be prepared by a priest in a state of purity effected by sunset in accordance with the written law. The Pharisees who insisted that a state of purity is also achieved by immersion [Tebul-yom], in accordance with the above rule, compelled the High Priest to readminister the ritual of the red heifer.

The Pharisaic order did not only ask of its members to abstain from any impurities in the administration of the household, but also to be strict in the observance of the law of tithes in the preparation of food. Delivery of a portion of the farmer's produce to the priestly and Levitical groups was made in two forms: Terumah (heave offering) and Ma'aser (a tenth). Terumah was portioned as follows: "Terumah Gedolah", a portion of any amount of grains [6]) to be delivered to the priests and "Terumath Ma'aser", a payment of the priestly tax from the Levite's portion [7]). Ma'aser was to be issued yearly to the Levitical groups [8]), in addition to a portion to the poor on every third or sixth of the sabbatical cycle, and a set amount

---

[1]) T. Yom. 1. 16 (182. 11).

[2]) M. Yom. 3. 2.

[3]) b. Yom. 30a and T. Kel. B.K. 1. 6 (569. 21 ff), the statement of Shimeon the Humble (c. 70 A.D.).

[4]) On the services of the Day of Atonement see M. Yom. 1. 1, on the preparations of the red heifer see M. Par. 3. 1 and on the difference of the two see T. ib. 3. 1 (631. 28).

[5]) T. Par. 3. 6 (632. 6 ff), on the Pharisaic interpretation see Sifre Num. § 124 (43b).

[6]) Num. 18. 12 (cf. Neh. 10. 38). The Mosaic law does not indicate the amount, see b. Hul. 137b, whereas the Academies prescribe an amount, see T. Ter. 5. 3 (32. 25).

[7]) Num. 18. 26 (cf. Neh. 10. 39).

[8]) Num. 18. 21 (cf. Neh. 10. 38).

converted into money to be enjoyed in Jerusalem by the farmer on the second or fifth year of the cycle [1]). The Passover festival of the fourth year marked the close of the first division in the sabbatical cycle [2]), a time of clearance [Bi'ur] when all back payments were to be settled. The individual settling the account enters the Temple on the noon of the last day of the holiday and reads the portion as prescribed in Deut. 26. 5-10.

The imposition of the Mosaic law on the farmer was very severe. In addition to the heavy taxes levied by the authorities, he had to share his produce with strangers. The removal of several grains as a payment to the priest did not affect his financial position and he was willing to comply with the rule in order not to be forced to pay a fine as prescribed in Lev. 22. 14. Yet a delivery of a tenth of his produce in addition to the other required payments was a financial burden. Thus a majority of the country folk—as in the days of their forefathers [3])—neglected the observance of the law of tithes. Their produce was given the name "Demai" by the Pharisaic teachers denoting a mixture of grains [4]), of which a part belongs to the Levites. Thus the farmer's goods were considered by the Pharisaic members ritually unfit to eat, and therefore forbidden by the Mosaic law.

At the close of the era the organized membership of the Pharisaic units is said to have numbered about six thousand [5]). This number indicates only the affiliated male members and probably the count assumed larger proportions. If we accept L. Finkelstein's assumption [6]) it can be said that one in every four city families was formally associated with Pharisaism. The Order asked of its members caution in the purchase of unprepared produce according to the laws of tithes. The members also had to submit to the rules of purity. In case a person, utensil, foodstuff or drink were defiled upon contact with one of the eleven categories of pollution, listed above,

---

[1]) See Deut. 14. 22-26, 15. 7-11 and Sin. Tob. 1. 7, 8.

[2]) M. M. Sh. 5. 6.

[3]) See Neh. 13. 10-13, the Levites did not receive their share.

[4]) Compare the Hebraic expression in Ex. 22. 28 דְּמָע. So found in the Copper Roll of the Qumran community. J. M. Sh. 56d explains the word to denote suspicion see further M. Jastrow, Dictionary of the Targumim (1903) I, p. 312, M. S. Zuckermandel in Glossar LXII of his edition of the Tosefta (1882) and A. Kohut in Aruch Completum, דמאי, explain it as a mixture.

[5]) Ant. XVII. 2. 4. § 42.

[6]) The Pharisees II, p. 609; See further J. Jeremias, Jerusalem zur Zeit Jesu, II, p. 122.

it was considered the first degree of impurity (or simply "first" (Rishon)). The contact with "the first" could produce "a second", and with the "second" a "third", and with the "third" a "fourth". A member of the Pharisaic order [1]) in the preparation of Ḥullin (commoner's food) had to be watchful for defiled objects of the first two degrees, in the preparation of Terumah (priest's food) of the three degrees and in the event of Qodesh (sacrificial food) of all four.

The procedure of initiation into the fold assumed the following order: The individual presents himself to a group of Pharisaic members, and vows to adhere fully to their code of observance [2]). He may prove himself in a preliminary test of conduct or he is to be given instructions in the code [3]). First [4]) he must accept the regulations pertaining his apparel and food purses. These objects are to be guarded against contamination arising from a contact with the "heads of impurity" or a defiled person. In such an event he must withstand a period of thirty days on guard against defilement of his drink and his apparel. The school of Shammai required for the latter a period of twelve months. The second step of initiation required the novice to be observant of the rules regarding the transmission of impurity through a lever—a difficult point of observance. The last two steps were directed to the laws of tithes and the rules of purity in the preparation of food. Thus, the member and his household must restrict their purchases to observant dealers and farmers, and at the same time be prevented from preparing their food with the assistance of defiled persons. In most cases the implication pointed at the boorish country folk.

The country people, removed from the vicinity of the Temple,

---

[1]) See M. Toh. 2. 4, 5, 6.

[2]) T. Dem. 2. 5 (47. 19) so in I Q S 5. 8-11.

[3]) T. Dem. 2. 10-11 (48. 4-8); see further Ch. Rabin, Qumran Studies, Ch. 1.

[4]) The steps of initiation are listed in J. Dem. 23a, T. ib. 2. 11 (48. 6) and 2. 1 (47. 10). The first step כְּנָפַיִם is explained by the commentaries on Jerushalmi (cf.

I. H. Weiss, D. D. Wed. I, p. 109) as regulations concerning the purity of the hands (יָדַיִם). I maintain that כְּנָפַיִם refer to apparel and food purses based on the following arguments: a) If כְּנָפַיִם denotes יָדַיִם why not state יָדַיִם ? b) M. Hag. 2.7 describes the Pharisaic rule on purity in reference to clothes (בְּגָדִים). c) Hag. 2. 12 speaks of כְּנַף בֶּגֶד in regard to the law of purity. d) Compare also the rule which distinguishes a member of the circle in M. Dem. 2. 3. e) The Essenes, too, presented an apron upon initiation, see Ch. D. Ginsburg, Essenes, p. 13. The regulations in reference to purity are recorded in M. Kel. 27-29.

admired the work of the Pharisees [1]) but could not abide by the strict code of conduct directed to their household and to their produce. A class division resulted, indirectly, in the 'Am Ha'areṣ (the country people) and the Ḥaber (the member [of the Pharisaic order]). As at the dawn of the era, in the days of Ezra, the 'Am Ha'areṣ representing the country people was divorced from the Judaic society; so in its twilight, the days of Pharisaic activity, the 'Am Ha'reṣ was segregated from his teachers. Yet the causes of this phenomenon in the two periods are different. In the days of Ezra the break was deliberately planned and was directed in the main at the assimilated or the non Jewish elements. In the Pharisaic days the separation was created unintentionally and superficially. The 'Am Ha'areṣ was permitted to join the Pharisaic order [2]), and was also accepted at their academies. Two of the great Pharisaic teachers, Shemaiah and Abtalion, were the sons of country people.

As long as the majority of the Pharisees lived about the Temple and its environs, they endeavoured to reduce the friction with their neighbours, the country people. A perimeter of trust of the purity of the utensils sold by the dealers and farmers had extended as far as Modin [3]). With the transfer of the Pharisaic academies to distant places after the destruction of the Temple, their behaviour and the stress on the code of purity caused bitter comments among the country folk, and, in turn, among the teachers as found in the Tannaitic writings.

ON JUDICATURE

Ezra [4]) acquired from the Persian king a decree granting the establishment of courts, the appointment of judges and the administration of justice through the penalties of death, expulsion, fines and imprisonment. Upon his arrival in Judea, an order was issued with the approval of the heads of state and the elders requiring the colonists to appear in Jerusalem under the penalty of excommunication and confiscation of properties [5]). The decision, presented at the gathering,

---

[1]) Bell. II. 8. 14 § 166

[2]) T. Dem. 2. 3 (47. 16). On the question of 'Am Ha'areṣ during the period see A. Büchler, Der Galiläische 'Am Ha'areṣ des zweiten Jahrhunderts, Wien, 1906.

[3]) T. Hag. 3. 33 (238, 19).

[4]) Ezr. 7. 25, 26. For the relationship of the Great Synagogue to the Sanhedrin see J. Levy, Die Präsidenten im Synderdium, M.G.W.J. 4 (1855).

[5]) Ezr. 10. 8.

asked for the immediate separation from the wives of non-Jewish parentage. This was to be enforced by the judges and elders at each town [1]). The above incidents point to the existence of a body of judges, probably appointed by Ezra and his associates [2]).

The Chronicler [3]), writing about a century later, presents the activities of Jehoshaphat, the king of Judea in the years of the first Jewish Commonwealth (c. 875-851 B.C.), in the colours of the institutions present in his days. He describes a judiciary system with a supreme-court, composed of priests, Levites and heads of the Israelite community situated in Jerusalem. Two administrators of justice were appointed at the head of the system; a priest responsible for the religious affairs and a commoner for domestic and national issues. Enforcement of the law was delegated to the Levites, the court's police force. The appointment of two administrators—as described by the Chronicler—did not, however, connote a separation of the political and religious elements. During the years of the Persian and Ptolemian rule the court composed of elders and priests, known as Gerousia [4]), was responsible to the High Priest who was, supreme in the theocratic government. Letters from Elephantine Jewry are addressed to "Jochanan the high priest and his companions, the priests of Jerusalem". Alexander the Great was approached by the high priest and his companions. The latter are described by Josephus[5]) as "a body of citizens" or in rabbinic tradition [6]) as "the nobles and counsellors" who simply represented the elders of the Gerousia. During the Seleucidian rule the sons of Tobias [7]) assumed political power over the Zadokite high priest. According to L. Finkelstein [8]) they were even instrumental in appointing the high priest.

The Hasmonaean victories, which resulted in the eviction of the Zadokite priests and the Hellenized Tobiads from administrative powers, also caused the rupture between the ecclesiastical or the ritualistic and the judicial and educational functions. The Gerousia,

---

[1]) Ib. 10. 14.
[2]) B. B.K. 82a. One of the innovations introduced by Ezra was that on Monday and Thursday, the market-days, the court was in session.
[3]) II Chr. 19. 4-11.
[4]) See Hoenig, G. Sanh. Exc. VII.
[5]) Ant. XI. 8. 5 § 329.
[6]) b. Yom. 69a and M.T. scholion 9 (p. 14).
[7]) See A. Büchler, Die Tobiaden und die Oniaden, Vienna, 1899.
[8]) The Pharisees II, p. 586; The number 71 of the Great Sanhedrin denotes 3×23 (members required for a smaller Sanhedrin) in addition to Nasi and Ab Bet-Din.

and its later equivalent the Sanhedrin, was independent in administering justice, interpreting the law and presiding over civil and capital cases. The high court was headed by a pair of teachers known as "zugoth". The first three "zugoth" were composed of priests as presidents (Nasi) and commoners as fathers of the court (Ab beth-din) [1]. The supreme court included members from the three Judaic classes and it was situated near the Temple in the Chamber of the Hewn-Stone [2].

The increase in responsibilities of law and order enlarged the judiciary system. At the head was the supreme-court (Συνέδριον, בֵּית דִּין הַגָּדוֹל) composed of seventy-one members responsible in extreme cases and court-briefs involving high personage [3]. The lesser courts of twenty-three presided over capital cases and were located in major towns. Two such courts were also situated in Jerusalem [4]. Settlements in civil matters were handled by the elders or the teachers-scribes in all parts of the country [5]. In cases of a higher nature the parties appealed to the higher courts [6]. Death penalties and banishment were administered for capital offences; flogging, imposition of fines and imprisonment for lesser crimes [7].

Since the legislative and judicial powers were vested in the hands of the law makers, the Sadducees and the Pharisees strove to assume control over these powers. In the later years of John Hyrcanus' reign (c. 100 B.C.), the golden era of the Hasmonaean rule, the Pharisaic teachers were ousted from the seat of judgement. John Hyrcanus [8], following the advice of a Sadducean sympathizer,

---

[1] See Hoenig, G. Sanh. ch. 4

[2] Ib. ch. IX; M. T. scholion, 10 (p. 16, 17) refers to the Pharisaic Sanhedrin as that of Israel in contrast to the Sadducean court.

[3] See M. Sanh. 1. 5 and 2. 1; See Hoenig, G. Sanh., ch. VIII.

[4] See M. Sanh. 11. 2.

[5] M. Ed. 2. 3 cites a civil case administered by an elder. See also M. Ket. 13. 1 (b. ib. 105 b) which mentions the names of judges or arbitrators in civil matters during the period, see further p. 138.

[6] M. Sanh. 11. 2 see also Sifre Deut. § 152 (104 b).

[7] Death punishment was administered in four forms: a) "stoning" described M. Sanh. 6 in cases recorded ib. 7.4 ff, b) "burning" described ib. 7. 2 in cases ib. 9. 1, c) "decapitating" described ib. 7. 3 in cases ib. 9. 1, and d) "strangling" described ib. 7. 3 in cases ib. 11. 1 ff. A sentence of "banishment" was issued in case death was caused accidently see M. Mak. 2, "flogging" described ib. 3. 12 in cases ib. 3. 1 ff and "imprisonment" as recorded in M. Sanh. 9. 5.

[8] See Ant. XIII. 10.5 and compare b. Kid. 66 a. The Pharisees remarked: "It is not befitting you to be the High Priest".

noted that the influence of the Pharisees in priestly matters was
undermining the Hasmonaean position as high priest. The Sadducees,
therefore, obtained the highest position in the state, a control over
the judiciary system. They adopted a strict code of justice: the application of the ancient rule of lex talionis. They issued [1]) a book of
laws spelling out the different capital offences and their related punishments. Josephus relates that the Sadducees ordered the death
penalty to a person who [2]) issued a false report on the status of the
high priest. The Pharisees opposed this severe sentence, "for they did
not think it right to sentence a man to death for calumny, and anyway
the Pharisees are naturally lenient in the matter of punishment".

The priests of the more prominent families exhibited a harsher attitude on the enforcement of the law. As far back as the outset of the era
Nehemiah, an eye witness, recorded [3]) the extortion and the mishandling of the Temple funds by the high priest and his associates. John
Hyrcanus on the advice of the priestly clan appointed two Sadducean
sympathizers, as administrators [4]) of the priestly taxes which were
collected by strong men. With the expulsion of the Pharisees from the
seat of justice, the Herodian period witnessed even greater displays of
force on behalf of the priestly families in the administration of religious
affairs. A period of near-terror and brutality among the inhabitants is
reflected in the following ballad [5]):

"Woe is me, for the house of Boethus: woe is me, for their clubs.
Woe is me, for the house of Kathros: woe is me, for their pen.
Woe is me, for the house of Annas: woe is me, for their whisper.
Woe is me, for the house of Ismael ben Piabi: woe is me, for
their fists.
For they are high priests and their sons the treasures; their sons-
in-law are Temple officers and their servants come and beat us
with their staves".

Jesus [6]) was also met by a band with swords and clubs, including the

---

[1]) As described in M.T. 4 (p. 8) and see scholion ad loc.

[2]) Ant. XIII. 10. 6 § 294.

[3]) Neh. 13. 4-14 and 5. 1-13 in his diary.

[4]) See J. Sot. 24a and J. M. Sh. 56d on the appointment of pair of administrators. These men, Eleazer ben Pehorah and Jehuda ben Pethorah, collected the taxes
by force. The former was a Sadducean sympathizer, who was responsible for
the expulsion of the Pharisees. See b. Kid. 66a (the variant, Eleazer ben Pe'orah)

[5]) T. Men. 13. 21 (533. 33-38) cf. b. Pes. 57a as transmitted by Abba Saul ben
Bitnith, a contemporary of Zadok's father, see M. Shab. 24.5 (c. 10-60 A.D.). See
further Klausner, Jesus, p. 337.

[6]) Matt. 26. 47 ff, Mk. 14. 43ff, Luk. 22.50, John 18.3.

High Priest's slaves, to be delivered to Caiphas' court for hearing. Josephus speaks in the same bitter way of the Sadducees attitude to law (see above). The high priest Ben-Zion [1]) during Archelaus' rule is said to have exercised excommunication and expulsion from the priestly matters on one of the families and the incident had to be discussed only in utmost secrecy. Even among the priestly Watches, the families in power denied their brethren the skins of the Temple's treasury allotted to them (T. Men. 13. 18, 19).

During the Herodian-procurators period the exhibition of forceful application of the law was limited to religious affairs and the administration of the Temple revenue. The priests were recognized by the Roman authorities as the leaders of the state. Their families, viz. the Boethusians, were associated with their predecessors, the Sadducees, the Zadokite clan. Their attitude towards law and order reflects also the Saducean stand in former days.

During the lifetime of Alexander Jannai I (103-78 B.C.) a reign of terror prevailed in which the Pharisees and the Teacher of Righteousness were persecuted. The cruellest Roman punishment, crucifixion, was administered to the opponents [2]) of the king. Josephus relates that while most of the teachers [3]) were hiding, the Pharisaic zealots opposing the monarchy persuaded Demetrius III (88 B.C.) to remove Alexander Jannai and to restore in his stead the former theocratic rule. With great difficulty the king was able to withstand the forces of Demetrius III. Upon the return of Alexander to Jerusalem, he put to death the Pharisaic instigators, and the people in anger surnamed him θρακίδας [4]). Alexander Jannai I, realizing the great influence excercised by the Pharisees over the masses, advised his wife Salom Zion [5]): "Do not fear the Pharisees nor the non-Pharisees. Do fear the hypocrites who pretend to be like the Pharisees; their deeds are the deeds of Zimri and they ask to be rewarded as Pinchas".

When Salom Zion ascended the throne, the Pharisees returned to power. The occasion is recorded as a day of celebration [6]). The Sanhedrin was headed by the capable Shimeon ben Shetach and his

---

[1]) M. Ed. 8. 7 and compare T. ib. 3.4 (459. 30 ff).

[2]) Ant. XIII. 14. 2 § 380.

[3]) For example the head of the Duumvirate fled to Alexandria, J. Hag. 17 d, and Shimeon ben Shetach was in hiding b. Kid. 66 a. So was the plight of the Teacher of Righteousness, see Pesher Nahum discussed pp. 107, 151.

[4]) See J. H. Allegro, Thrakidan, in Palestine Exploration Quaterly, 1959.

[5]) b. Sot. 22 b, cf. Ant. XIII. 15. 5.

[6]) M. T. scholion 10 (p. 16), cf. Ant. XIII. 16. 2.

elder colleague, Jehudah ben Tabbai; the third "pair" in the rabbinic tradition. Their first act was to abolish the harsh code of laws enacted by the Sadducees. Cases before the court were not to be resolved by applying the written unaltered rules; instead they were to be judged each on its own merit. A tribunal can no longer take matters in its own hands, the voice of the people must be heard. Hence judges must rely solely on the testimony of public witnesses. Circumstancial evidence cannot be considered [1]). A testimony is to be presented by two eye witnesses, so their statements can be collaborated upon investigation [2]). A separation is to exist between the executors of justice and those responsible for the presentation of evidence; therefore, no witness is to serve as a judge [3]).

In opposition to the Sadducean stand, Shimeon ben Shetach stressed the importance of public witnesses. In former days the Sadducean court executed punishment according to the prescribed rules enacted by the legislators, absolving the greater participation of the eye witness. The court of Shimeon ben Shetach formulated the verdict from the hearing based on public testimony. Thus, the Pharisaic heirs taught [4]): "A Sanhedrin executing capital punishment once in seven years is considered a murderous court".

To demonstrate the fallibility of the Pharisaic stand on jurisprudence a band of mockers [5]), presumably Sadducean sympathizers, brought false testimony against Shimeon's son. The court presided over by Shimeon found the son guilty. As it was about to carry out the death penalty, the witnesses declared the testimony false. The son turned to his father and said: "Father if you wish to bring about reforms, then use me as a threshold". The head of the tribunal witnessed the execution of his beloved son, an heroic example in promulgating the new legislation, namely, the credibility of the public witnesses in court.

The complete reliance on the testimony of strangers did create a measure to prevent similar damage. A stricter interpretation of the law of false-witnesses was introduced by Shimeon. The Mosaic law

---

[1]) J. Sanh. 22 b.

[2]) Daniel demonstration of false testimony (Sus., LXX, 33-43) is to be compared to a similar demonstration by the youth, Yochanan ben Zakkai, see M. Sanh. 5. 2.

[3]) See b. R. H. 26 a, a controversy between R. Tarfon and R. Aqiba (c. 100 A.D.). Both affirm the older view that no witness can be a judge.

[4]) M. Mak. 1. 11, cf. M. T. scholion 6 (p. 12) which explains that only in extreme cases was capital punishment administered.

[5]) J. Sanh. 23b. This case gave rise to the rule: "Once a testimony was delivered and accepted in court, it cannot be altered", see b. Sanh. 44b.

[Deut. 19. 18, 19] declares: "Behold the witness is a false witness . . .
then shall ye do unto him as he had purposed to do unto his brother".
The Sadducees identified the above punishment with the rule of lex-
talionis as expounded in the Mosaic law [ib. 19. 21]. Therefore, the
execution of false witnesses could take place only if the sentence
had been carried out on the accused. Shimeon broadened the scope
of the law. He administered the death penalty for false testimony as
long as it was accepted in the court, even though the sentence was not
carried out on the accused [1]).

The era before Shimeon's reforms witnessed the execution of the
Sadducean opponents in the cruellest fashion, crucifixion. The
emphasis on severe punishments was introduced by the Sadducees
for lesser offences. Even in later years when the Sadducean adherents
were in control of the Temple, they administered cruel punishments on
their fellow members. When a priest was found serving in the Temple
in a state of impurity, the priestly youths [2]) would split his skull with
clubs. On one occasion [3]), a priestly daughter who had committed
adultery was burned at the stake, and the Talmudists interpreted it to
be the action of the Sadducean court.

The policies of the new administration under Shimeon's guidance
were also directed to a more humane form of penalty. Shimeon is said
to have executed seventy witches in Askelon [4]), administering an
easier form of death, hanging. The Tannaitic description of the
four modes of death penalty to execute in a more humane fashion [5])
is based on the early reforms of the Sanhedrin. One of the forms,
strangling [6]), was executed on Hyrcanus II following a Sanhedrin
session convoked by Herod the Great. Josephus declares [7]): "It did

---

[1]) See M. Mak. 1. 7, cf. b. ib. 5b and Mech. on 23. 7 (p. 105b).

[2]) M. Sanh. 9. 6.

[3]) M. Sanh. 7. 2, T. ib. 9. 11 (429. 30); note the presence of Zadok, a priest,
at the execution.

[4]) According to the rule á witch is stoned, M. Sanh. 7. 4; yet Shimeon administered a lesser form of punishment "hanging". See J. Sanh. 23c, This was
even in later generations regarded as an extraordinary case, see M. T. scholion 6
(p. 12). Cf. Ant. 13. 16. 2 § 410 (σφάττουσι, decapitating).

[5]) See Sifre Deut. § 221 (114b), which states: "All those who are sentenced to
stoning are hanged: can it be that the court will hang the accused while he is
alive as it is customary with the other governments (the Romans), therefore it is
written "and he is to be killed". The accused must not suffer the ordeal of crucifixion. See further S. Zeitlin and N. Wieder on the phrase יתלה אנשים חיים in Journal
of Jewish Studies, vol. VIII, 1957, pp. 117-121.

[6]) Ant. 15. 6 3 § 176.

[7]) Ant. 13. 10. 6 § 294.

not seem right to punish reproaches with death, and indeed the Pharisees even upon other occasions are not apt to be severe in punishments". The tendency to be lenient in cases of capital punishment was
based on a democratic concept reflected in the Mosaic law. The accused
is an equal of his brothers [1]). Thus in later generations [2]) the former
rule: "Select an easier death", was linked with the golden rule: "Love
thy neighbour as thyself". Every effort was made for an acquittal [3]),
and in case the defendant was found guilty, steps were taken to alleviate
the pain of death. A custom prevailed among the wealthy women
of Jerusalem to deliver to the condemned a potion to deaden his
senses before the execution [4]). Jesus before his crucifixion is said to
have been offered a potion of wine mixed with a grain of myrra [5]),
confirming the above practice.

The status of the individual was also raised with the restoration of
the Pharisaic teachers to the legislative powers. One of the bitter
controversies between the two parties concerned the position of the
slaves, a submerged group, in civil matters. Although a slave in a
Jewish home was subject to the humane Mosaic laws [6]), the Sadducees [7]) maintained, as was the common practice, that a slave or maid
was to be considered the master's property. In cases of damage they
were placed in the same category with an ox or an ass, thereby holding
the owner responsible for their actions. The Pharisees, on the other hand
ascribing to the slave the same status as that of a Jewish woman,
considered him responsible for his actions. The subservient status of
the individual does not affect him as a human being. He is considered
as he would have been in different circumstances. Thus, if he was set
free he had to pay for all the damages done in the past [8]). The same
democratic principle determining the position of the slave is noted in
the attitude of the later Pharisaic masters [9]).

The status of women was also improved during the Pharisaic
return to power. From early times the woman was financially secure

---

[1]) See Sifre Deut. on 25. 3 § 286 (p. 125a), M. Mak. 3. 15.
[2]) See T. Sanh. 9. 11 (429. 32) in the name of R. Jehudah, the disciple of R. Aqiba.
[3]) M. Sanh. 5; 6. 1.
[4]) b. Sanh. 43a.
[5]) Matt. 27. 34, Mk. 15. 23.
[6]) See Ex. 21. 1-11, Deut. 15. 12-18, 23. 16, 17.
[7]) M. Yad. 4. 7.
[8]) See the rule in M.B.K. 8. 4. A slave is equated in the Jewish law with the
religious status of a woman.
[9]) For example M. Ber. 2. 6. about Tabbai, the slave of R. Gamliel II, J. Ber.
5b about the maid of R. Eliezer.

under the Judaic institution of the Ketubah, a marriage document guaranteeing payment in case of divorce. Prior to Shimeon's administration [1]), a security endorsing the woman's rights to the Ketubah was placed in the father-in-law's house. Since the value of the security depended on the husband's financial position, a wife of a wealthy man, viz. the wives of the Sadducees and the aristocrats, obtained a greater payment in case of divorce than did the wife of a plebeian. Shimeon ben Shetach introduced a clause in the Ketubah stating [2]): "All the properties in my possession are held responsible to your Ketubah". This insertion became known as "the court's clause". Other clauses introduced in the Ketubah were probably initiated in the days of Shimeon. The employment of the Ketubah's text in the schools of Shammai and Hillel [3]) for halachic exegesis points to the early dating of the clauses.

Another "court-clause" in the document states [4]): "Male children that you will bear me, shall inherit the monies of your Ketubah in addition to the allotted shares partitioned in the estate with their step-brothers; female children that you will bear me, shall remain in the house and shall be supported from my properties until they shall be wedded." This insertion was directed at a controversial point existing between the two parties. The Sadducees [5]) maintained that a daughter had the same right of inheritance as a son; while the Pharisees declared that the son's daughter precedes the daughter of the deceased in the order of inheritance. The Pharisees explained their position with an halachic exegesis similar to the one mentioned above in reference to the levirate marriage. The Mosaic law reads (Num. 27. 8): "In case a man dies and there was no son unto him [וּבֵן אֵין־לֹו], then ye shall cause his inheritance to pass unto his daughter". The reading also implies the form עַיֵּין־לֹו (hold an inquiry concerning him) [6]), namely, anyone surviving his son is preferred to the daughter. The Pharisees maintained that the individual assumes full rights over

---

[1]) B. Ket. 82b, J. ib. 32b, c (a marriage document was uncovered at the Dead Sea area, Discoveries II pp. 109-117). See also M. Gaster, Die Ketubbah bei den Samaritanern, M.G.W.J. 54 (1910).

[2]) As related in the rabbinic sources mentioned above, see M. Ket. 8. 8 and the explanation by the Tosefite Rabbi Issac at the end of b. Ket. 82b. Compare T. Ket. 12. 1 (274. 3-5).

[3]) J. Yeb. 14d.

[4]) M. Ket. 4. 10, 11.

[5]) M. T. scholion 5 (p. 10), cf. b. B.B. 115b; On this point Jesus seems to have sided with the Sadducees, see b. Shab. 116b.

[6]) B. B.B. 115a see also Sifre Num. §§ 133, 134 (49a-50a).

his properties. His estate is to be handed over to those who will represent him in name and action, i.e., his son. As long as he is alive he can also select the proper mate for this daughter knowing that his properties will be transferred to the party of his choise. In case of his death, the daughter is still secured financially by the Ketubah before she chooses to marry [1]). Upon her marriage she is, in turn, supported by her husband, whereas the orphans left by the son of the deceased have only their grandfather's properties as their support.

The same mode of interpretation was applied by the Pharisees [2]) to the rule in the Priestly Code [Lev. 22. 13]: "In case a priest's daughter will be widowed or divorced and there is no child unto her [וְזֶרַע אֵין לָהּ] then she may return to her father's house as in the days of her youth, from the bread of her father she can eat." The additional reading of עַיֵּין לָהּ implies hold an inquiry concerning the daughter's descendants.

Thus, the Pharisees denied a priest's daughter the support from the priests' granary as long as a child is alive, even though he may be that of her deceased son. The Sadducean priests affected by the above ruling naturally denied the application of oral interpretation to the written law.

A denial of the oral tradition by the Sadducean teachers is also noted in the Pharisaic interpretation of the Mosaic law concerning Ḥaliṣah (the removal of a shoe, a ceremony taking place in lieu of the levirate marriage). The law states (Deut. 25.9): "Then shall his brother's wife draw nigh unto him in the presence of the elders and loose his shoe from off his foot and spit in his face [וְיָרְקָה בְּפָנָיו]". The last words are explained literally [3]) by the Sadducean teachers to mean the levirate woman is to eject spit directly on the face of her brother-in-law, that is, to register abuse in court to a brother who does not adhere to the primitive law of levirate marriage. The Pharisees, who in general encouraged the woman to follow the ceremony [4]) rather than resort to a levirate marriage, interpreted the last words to denote a visible spit ejected before the court. Thus in the issuance of a Ḥaliṣah document a phrase was inserted in early days, saying [5]): "And she had removed the shoe of his right foot and spat before us (the court) spit visible on the ground".

---

[1]) As explained in b. Ket. 52b.
[2]) b. Kid. 4a, compare Sifra on 22. 13 (97c).
[3]) See M.T. scholion 4 (p. 9), compare Sifre Deut. § 291 (126a).
[4]) M. Bech. 1. 7, compare b. Yeb. 39b.
[5]) J. Sanh. 19a, compare T. Yeb. 12. 15 (256. 12).

THE FESTIVALS

The structure of a Jewish liturgical year was developed in the Mosaic law and in the prophetic teachings. Its aim was to consolidate the Jewish nation and, at the same time, to preserve the unique background of the Jewish heritage and religion. Through the institution of sacrifices and a body of priests the Temple was to maintain the prescribed regulations governing the liturgical year, and at the same time, serve as an organ of centralisation. Every day from morning until evening acquired a religious significance through the offering of the "Tamid". The Sabbath and the New-Moon Day were a cause for additional sacrifices. The other major festivals indicated a time of celebration with public participation and a reason for offering numerous sacrifices [1]).

For the duration of the Second Commonwealth era, the Temple's liturgical year was composed of [2]): the week day, the Sabbaths, the New-Moon Days, the day of slaughtering the paschal lamb, the day of offering the Sacred-Sheaf, the week of the unleavened bread [the second paschal ceremony] [3]), the day of Pentecost, the New Year Day, the Great Fast-Day, the week of Booths with the additional day of Aṣereth (Assembly).

The position of the three pilgrim-feasts in the liturgical year was governed by the agricultural season, commencing with the Feast of Unleavened Bread in the month of the Ears (Abib) near the spring equinox. It indicated a lapse of half a solar year. On the other hand, the celebration of a New-Moon Day and the commencement of Passover and Tabernacles at the full moon points to the usage of a lunar year. Regulating the Temple services according to different calendar schemes necessitated a knowledge of intercalation and astronomical calculations. Thus, from days of antiquity the fixing of a calendar, an esoteric lore, became a prerogative of the priesthood.

During the Second Jewish Commonwealth, the priests acquaint-

---

[1]) See further the article "Sacrifices" by E. G. Hirsch in J. Enc.

[2]) As enumerated by Philo, De Sp. Leg. II. 11 § 41 see also Ant. 3. 10. 1-6 The important days of the year are listed in the covenant, Neh. 10. 34; compare the list of sacrifices on important occasions in Num. 28, 29.

[3]) The second or minor Passover is described in Num. 9. 1-14 which falls on the full-moon of Iyyar. See M. Pes. 9, M.T. 2 (p. 5) and the list of the Dead Sea calendar presented on p. 70. In the days prior to the Destruction the following festivals can be included: "The Festival of Dedication", see II Macc. 1, 2. 1-18 and "Purim" or "the Day of Mordechai", see II Macc. 15. 36 and Es. 9. 26.

ed with the Babylonian astronomical lore [1]) perfected a system regulating the liturgical year. They introduced a division of the priestly
families into twenty-four Watches. Each Watch was responsible for a
week of Temple duties [2]), commencing with the afternoon services
of the Sabbath and ending with the Mussaf (additional [mid-day]
service) of the following Sabbath. The three major pilgrim-feasts,
marked with greater Temple activity, were maintained by joint
participation of all the Watches [3]). The close of the seven weeks
from "the day you first put the sickle to the standing grain", the
beginning of a pentecontad of the Assyrian calendar [4]), was marked
by the feast of the First Fruits which usually coincided with the
end of the wheat harvest. On that day [5]) the wave-offering of the
two leavened loaves was enjoyed by all the Watches. That day according to the priestly reckoning always fell on a Sunday [6]). Its arrival
indicated the close of the activities of the first eight family courses and
the beginning of the activities of the last sixteen Watches [7]). Thus,
the Temple services from spring until autumn was fixed by the priestly
divisions. The Chronicler, projecting the institution of his days to that
of the former Temple, states (II Chr. 8. 13. 14): "Concerning the daily
duties, it is to offer according to the commandment of Moses, on the
Sabbath and on the New-Moons and on the appointed seasons, three
times a year, even in the Feast of Unleavened Bread, in the Feast of
Weeks and in the Feast of Tabernacles. He (Solomon and, in
fact, the institution appears only during the Second Temple period)
appointed . . . the courses of the priests to their services and the Levites
to their charges, as the duty of every day required".

The administration of the Temple services, the supervision over
religious rites and matters, and the regulating of a calendar year were
vested in the hands of the priests during the Zadokite ministry. Letters
were issued to diasporaean Jewry on the date of observance of the
Festival of the Unleavened Bread. Only with the Maccabean upheavel,

---

[1]) R. Jochanan maintains that the names of the Hebrew months were
adopted in Babylonia, see J.R.H. 56d—On Jewish Calendar see Schürer, G.J.V. I,
Beilage III; J. B. Segal, Vetus Testamentum VII, p. 250 ff.
[2]) T. Suk. 4. 24, 25 (200. 11-13).
[3]) M. Suk. 5. 6, 7.
[4]) See H. and J. Lewy, The Week and the oldest West Asiatic Calendar, H.U.C.
A. XVII.
[5]) M. ib. 5. 7 the Wave-Offering, as described in Lev. 23. 17.
[6]) M.T. scholion 1 (p. 4, 5) and b. Men. 65a.
[7]) The division of eight and sixteen is mentioned in I Chr. 24. 4, 6.

did the priestly caste lose its former all-embracing powers. The religiously inspired masses under the banner of the zealous Hasideans and Hasmonaeans rededicated the Temple and restored the services after a cessation of three and a half years. They cleansed the courts removing all defiled objects, and also ousted the Hellenized autocratic priests. The high priesthood itself was delegated to the Hasmonaean family in accordance with the public wishes. The Temple became the house of the people, and the teachers came from their ranks. The same teachers, who had advocated a strict code of separation and purity, directed also their attention to the masses, bringing them into closer harmony with the Temple services and the yearly festivities. Owing to the liberal approach of the Pharisees, they became popular and were admired by the people [1]).

The commoners acquired a greater say in priestly matters. They formed "Guard-Corps" (Ma'amadoth) [2]) whose duties were to be present at all Temple services. Each week the arrival of the new priestly Watch and that of the commoners' representation was a cause for public concern and celebration. The commoners included women and slaves who were also permitted to slaughter [3]) their own sacrifices. In former days, the Chronicler relates [4]) that the rites of the paschal lamb, from the moment of slaughtering until its roasting, were solely the duties of the priests and the Levites, as is the case with the Samaritans. Even in cases such as leprosy, where the Mosaic law requires the priest to examine the afflicted, the duty was transferred to the local elders. The elder [5]) examined the plagued body, then informed the priest of his findings. The priest's sole duty was to ascertain the diagnosis verbally.

The members of the priestly clans, viz., the house of Zadok and the house of Boethus, were the bitter rivals of the Pharisaic school. They upheld the priestly lore of the past opposing the newer innovations introduced by the Pharisaic teachers. The important controversies included the calendar and the regulations concerning the festivals. The rise of Pharisaic popularity and the inclusion of commoners in the Temple corps compelled the Sadducees to adopt the Pharisaic regulations in time of worship [6]).

---

[1]) Bell. II. 8. 14 § 166, Ant. XIII. 10. 6 § 298; 15. 5 § 401.
[2]) M. Taan. 4.2 .
[3]) M. Zeb. 3. 1.
[4]) II. Chr. 35. 10-13.
[5]) M. Neg. 3. 1 see p. 124.
[6]) As described in the story recorded in T. Yom. 1. 8 (181. 1 ff).

THE CALENDAR

During the Hasmonaean period the Essenes issued their own calendar declaring the priestly calendar misleading [1]). Their calendar [2]) was based on a solar year of 364 days. The year consists of four quarters. Each quarter contains three months, the first two of 30 days each and the last month of 31 days. The first day of the first month, Nisan, falls on a Wednesday, therefore no holiday can occur on a Saturday thus upholding its sanctity. Since each priest's Watch is responsible for a week's activity in the Temple, the 52 weeks are divided into 2 times 24 Watches, and in the intervening 4 weeks the last 4 Watches serve. The whole solar year is divided into 52 [3]) divisions of commoners' courses as introduced by the Pharisees.

The calendar appears as illustrated on page 71.

According to this scheme the day of Pentecost falls on the 15th of Siwan, the middle of the month, as is the case with the first day of the other two pilgrim festivals. This day was celebrated by Abraham as the Day of the First Fruits according to the book of Jubilees [4]). Pentecost, therefore, was fixed by a count of seven weeks after the Sabbath following the Feast of Unleavened Bread [5]).

The list of Watches found in the Qumran area confirms this calendar, since the above calendar was permanently fixed. It states [6]): "On the first year, her festivals: On 3 of Mauziah: the Passover (14th of Nisan)

[On 1] of Jedaiah: the Wave-Offering [of the Omer] (26th of Nisan) *

[On 5] of Seorim: the [Second] Passover (14th of Iyyar)

On 1 of Jeshuah: the Feast of Weeks (15th of Siwan)

[On] 4 of Mauziah: the Day of Remembrance ** (1st of Tishri)

[On] 6 of Jehoiarib: the Day of Atonement (10th of Tishri)

[On 4 of] Jedaiah: the Feast of Booths (15th of Tishri)".

Note: The numbers represent the days of the week starting with Sunday.

* According to the Pharisees this day falls on the 16th of Nisan with which the count of weeks begins (b. Men. 65).
** The name for the New Year (Lev. 23.24).

[1]) The Essene Day of Atonement was rejected by the priests, I Q.P. Hab. 11. 5-8. Compare the warning in Jub. 6. 32-38, and C. D. 6. 17-19.

[2]) See Jub. 6. 23 ff and E. En. 72. 32. Compare the calendar by Mlle. A. Jaubert in Le Calendrier des Jubilés, Vetus Testamentum, III (1953), p. 253.

[3]) I Q.M. 2. 1-5, where also the 26 Watches are mentioned, i.e., $2 \times 26 = 2 \times 24 + 4$.

[4]) 15. 1; Cf. Goudoever, Bibl. Cal., p. 103, the dates of Ezra Apocalypse.

[5]) See Goudoever, Bibl. Cal., p. 25 ff.

[6]) J. T. Milik in V.T. Supplement, IV (1957), p. 17 ff. and in "Dix Ans de

Left table

Names of the 24 watches	Sunday	Monday	Tuesday	Wednesd.	Thursday	Friday	Saturday	Month
Mauziah	29	30	31	1	2	3	4	Elul
Delaiah	22	23	24	25	26	27	28	Elul
Gamul	15	16	17	18	19	20	21	Elul
Yachin	8	9	10	11	12	13	14	Elul
Jechezeqel	1	2	3	4	5	6	7	Ab
Petahiah	24	25	26	27	28	29	30	Ab
Aphses	17	18	19	20	21	22	23	Ab
Hezir	10	11	12	13	14	15	16	Ab
Immer	3	4	5	6	7	8	9	Ab
Bilgah	26	27	28	29	30	1	2	Tammuz
Jeshebeab	19	20	21	22	23	24	25	Tammuz
Huppah	12	13	14	15	16	17	18	Tammuz
Yaqim	5	6	7	8	9	10	11	Tammuz
Eliashib	29	30	31	1	2	3	4	Tammuz
Shechaniah	22	23	24	25	26	27	28	Siwan
Jeshuah	**15**	16	17	18	19	20	21	Siwan
Abijah	8	9	10	11	12	13	14	Siwan
Haqqoş	1	2	3	4	5	6	7	Siwan
Mijahin	24	25	26	27	28	29	30	Iyyar
Malchiah	17	18	19	20	21	22	23	Iyyar
Seorim	10	11	12	13	**14**	15	16	Iyyar
Harim	3	4	5	6	7	8	9	Iyyar
Jedaiah	**26**	27	28	29	30	1	2	Iyyar
Jehoiarib	19	20	21	22	23	24	25	Nisan
Mauziah	12	13	**14**	15	16	27	18	Nisan
Z	5	6	7	8	9	10	11	Nisan
Y				1	2	3	4	Nisan

Right table

Names of the 24 watches	Sunday	Monday	Tuesday	Wednesd.	Thursday	Friday	Saturday	Month
Z	5	6	7	8	9	10	11	Adar
Y	29	30	31	1	2	3	4	Adar
X	22	23	24	25	26	27	28	Adar
W	15	16	17	18	19	20	21	Adar
Delaiah	8	9	10	11	12	13	14	Adar
Gamul	1	2	3	4	5	6	7	Adar
Yachin	24	25	26	27	28	29	30	Shebat
Jechezeqel	17	18	19	20	21	22	23	Shebat
Petahiah	10	11	12	13	14	15	16	Shebat
Aphses	3	4	5	6	7	8	9	Shebat
Hezir	26	27	28	29	30	1	2	Shebat
Immer	19	20	21	22	23	24	25	Tebeth
Bilgah	12	13	14	15	16	17	18	Tebeth
Jeshebeab	5	6	7	8	9	10	11	Tebeth
Huppah	29	30	31	1	2	3	4	Tebeth
Yaqim	22	23	24	25	26	27	28	Kislew
Eliashib	15	16	17	18	19	20	21	Kislew
Shechaniah	8	9	10	11	12	13	14	Kislew
Jeshuah	1	2	3	4	5	6	7	Kislew
Abijah	24	25	26	27	28	29	30	Marcheshwan
Haqqoş	17	18	19	20	21	22	23	Marcheshwan
Mijamin	10	11	12	13	14	15	16	Marcheshwan
Malchiah	3	4	5	6	7	8	9	Marcheshwan
Seorim	26	27	28	29	30	1	2	Marcheshwan
Harim	19	20	21	22	23	24	25	Tishri
Jedaiah	12	13	14	15	16	17	18	Tishri
Jehoiarib	5	6	7	8	9	**10**	11	Tishri

Découvertes dans le Désert de Juda", Paris, 1957, p. 72. See, also, S. Talmon, The Calendar Reckoning of the Sect from the Judaean Desert, Scripta Hierosolymitana, IV, 1958.

A fragment further states: "On the 16th (of Iyyar) the Week of Malchijah". Thus the Qumran findings do follow the scheme offered by the author of Jubilees [1]). The Watch family of Mauziah appears to have occupied an important position in the calendar. With Mauziah began the important holidays in Nisan (Passover) and in Tishri (The New Year). Is it possible that the Teacher of Righteousness, a priest [2]) mentioned in the Qumran writings, was a member of the priestly family, Mauziah?

Year I. Intercalated month (Weadar)

Sunday	27	4	11	18		8			2	9	16	
Monday	28	5	12	19					3	10	17	
Tuesday	29	6	13	20					4	11	18	
Wednesday	30	7	14	21					5	12	19	
Thursday	1	8	15	22					6	13	20	
Friday	2	9	16	23	14				7	14	21	29
Saturday	3	10	17	24			1		8	15	22	
	Nisan				Iyyar	Siwan			Tishri			Shebat

Year II Regular month (Adar)

Sunday	29	7	14	21		11		5	12	19
Monday	1	8	15					6	13	20
Tuesday	2	9	16		14			7	14	21
Wednesday	3	10	17				1	8	15	22
Thursday	4	11	18				2	9	16	23
Friday	5	12	19				3	10	17	24
Saturday	6	13	20				4	11	18	25
	Nisan				Iyyar	Siwan		Tishri		

Year III Regular month (Adar)

Sunday	25	3	10	17		7	1	8	15	22
Monday	26	4	11	18			2	9	16	
Tuesday	27	5	12	19			3	10	17	
Wednesday	28	6	13	20			4	11	18	
Thursday	29	7	14	21			5	12	19	
Friday	1	8	15	22			6	13	20	
Saturday	2	9	16	23	14		7	14	21	
	Nisan				Iyyar	Siwan		Tishri		

---

[1]) Contrary to the opinion of J. Morgenstern, Vetus Testamentum, V, p. 34 ff; See J. T. Milik, op. cit., p. 71 n. 1.

[2]) I Q. p. Hab. 2. 8.

Another fragment represents a synchronism which enables us to establish the official calendar, perhaps that of the Sadducean priests [1]. It states: "On the 6th (i.e., Friday) of Jechezeqel, the 29th, is on the 22nd of the eleventh (month, i.e., Shebat)." The date, 22nd of Shebat, according to the calendar on p. 71, does fall on Friday of the week of Jechezeqel. The priestly calendar was, on the other hand, a luni-solar calendar, i.e., 354 days per year, according to the phases of the moon (E. En. 79), in addition to 30 days intercalated once every three years after the last month, Adar ($3 \times 364 = 3 \times 354 + 30$). If the Friday of Jechezeqel was Shebat 29th of the priestly calendar, therefore, the beginning of the Year, the 1st of Nisan, falls on Thursday. A year reckoned every odd month 30 days, and 29 days for those with even numbers. The calendar appears on page 72.

Passover of the 3rd year was celebrated on Thursday, as recorded in the Synoptic Gospels [2], whereas the Second Passover was celebrated on Friday of the first year (The Passover? of John). John (7. 37 and 9. 14 deleting 8. 1-11) further relates that the last day of Booths was a Sabbath as shown in the above calendar of the first year. Pentecost falls, always, seven weeks after the Sabbath of the Feast of Unleavened Bread [3]. Thus, in the third year Pentecost arrives on the 7th of Siwan (compare the statement of R. Jose, b. Shab. 86b) and in the second year on the 11th [4]. Nicholas (Ant. XIII. 8.4 § 251) relates that Hyrcanus I marching with his troops under Antiochus VII caused the whole army to be delayed for two days because the Jews could not travel either on the Sabbath or on the Sunday, which according to the priestly calendar was the day of Pentecost.

During the Herodian period, the Pharisees contested the priestly calendar. They insisted [5] that each month should be calculated separately according to public testimony declaring the arrival of the new moon. The Boethusian priests naturally contested the Pharisaic

---

[1] See further E. Vogt, Kalenderfragmente aus Qumran, Biblica 39 (1958), p. 72 ff.

[2] See Mk. 14. 12 (14th of Nisan) and 15.1 (15th of Nisan, day of crucifixion) which was Friday (v. 42), so Luke and Matthew. Compare a similar dating of Passover in S.O.R. 5 (p. 34, 35). According to John the day of crucifixion is Friday, yet it was the 14th of Nisan (18. 28).

[3] See Goudoever, Bibl. Cal., p. 19 ff.

[4] See further Goudoever, op. cit., p. 27 and p. 61.

[5] M.R.H. 2. 6, 7, 8. For rabbinic material concerning the reckoning of the year see B. Zuckermann, Materialien zur Entwicklung der altjüddischer Zeitrechnung im Talmud, Breslau, 1882.

innovation and even hired [1]) false witnesses to alter the astronomical reckoning. The Pharisees maintained that the issuance of a yearly calendar should arise from the heads of the academy [2]), therefore the Pharisees determined the dates of the great festivals. Rabban Gamliel I, a contemporary of Paul, is said to have issued letters to diasporean Jewry determining the calendar for the coming year and informing them of the designated festivals, a prerogative of the priests in the early days.

THE TAMID

The most important sacrifice regulating the Temple services was the Tamid (daily, once in the morning and once in the evening) offering. It represented the beginning and the close of the daily activities [3]). The absence of a Tamid offering indicated the capitulation of the Temple [4]) and, therefore, even in the gravest situations the Tamid was still maintained [5]). During the Zadokite period the high priest naturally assumed the responsibility for the costs of the Tamid lambs. Thus, the Temple services, which in turn directed the religious affairs of the masses, was completely vested in the high priest's hands. The high priest followed the prescribed rule designated in Ezekiel's priestly code [6]).

The Pharisees during the Hasmonaean period insisted that the Tamid lamb be purchased from the public collections [7]). The Temple is the house of the people. The services are to follow a democratic rule, namely the supervision of the Temple affairs is to be placed in the hands of the public representatives [8]) and, therefore, the important sacrificial animals are to be bought from public funds. The day which instituted this democratic rule was designated as a day of celebration.

---

[1]) J. R. H. 57d on M. ib. 2. 1 and T. ib. 1. 15 (210. 10).

[2]) Mech. on 12. 2 (4a) and T. Sanh. 2. 6 (416. 27ff). R. Gamliel I and the elders were responsible for the letters instructing the diasporean Jewry on intercalation. T. ib. 2. 15 (418. 6) denies the right to a king or a high priest to be seated in the session on intercalation.

[3]) The Tamid, at daybreak, begins the daily services in the Temple, see M. Tam. 3. While the Tamid of "Between the Evenings" closes the services, see b. Yom. 33a

[4]) As in Dan. 8. 13, 9. 27, 12. 11.

[5]) As described in b. Sot. 49b and Ant. XIV. 4. 3.

[6]) See Ez. 46. 13, 14 according to LXX reading, "He shall do", corrected by the Pharisaic scribes as "Thou shall do", see L. Finkelstein, Pharisees II, p. 683 n. 4.

[7]) M. T. scholion 1 (p. 4) and b. Men. 65a; compare Ant. III. 10. 1 § 237, Cont. Ap. II § 77.

[8]) See Sifre Num. § 142 (53a).

The Sabbath

One of the articles of the Great Assembly's covenant states [1]: "And the country people bring wares or any victuals on the Sabbath day to sell, we will not buy of them on the Sabbath nor on a holy day", a restriction already declared by the earlier prophets [2]. Nehemiah [3] appointed Levites to enforce the law as recorded in the article. Agatharchides of Cnidon (2nd cent. B.C.) states [4]: "The people known as Jews . . . have a custom of abstaining from work every seventh day. On those occasions they neither bear arms nor take any agricultural operation in hand, nor engage in any other form of public services, but pray with outstreched hands in the temples (synagogues) until the evening. Consequently, because the inhabitants instead of protecting their city (Jerusalem) persevered in their folly, Ptolemy son of Lagus (305-283/2 B.C.) was allowed to enter with his army, the country was given over to a cruel master". In the same manner, Antiochus Epiphanes stamped out the stubborn resistence on the Sabbath day [5].

A code of twenty-two works forbidden [6] on the Sabbath is known to have existed in the early days of the Hasmonaean period, and a code of thirty-nine [7] is recorded by the later Pharisaic teachers. It is recorded [8] that the women present at Jesus' death abstained from purchasing and from preparing the embalment for the dead body on the Sabbath. Even though rubbing a dead body with ointment was permitted [9], purchasing on the Sabbath was forbidden, as was grinding considered by the Rabbis a labourious act.

It is true that the Pharisaic teachers created a strict code governing Sabbath activities which was compared to "mountains hanging on hairs" [10] (restrictions based on the oral law with little reference to the written law). Yet a rule of leniency existed in a question of life and death. A first step was taken by the Hasmonaeans in permitting work

---

[1]) Neh. 10. 32.
[2]) See Am. 8. 5, Jer. 17. 21-24.
[3]) Neh. 13. 14-22.
[4]) Cont. Ap. 1. 22 §§ 209, 210 and Ant. 12. 1. 1 § 6.
[5]) I Macc. 2. 29-37, Ant. 12. 6. 2 § 274.
[6]) Jub. 2. 23 see Ch. Albeck, "Das Buch der Jubilaeen und die Halacha" in 47. Bericht der Hochschule für Wissenschaft des Judentums in Berlin (1930).
[7]) M. Shab. 7. 2.
[8]) Luk. 23. 56, Mk. 16. 1 see Billerbeck, Kommentar II, pp. 52, 53.
[9]) M. Shab. 23. 5.
[10]) M. Hag. 1. 8, T. ib. 1. 9 (233. 18).

on the Sabbath in case of national strife. Judas and his associates declared [1]: "Whosoever attacketh us on the Sabbath day let us fight against him that we may not in any case all die, as our brethren died in their hiding places"—a rule adopted by the heads of the Pharisaic academies. A second step permitting work to save the life of the individual was introduced by the Pharisaic teachers, Shemayah and Abtalion (c. 40 B.C.) [2]. A third step permitting the doctor to heal the sick on the Sabbath was an issue of debate at the time of Jesus. Jesus [3] himself maintained that healing is not work but a removal of the patient's ailments. At the schools in Jamnia [4] certain medicaments were permitted also on the Sabbath. The Sabbath laws, as early as Nehemiah's time [5], affected the free transfer of items and food products between estates. The Pharisees [6], in order to reduce the hardship involved in the prohibition of transfer of goods, have enacted "the application of Erub" (a formal merging of estates is created by placing a quantity of food a) 2000 cubits from the town boundary, so as to extend the Sabbath limit by that distance, b) in a room or in a court-yard to enable all the residents to carry to and fro in the court-yard on the Sabbath)—an enactment circumventing the rigourous Sabbath law.

The Pharisaic rule was contested by the Sadducees [7], who abided by the letter of the law and negated the introduction of innovations not recorded in the written tradition.

The Pharisaic teachers also designated the day of rest as a day of festivities and spiritual undertakings. On the Sabbath day the Law was read, prayers were recited and sermons delivered. The day was welcomed with the kindling of lights [8], a daily custom prevailing in the Temple. The Sadducean priests, naturally, contested the application of the above custom since kindling of lights was a priestly prerogative and a part of the Temple services not to be introduced in

---

[1] I Macc. II. 41 refer to M. D. Herr on "The Problem of War on the Sabbath in the Second Temple Era and Tannaitic Times," Tarbiz, 30. pp. 242 ff, 341 ff.

[2] b. Yom. 35b. The explanation of R. Eliezer (c. 100 A.D.), T. Shab. (16) 15. 16 (134. 13) is identical with that of Jesus, John 7. 22, 23.

[3] Luk. 13. 10-17, a reply to the Synagogue head that healing is not work, see further p. 170.

[4] As at the time of birth and circumcision, M. Shab. 18. 3, see further T. Shab. (13) 12. 9, 10, 11, 12 (127. 10-20).

[5] Neh. 10. 32, 13. 15 ff.

[6] See L. Finkelstein, Pharisees I, p. 135 ff.

[7] M. Erub. 6. 1.

[8] See Finkelstein, Pharisees I, p. 130 ff, and refer to Cont. Ap. 2. 39 § 282.

the people's homes. On the Sabbath the family feasts over bread and wine. The Sabbath day was designated by the Pharisees as a day of joy among the country folk removed from the Temple courts and Jerusalem [1]).

THE DAY OF ATONEMENT

The tenth of Tishri was designated a unique day for the people and for the Temple. This is the day when the Most High sits in judgement and atones His creation, an occasion marked by the people with fasting and supplication. On this day the high priest was permitted to enter the Holy of Holies (the sacred compartment of the Temple) [2]) which was otherwise entered only on penalty of death. Therefore the high priest presided over the Temple services of the day and administered the religious ceremony.

The Pharisees, representing the voice of the people on Temple matters, insisted that the day's program be conducted according to their prescribed rules. The high priest was considered merely the representative of the people and the Pharisaic court [3]). He was isolated for a week of preparation and instruction and took an oath to adhere to the Pharisaic teachings [4]). During the services he had to undergo five ritual baths and ten washings of the hands and feet—a strict rule of purification [5]). The preparation of the incense had to follow the Pharisaic interpretation which required the preparation of the incense in the holy enclosure, a controversial point between the Sadducean and Pharisaic teachers [6]). Lev. 16. 2 (which describes the services of the Day of Atonement) states: "For in a cloud אראה (I shall be seen or I shall appear) upon the curtain". The Sadducees maintained that the cloud denotes the cloud of smoke caused by the incense with which the high priest approached the curtain. Thus, the high priest enveloped in a cloud of smoke created a mystical appearance in the eyes of the superstitious audience. The Pharisees explained that the cloud referred symbolically to the cloud of Yahweh which hovers above the curtain [7]). The high priest was instructed to prepare the incense in the enclosure and not to create thereby a dramatic appearance.

---

[1]) See further the collection of rabbinic material in Der Sabbat by M. Zobel (Schocken Verlag/25) Berlin, 1935.
[2]) See Ant. III. 10. 3, Bell. 5. 5. 7 § 236.
[3]) M. Yom. 1. 5 and b. ib. 19a.
[4]) M. ib. 1. 1-5.
[5]) M. ib. 3. 3.
[6]) See J. Yom. 39a, b, T. ib. 1. 8 (181. 1-9), b. ib. 19b.
[7]) See Mech. on 12. 25 (16a) which compares Lev. 16. 2 with I Kin. 8. 12.

The Feast of Passover

The Mosaic code indicates that the fourteenth day of Nisan "between the evenings" is the Feast of the Paschal Lamb and the following seven days, from the 15th to the 21st, are to be observed as the Festival of the Unleavened Bread. The existence of two distinct feasts, yet interrelated, is noted in the post-exilic writings [1]. Ezekiel states [Ez. 45. 21]: "In the first month (Nisan) on the fourteenth day of the month, ye shall have the Feast of the Paschal Lamb, a feast of seven days: unleavened bread shall be eaten." The exiles returning to Judea observed the Feast of the Paschal Lamb on the fourteenth, and the Feast of Unleavened Bread on the following seven days. The Chronicler, conveying the institutions of the Second Temple, states [II Chr. 35. 17]: "The Children of Israel ... kept the Feast of the Paschal Lamb at that time and the Feast of the Unleavened Bread seven days". The high priest Joḥanan (c. 400 B.C.) [2] informs the Jews of Elephantine to observe the Feast of the Paschal Lamb on the 14th and the Feast of the Unleavened Bread from the 15th to the 21st. The author of Jubilees (49. 10, 22), describing the ceremonies of the Hasmonaean period, speaks of the preparation of the Paschal Lamb and the Feast of seven days separately. Mark (14. 1) indicates also a distinct day for the preparation of the lamb as the start of the Feast of the Unleavened Bread. Only in the years following the destruction of the Second Temple, and the consequent disappearance of the Paschal Lamb ceremony, do the Tannaitic writings refer [3] to the Feast of the Unleavened Bread as Pesach (the Feast of the Paschal Lamb).

The preparation of the Paschal meal required the selection of a group and a place for the feast where the ceremony of the lamb slaughtering took place. The period designated in the Mosaic law for the preparation of the ceremony is "between the evenings". The author of Jubilees [4] explains "between the evenings" as the time between the "last third" of the day (two o'clock in the afternoon) and the approach of the evening. The Sadducees, as did the former Samaritans and the later Karaites [5], appointed the onset of evening as the time for slaughtering. The Pharisees, on the other hand,

---

[1] Refer also to Ant. III. 10. 5.

[2] A. Ungnad, Aramäische Papyrus aus Elephantine, pap. 8.

[3] See M. Shek. 3. 1 and M.R.H. 1. 2 (On Passover see Billerbeck Kommentar, IV. 1, Exc. 4). Mk. 14. 1 reads πάσχα καί τά ἄζυμα but not Luk. 22. 1: τῶν ὀζύμων ἡ λεγομένη πάσχα (a later explanation).

[4] Jub. 49. 10, 11.

[5] See Goudoever, Bibl. Cal., p. 9 n. 13.

permitted the preparation to begin in the afternoon after six hours (mid-day) [1]. They designated the closing time for the offering of the afternoon Tamid (about three o' clock) as the time of slaughtering the lamb [2], allowing ample time for the public to prepare the feast. The Gospel according to John, aware of the Pharisaic tradition, indicates [3] that Jesus was the Paschal Lamb, since the ordeal of crucifixion lasted from the 6th to the 9th hour (from midday until three o'clock) [4]. The time of Jesus' death coincided with the time when the Paschal lamb was slaughtered. Thus, this Gospel in contrast to the Synoptics describes the ordeal taking place on the 14th of Nisan, the day of the Paschal Lamb.

THE SEASONAL FEASTS

Palestine is described as a "land flowing with milk and honey", where the inhabitants derive their livlihood from agriculture, and the wealth of the country. The activities of the agrarian society was, from days of old, confined by the Temple activities. The covenant of the Great Assembly [5] bound the inhabitants to the Temple through yearly payments of the third a shekel, the continual delivery of offerings, the periodical allotment of woods for the altar, the delivery of the prescribed gifts from herds, vineyards, fruits, wheat, oil and dough, in addition to the yearly tithes. The author of Jubilees [6] speaks of the four days designating the start of each season as days of celebration. The book of Tobit describes [7] the manner of observance of the different priestly taxes and other allotments during the Persian period. The Pharisaic code designated four days of the agrarian year as the starting days of the different seasons, and the three yearly periods [8] for the Temple collection.

The three major Jewish festivals: Passover, Pentecost and Tabernacles, are bound by the agricultural seasons. They served as days of pilgrimage at which time the Most High was sought to bestow His

---

[1] M. Pes. 5. 3, compare Sifra on 23. 5 (100b).

[1] M. Pes. 5. 1. Cf. Ant. XIV. 4. 3 § 65.

[3] John 1. 29. The lamb for the Passover was prepared four days prior to slaughtering (b. Ara. 13b; Mech. on 12. 6 (6a)). Compare Jesus' entry into Jerusalem, John 12. 1, 12.

[4] Matt. 27. 45, Luk. 23. 44, Mk. 15. 33 and John 19. 14.

[5] Neh. 10. 33-40.

[6] Jub. 6. 23.

[7] Vat. Tob. 1. 6-8, Sin. Tob. 1. 6-8.

[8] M.R.H. 1. 1, M. Shek. 3. 1.

blessings on the produce of the land. The beginning and the end of
the wheat-harvest season are designated "from the time the sickle
is put to the standing grain" until the Feast of the First Fruits. The
"time the sickle is put to the standing grain" arrives on "the morrow
of the Sabbath", which according to the Pharisees denoted the second
day of the Feast of the Unleavened Bread. On that day, the occasion
of a great gathering of the masses, the "Omer" (the sheaf of barley) is
offered to permit the consumption of new wheat. A regulation
prescribed in the Code of Holiness [Lev. 23. 14]: "Ye shall eat neither
bread nor parched corn, nor fresh ears . . . until ye have brought
the offering to your God". In the presence of the Pharisaic delegates [1]
the grain for the "Omer" was harvested on the first day of the Feast
and brought in baskets to the temple court. There they were parched,
crushed and purified. An "Issaron" (a measure of a tenth) was prepared
for the early morning of the next day to be waved and then offered.
After the Temple ceremony the flour of the new wheat was permitted
to be sold in Jerusalem's markets [1] and the people could enjoy the
new blessed wheat [3].

At the end of a fifty day period from the day of the "Omer" the Feast
of the First Fruits occurs. On that day a wave-offering of two loaves
was presented in the Temple, permitting the meal-offering on the
altar [4]. The author of Jubilees [5] relates that on the Feast of Weeks
Rebecca baked fresh cakes from the new harvest; thus indicating the
priestly rule that on this day the priestly Watches can enjoy the fresh
leavened loaves. The houses of Zadok and Boethus preferred the
arrival of the Feast of Weeks to fall on a Sunday, designating the
beginning of the last 16 Watches.

The autumn season indicated the arrival of the Feast of Tabernacles.
The festival arrives on the onset of the rainy season and was, therefore,
designated by the Pharisaic school as a period of judgement for rain [6].
The Pharisees introduced certain ceremonies [7] to indicate a form of a
request to the Most High for a rainy and a fruitful season. On each
day of the festival a water libation was poured on the altar. A public
procession encircled the altar, which was decorated with willow

---

[1] M. Men. 10. 2, 3, 4, compare Ant. III. 10. 5 § 251.
[2] M. Men. 10. 5, 6.
[3] As described in Lev. 23. 14 and Jos. 5. 10-11.
[4] M. Men. 10. 6.
[5] Jub. 22. 4.
[6] M.R.H. 1. 2, b. Taan. 2b, T. Suk. 3. 18 (198. 2).
[7] M. Suk. 4. 5 ff, 5. 1. Cf. Ant. III. 10. 4.

branches, on the first six days of the festival. The men carried in their hands a citron, a palm branch, myrtle and willow branches. On the seventh day, the procession marched seven times around the altar crying "Hoshanna" (help us) and the willow branches were beaten at the altar.

On these three agricultural festivals the Pharisaic teachers with their innovations and interpretation of the Mosaic legislation sought to introduce the country people to the Temple-worship and appealed to the people to participate in the services. The priestly Sadducees, naturally, contested the innovations which created an intrusion of the public participants at the priest's services. The public, on the other hand, embraced the Pharisaic teachings and on one occasion, it is told, they had stoned a Sadducean sympathizer with their citrons [1]).

EDUCATION

From post Exilic times the Hebrew lore and wisdom were vested in the hands of the priests. Ezekiel, the spokesman of the Babylonian Exile, was a priest-prophet as were some of his predecessors. The Code introduced by Ezekiel was adopted by the Zadokite families. Haggai, a prophet at the time of the erection of the Second Temple, approached the priests for information concerning the rules of purity [2]). Ezra, a century later, with whom the Judaic religion received a new shape, was of noted priestly extraction. His assistants were, in the main, of Levite or priestly descent whose duties were to teach and promulgate the Mosaic teachings. The Chronicler, portraying the activities of the Persian period, records [3]) that a group of Levites and two priests in the company of state representatives travelled about the Judean towns proclaiming and expounding the Mosaic lore. A group of seventy two scholars, among them priests educated in Greek and Hebrew lore, was sent by the High Priest Elazar to the court of Ptolemy Philadelphus (285-247 B.C.) to render a Greek translation of the Pentateuch [4]). The prominent thinker and writer, Jesu ben Simeon the son of Sira, was of priestly stock [5]) and the head of a school. During the Hasmonaean period education and Judaic knowl-

---

[1]) M. Suk. 4. 9, b. ib. 48b and T. ib. 3. 16 (197. 22). Cf. Ant. XIII. 13. 5 § 372.
[2]) Hag. 2. 11-13.
[3]) II Chr. 17. 7-9.
[4]) Arist. § 46 and compare b. Meg. 9a.
[5]) See Segal, Sir., introduction, p. 2 n. 11.

edge appear to have been restricted to a limited group. The leaders
and spokesmen of the Three Orders were of priestly and aristocratic
families.

With the rise of the Pharisees to legislative and judiciary powers
in the days of Salom Zion and Shimeon ben Shetach democratic
rule prevailed. The law and religious lore became the inherited
knowledge of the commoners. Schools [1]) were founded for the
education of the laity's children. Two men, products of such schools,
were Shemayah and Abtalion [2]) who rose to the position of leadership in the Pharisaic circles. They are addressed by the High Priest
as "sons of the folk" (בְּנֵי־עַמְמִין) [3]) which, according to tradition and
the opinion of some scholars, indicates sons of proselytes [4]). In my
opinion the statement denotes the children of commoners. They
founded an academy which drew students from the poor and from
far away places [5]). A Babylonian student, Hillel, in the days of Herod
rose to the presidency of the Sanhedrin and of the academy [6]). Hillel's
academy adopted a liberal stand on the entrance requirement into
the Pharisaic circle. The period of initiation was reduced to thirty
days [7]) as compared to the longer period required by other circles.
Anyone, regardless to his background, was permitted to enter the
academy. The academy adopted the rule [8]): "There was many a sinner
in Israel and in their acceptance of Torah-study they turned out to be
pious, righteous and upright". In Hillel's days the aristocratic teacher,
Menachem [9]), resigned from the vice presidency of the Sanhedrin—
probably as a form of protest. The rabbinic tradition states [10]): "With
him (Menachem) have departed 80 pairs of disciples dressed in σηρικόν
(silk) embroidered with gold". Shammai, a zealous teacher, assumed
the position left vacant by Menachem and at the same time became the
head of the second academy. The doors of Shammai's academy were
open only to the select few, those of noted aristocratic families, and

---

[1]) J. Ket. 32c. The innovation of Shimeon ben Shetach.

[2]) See further the article "Shemaja und Abtalion" by W. Landau, M.G.W.J., 7
(1858).

[3]) B. Yom. 71b.

[4]) See b. Git. 57b and I. H. Weiss, D.D. Wed. I, p. 140 n. 1.

[5]) b. Yom. 35b.

[6]) J. Pes. 33a.

[7]) T. Dem. 2. 12 (48. 8, 9), compared to the yearly requirement of Shammai's
academy and two years of the Essenes. Cf. b. Bech. 30b.

[8]) I A.D.N. 3 (p. 7b).

[9]) M. Hag. 2. 2.

[10]) J. Hag. 77d and b. ib. 16b.

to students who could prove themselves to be wise and humble [1])—
the accepted rule of the past.

During the closing years of the Second Jewish Commonwealth,
the teaching of Hillel [2]): "In a time when the people are embracing
the teachings, then do disseminate them... if thou seest a generation
which is eager for the knowledge of Torah, disseminate it", was
realized. Joshua ben Gamala [3]), the high priest serving several years
before the destruction of the Temple, appointed elementary teachers
in each district and every town. No wonder Josephus [4]), the Jewish
historian in the days following the destruction of the Temple, relates that the Jewish religion and its sacred writings were known
and familiar among the people, young and old. The liberal stand on
education explains the reason after the Destruction the leadership of
a restored academy at Jamnia was placed in the hands of a man of
no special family background, Jochanan ben Zakkai.

The establishment of Pharisaic circles during the early part of the
Hasmonaean period appears to be terminated as a unique society
with the Jamnia period (70-132 A.D.) [5]). After the destruction of the
Temple Jochanan ben Zakkai, a disciple of Hillel, transferred the
Jerusalemian academy to Jamnia with the approval of the Roman
emperor [6]). This Pharisaic teacher [7]) is noted for his polemics with
the Sadducean-Boethusian sympathizers. After his death the presidency was restored to the Hillelic line, Rabban Gamliel II [8]). He is
known to have abided by a strict rule in preparing his meals in the
Pharisaic manner [9]). Upon the betrothal of his daughter, he required

---

[1]) I A.D.N. 3 (p. 7b). It should be indicated that after the destruction of the
Temple when Christianity became an important sect, the Shammaites stand was
maintained by Gamliel II of Hillel's descent, see b. Ber. 28a. This attitude had caused the master's impeachment whereby Hillel's rule was reinstated.

[2]) T. Ber. 7. 24 (17. 16), b. ib. 63a and see Epstein, Meb. Les. Hat., p. 17 who
cites Hieronymus describing Hillel (?) as "dissipator" = מְפַזֵּר.

[3]) B. B.B. 21a. These teachers were most probably supported from the Temple's
treasury (J. Shek. 48 a).

[4]) Cont. Ap. I §§ 42, 43.

[5]) I designate "the Jamnia Period" as the period of the Academy's activity
at Jamnia until the Bar-Kosiba revolt. After the unsuccesful revolt the academy
was transferred to Usha, see I. H. Weiss, D. D. Wed. II, p. 130.

[6]) B. Git. 56b, R. Jochanan according to rabbinic tradition (J. Ned. 39b,
b. Suk. 28a) was a disciple of Hillel.

[7]) For example, M. Yad. 4. 6, T. ib. 2. 9 (684. 2) and M. T. scholion pp. 4, 10, 13.

[8]) See I. H. Weiss, D. D. Wed. II, p. 65.

[9]) T. Hag. 3. 2 (236. 18).

his son-in-law to comply with the same code[1]). Questions relating to the strict practices of the Pharisaic society were presented to the academy [2]). Several years after his death the Bar-Kosiba revolt broke out (132 A.D.) with the support of Rabbi Aqiba, a distinguished member of the academy [3]). The revolt failed and the Jews were persecuted by Hadrian, the Roman emperor. Jerusalem, which now received the name Aelia Capitolina, was banned to any Jew on penalty of death. Heavy restrictions were placed on the Jews and thus, the generation after the revolt was named by the Rabbis "the generation of religious persecution" [4]). The Bar-Kosiba revolt resulted in the death blow for the Judaic [5]) and Pharisaic communities. Thus, the rabbinic tradition states [6]): "With the death of Rabban Gamliel the Elder (that of Jamnia) the practice of a code of purity and separation has terminated".

---

[1]) T. A. Z. 3. 10 (464. 6).

[2]) T. Kel. B.B. 2. 4 (592. 5) Aquila, a proselyte, had during Gamliel's lifetime accepted the Pharisaic membership, see T. Hag. 3. 3 (236. 19).

[3]) J. Taan. 68d.

[4]) See G.R. on 8. 21 (319) and Cant. R. on 2. 5 (106): דּוֹרוֹ שֶׁל שְׁמָד· For the expression cf. I Q.p.H. 5. 7, 8; C.D. 12. 23: קֵץ הָרִשְׁעָה·

[5]) See Y. Yadin, Bar kokhba (1971).

[6]) M. Sot. 8. 17 compare the reading in b. Meg. 21a omitting the title "Elder" which usually designates his grandfather Gamliel I. R. Gamliel II is also called "the elder", a title for a member of the academy, see T. Shab. 7 (8). 18 (119. 3).

PART C

THE WRITTEN AND ORAL TRADITION DURING THE HASMONAEAN AND HERODIAN PERIODS

Exposition

The era preceding the establishment of the Pharisaic order encompassed the closing stages of the prophetic activities and the period of the teachers-scribes. This era created a preparatory stage for the coming period through the collection of the Holy Writings and the establishment of the Pentateuch as a religious and a civil code. The later generations looked upon the era as an era of inspiration, when men were still guided by the Holy Spirit. These men, who are not mentioned in rabbinic sources by their names, are referred to metaphorically as "'Eshkoloth"; a vague term [1]) that can be interpreted from the Hebrew as "grape clusters", from the Greek as scoliast or more probably a combination of the words אִישׁ שֶׂכֶל (a man of keen knowledge) [see Ezr. 8. 18]. Nevertheless the general meaning is understood: these men of great mental productivity and versatility were responsible for the transmission of both the oral and written tradition with no defects—as the rabbinic tradition states [2]): "All the "'Eshkeloth" who arose for Israel from the days of Moses to the days of Jose ben Joezer of Ṣeredah (the first known Pharisaic teacher) one can not find in them any blemish, but from then on one can find in them a blemish". The preceding era witnessed a consolidated authority with no disagreements and controversies among the Scribes, whereas during the Hasmonaean period two fronts, the Sadducees and the Pharisees, emerged in the center of learning.

Even among the Pharisees there existed a difference of opinion. The first important controversy among the Zugoth, the Pharisaic heads, commenced between Jose ben Joezer and Jose ben Jochanan. Tradi-

---

[1]) See Hoenig, G. Sanh., p. 28 and exc. XV.
[2]) b. Tem. 15b renders an explanation attributed to Samuel (200 A.D.): "All the Eshkoloth who arose for Israel used to teach the Law even as Moses" and in b. Sot. 47b Samuel explains Eshkoloth as "a man ('ish) in whom is everything", i.e., a man of full authority with regard to the Jewish law. See also T.B.K. 8. 13 (362. 9-11), the reading 'ishkeloth, and J. Sot. 24a.

tion relates [1]): "In the early days there was no conflict but in semikah. There were five Zugoth; three of the first Zugoth who maintained "not to apply semikah" were Nesi'im (heads of the court or academy), whereas their seconds (who maintained "to apply semikah") were Aboth Beth-Din (fathers or second in position in the court or academy) while the two of the last Zugoth who maintained "to apply semikah" were Nesi'im and their seconds were Aboth Beth-Din". S. Zeitlin [1]) explains that the semikah controversy dealt with the reliance upon the authority of the sages who introduced new laws —an important issue debated also among the Pharisees and Sadducees. Following S. Zeitlin's assertion, S. B. Hoeing [3]) states: "Hence the basic conflict in the early Great Sanhedrin was conservatism (opposition to the introduction of new laws and innovations by the sages) versus liberalism (reliance upon the authority of the Hakamim (teachers) in addition to that of the Torah), i.e., "strict constructionism" versus "flexible constructionism" in the interpretation of the law".

With the establishment of the Hasmonaean dynasty, the Pharisees numbering members from the three Judaic classes vehemently opposed the old ruling priestly class, the Sadducees. In the early days of the Pharisaic order, the priests occupied the seat of the presidency and, consequently, controlled the interpretation of the Law through the voice of the majority. Naturally, the priests adopted the conservative attitude—as was the common rule with the Saducean priests. The Nasi of the first Duumvirate (Zugoth), Jose ben Joezer, was a priest [1]). He expressed the view [1]): "Only the one who comes in contact with a dead body is defiled" based on the strict interpretation of the law in Num. 19. 16: "Whosoever touches a sword-slain body or a dead body [בַּחֲלַל־חֶרֶב אוֹ בְמֵת] (i.e. one who dies naturally and one who is killed) or a bone of a man, or a grave shall be unclean seven days". He was considered by later generations too lenient. The late Pharisaic school, applying a loose interpretation of the law— reading the words בַּחֲלַל־חֶרֶב not in their construct form but as two separate substantives, a slain body and a sword—maintained that the

---

[1]) T. Hag. 3. 8 (234. 27-235. 3) and compare J. ib. 77d and b. ib. 16b.
[2]) "The Semikah Controversy Between the Zugoth", J.Q.R., VII (1917), p. 499 ff.
[3]) G. Sanh., p. 48, see n. 9.
[4]) M. Hag. 2. 7.
[5]) M. Ed. 8. 4.

articles of the corpse cause contamination [1]). The Nasi of the second Duumvirate, Joshua ben Perahiah, was also a priest [2]). He ruled [3]) that wheat imported from Alexandria is susceptible to contamination. He referred to the rule in Lev. 11. 38: "If water is put [וְכִי יֻתַּן־מַיִם]

on a seed and ought their carcasses fall thereon, it is unclean unto you" and the wheat in Egypt is watered by means of a water wheel. The Pharisaic colleagues refuted Joshua's decree. They maintained that wetness makes the seed to be ritually susceptible for defilement only upon the intention of the owner. The Mishnah (Mach. 1. 1) sets the rule: "Any liquid which came in the beginning with (owner's) consent, though it was not in the end with consent or which was at the end though it was not at the beginning with consent comes under the law of כִּי יֻתַּן"—a rule accepted by the academies. The explanation

of the law is presented by the Amora Rab Pappa (375 A.D.) [4]) as follows: יתן can be read either as יֻתַּן (being put) or as יִתֵּן (will put), i.e.,

water caused by nature (e.g. rain) can cause the seed to become susceptible for defilement, יֻתַּן as יִתֵּן, water put by man: in both cases

the moistening of the produce must be with the owner's consent. The head of the third Duumvirate was in the original body, Jehuda ben Tabbai [5]). He administered the death penalty to a person bearing false testimony even though the death sentence was not carried out on the accused—following the Pharisaic stand on the law of false witnesses. In this case, Jehuda demonstrated a strict interpretation of the Mosaic rule (Deut. 19. 16): "If an unrighteous witness (עֵד) rise up against

any man to bear perverted testimony . . . you shall do unto him as he has planned to do to his brother"—the law refers to one witness since the rendering is in the singular case, עֵד. His colleague, Shimeon ben

Shetach, reprimanded Jehuda's action basing his argument on a loose interpretation of the law—since [6]) "the Mosaic law decrees (Deut. 17. 6) a death penalty can be administered on the testimony of two witnesses

---

[1]) Sifre Num. § 127 (45b) and b. A.Z. 37b.
[1]) See Sifre Zuta, p. 302, unless Joshua directed the ceremony.
[3]) T. Mach. 3.4 (675. 21) and refer to L. Ginzberg, On Jewish Law and Lore, p. 81.
[4]) b. B.M. 22b
[5]) J. Hag. 77d.
[6]) See Mech. on Ex. 23. 7 (105b), b. Mak. 5b which is based on b. Sot. 2b and Sifre Num. § 7 (4a).

so the death penalty is to be meted out to the bearers of false testimony, namely two".

During the Hasmonaean period the Pharisaic leaders, the first three Duumvirates and the Sadducees were in conflict over the issue of reliance on the words of the sages. Josephus [1]) describes the conflict: "The Pharisees had passed on to the people certain regulations (Halachoth) handed down by former generations and not recorded in the laws of Moses for which they are rejected by the Sadducean camp". The Great Sanhedrin [2]) was the body which regulated the religious life of the Jews and gave sanction to religious practices in accordance with the Bible (the constitution) and its interpretation. During this period the Pharisees struggled to assume control over the judiciary enabling them to introduce their form of interpretation of the Law. They were met with strong opposition from the Sadducees, and in the last years of Hyrcanus I and in the days of his successor Alexander I Jannai (100-76 B.C.) the Pharisees were ousted from the Great Sanhedrin. Only in the days of Salom Zion [3]), the last important Hasmonaean ruler (76-67 B.C.), the Pharisaic leader, Shimeon ben Shetach, assumed the presidency and thus obtained complete control over the Great Sanhedrin. He advocated, as illustrated above, flexible constructionism in the interpretation of the Law. Even his colleague, Jehuda ben Tabbai, the strict constructionist, subscribed to the teachings and reforms introduced by Shimeon. With the administration of Shimeon a new approach to the examination of the Mosaic laws was introduced which in turn laid the foundations for a new school, the School of Exposition (בית המדרש).

After the death of Salom Zion her sons, Aristabulus II and Hyrcanus II under the influence of Antipas, were in conflict over the leadership of the state. This internal strife was destined to have a most far reaching effect upon the Jewish nation [4]); Judea was finally incorporated into the Roman province Syria and Herod, a non-Hasmonaean, gained the leadership of the state with the approval of the Roman emperors. Due to the internal change in the Judaic government, the Pharisees who were the former legislators became instead the heads of the

---

[1]) Ant. XIII. 10. 6 § 297 and compare Philo in Eusebius, Praep. Evang. 8. 7. 6 (Tobit observes both written and oral laws, see Pfeiffer, History of New Testament Times, p. 266).

[2]) Hoenig, G. Sanh., part 1, ch. X.

[3]) M. T. scholion 10 (16). Cf. Ant. XIII. 15. 2 § 408.

[4]) Cf. Ant. XIV. 4. 5 § 77.

academies, the Schools of Exposition. Shemaiah and Abtalion, the
Pharisaic leaders, founded the great academy in Jerusalem where
Hillel, a Babylonian, was enrolled as one of the students. For the
first time the heads of the academy are identified by a contemporary
as Darshanim [1]), men of exposition. Hillel, upon the death of his
teachers, assumed the presidency of the academy. He continued in the
path of his teachers [2]) and was responsible for the introduction of
seven rules of exposition [3]), rules employed in earlier days.

The above report concerning the semikhah controversy indicates
the change that evolved with the last two Duumvirates. The Nesi'im
of the Academy adopted the application of loose interpretation of the
Mosaic Law. It is recorded that Shemaiah and Abtalion [4]) administered
the "bitter waters" to an adulteress who was a manumitted bondswoman. They maintained that the Mosaic law on the adulteress (Num.
5. 11-31), addressed to "the children of Israel", does not refer only
to the Israelites but also to freed slaves, since freed slaves who are
proselytes [5]) are considered in Jewish law children of the covenant
(בני ברית). Shammai also adopted the oral tradition in the interpretation
of the law. He maintained [6]) that in case person A sends person B to
kill person C, person A is responsible for C's death. Shammai pointed
to an oral tradition transmitted from the days of Haggai based on
II Sam. 12. 9—Nathan speaking to David says: "Thou hast slain
(Uriah) with the sword of the children of Ammon". In the same
manner Shammai adopted the decree issued by the early Hasmonaeans
permitting work on the Sabbath in case of defensive war. He pointed
to the interpretation of the law [7]) (Deut. 20. 20): "Thou mayest build
bulwarks against the city that maketh war with thee, until it falls"—as
long as necessary even on the Sabbath.

The written tradition was processed in the "era of inspiration", the
era preceding the period of the Pharisaic Duumvirates. The Scribes
of the era classified the Scriptures according to their authoritative
nature and their order of development—the Torah (the Mosaic law),
on one hand, and the Qabbalah (the written tradition), on the other

---

[1]) b. Pes. 70b. Cf. Bell. I. 33. 2 § 649 (ἐξηγουμένοις τοὺς νόμους), and ib.
11. 8. 14 § 162.
[2]) See J. Pes. 33a and M. Ed. 1.3 (Hillel transmits halachah from his teacher).
[3]) See T. Sanh. 7. 11 (427. 4-7), I A.D.N. 37 (55b).
[4]) M. Ed. 5. 6.
[5]) See Sifra on 12. 2 (57c) derives from אִשָּׁה to include a freed bondswoman, so
in Num. 5. 12 see Sifre Num. § 7 (3b).
[6]) b. Kid. 43a see I.H. Weiss, D.D. Wed. I p. 142.
[7]) b. Shab. 19a and compare Sifre Deut. § 204 (111b).

hand, encompassing the works of the prophets and other writings produced and edited in the era. These Holy Scriptures are composed of: codes of law; books of historical nature composed of legends, tales and genealogical records; books of prophetic knowledge; books of wisdom composed as philosophical dialogues and sayings; poetic, and liturgical works. These books were recognized by later generations as the products of heavenly inspired men, and thus have become the accepted authority on law and wisdom. They were instruments employed during the coming periods in two interrelated ways: a) as books guiding the writers of newer works in their style, purpose and type of composition, b) as texts for further analysis and exploration, thereby expanding the limits of the law and those of other branches of study.

THE WRITTEN TRADITION AS A GUIDE FOR THE WORKS OF THE HASMONAEAN-HERODIAN PERIOD

On Codes of Law

The Mosaic Law is composed of negative and positive precepts, penal sentences, a code of conduct for the military and priestly organization, the monarchy and community. The Sadducean law makers, following the Mosaic example, produced a "Book of Ordinances", a code of civil and capital offences and their penal sentences. The Teacher of Righteousness, who was the disappointed priestly scribe, also created books to guide the newly founded Essene communities: a code of military conduct, a code of rules for members with penal sentences. The Pharisees who established their own societies opposed, on the other hand [1]), the creation of new books in general and codes and manuals of law in particular.

The last verses in Ecclesiastes, which appear to be an additional note [2]), were inserted as a canonical ending for the last division of the Holy Scriptures, the Hagiographa, and more precisely for the complete structure of the Old Testament. This epilogue echoes the Pharisaic stand on three points a) free will, determination and Providence, b) the issuance of new books, c) oral tradition [3]). Concerning the

---

[1]) M.T. scholion 4 (8), refer to J. S. Bloch, Einblicke in die Geschichte der Entstehung der talmudischen Literatur (Vienna, 1884). For a different opinion see H. L. Strack, Introduction ch. 2 § 2.

[2]) The book opens with "Vanity of Vanities", Ch. 1.2, and closes with the same, Ch. 12. 8.

[3]) See p. 116 ff.

first point the epilogue states [Ecc. 12. 13, 14]: "Fear God, keep His commandments, for this is the whole (duty) of man. For God shall bring every work into judgement with every secret thing whether it be good or whether it be evil". Josephus attests to this Pharisaic view stating [1]): "For they believe that everything is done by fate, but on the other hand, they do not deny that the will of man is determined by this, saying this is a decree of God, that the end result is based on its (fate) outcome and the will of man which embraces virtue and iniquity". Rabbi Haninah (b. Ber. 33b) states the same view: "Everything is in the hands of Heaven (God) except the fear of Heaven".

On the issuance of new books and writings, the epilogue states [2]) (Ecc. 12. 12): "And furthermore, my son, be admonished of making many books endlessly". The opposition to Apocryphal and Apocalyptic writings is noted in the exclusion of these books from the academies. Rabbi Aqiba, a noted Pharisaic teacher at the Jamnia academy, was severe with the readers and possessors of Apocryphal writings. He included [3]) these transgressors with "the class of men who will not receive a share in the world to come". Shimeon ben Shetach[4]), a Pharisaic leader of the Sanhedrin, abolished the Sadducean "Book of Ordinances", accepting only the Mosaic Books and their interpretation with the oral tradition along side. The rule that existed between the times of the two Pharisaic teachers was "Do not commit to writing the Halachoth (the norms)", i.e., the derived Halachah from the Written Law is restricted to the walls of the academies where it is debated and discussed and is not to be issued in the form of a new code. Even liturgical pieces [5]) were orally transmitted, and men who put them in writing were not favoured by the Pharisaic teachers.

The erudition produced in the Pharisaic academies during the last century of the Temple era was orally transmitted in the form of old sayings, tales, reported incidents, decisions, aggadic and halachic discourses. A rule ascribed to the times of the Duumvirates was [6]) "a saying transmitted orally must be reproduced with the name of

---

[1]) Ant. XVIII. 1. 3 § 13 compare Bell. II. 8. 14 § 163. See Simhoni, Toledoth Milhemeth Hayehudim 'im Haroma'im (1957), p. 422 n. 14, and Finkelstein, Pharisees, p. 203 ff.

[2]) See Ecc. R. on 12. 12 (315) and N. Krochmal, More, p. 43.

[3]) M. Sanh. 11. 1 and the discussion in b. ib. 100b.

[4]) M. T. scholion 4 (p. 8).

[5]) T. Shab. (14) 13.4 (128. 28 ff.).

[6]) Tanh. Num. Bamidbar § 27 (11a), See Elieser ben Yehuda, Introduction to his Dictionary, p. 146 ff.

the person responsible for the saying". Hillel [1]) transmitting a halachah from his teachers, maintained that it was reproduced in accordance with the teachers' phraseology. On occasions [2]) the disciples recorded the halachah in their private note-books. The destruction of the Temple caused the great academies of Hillel and Shammai to close and the oral tradition became vulnerable to erasure and coloration. The Pharisaic teachers and the students of the academies assembled at the Jamnia academy under the leadership of Rabban Jochanan ben Zakkai. There a decision was reached unifying the scholarly efforts of the two former academies and at the same time accepting the decisions of one school, that of Hillel. For the first time the oral tradition was collected [3]). The students presented the decisions of the former teachers and testified to the validity of the material [4]). The opinions of both former academies were recorded and efforts were made to preserve the original form of the statements. Some of the contemporary teachers who lived during the last years of the Second Temple era preserved and edited the regulations and descriptions of the Temple services—subjects that can be forgotten with time. Shimeon of Mispeh edited [5]) the order of the services on the Day of Atonement, and some authorities ascribed to him the composition of the Tamid services. Rabbi Eliezer ben Jacob I [6]) edited a treatise on the composition and measurements of the Temple and its courts. In the same manner[7]) compilations were made of the Paschal Lamb's and the Festival of Booths ceremonies, the rites for a suspected adulteress, the bringing of the first fruits and the laws of purification and sacrifices.

A generation later, under Rabbi Aqiba's guidance, the first codification [8]) of the entire oral law, known as Mishnah of Rabbi Aqiba, was produced and revised during his lifetime. The Hadrian persecutions resulting from the unsuccessful Bar-Kosiba's revolt caused the transfer of the Academy to the northern town of Usha and

---

[1]) M. Ed. 1. 3, see M. Schachter, The Babylonian and Jerusalemian Mishna Textually Compared (Jerusalem 1959) in the Introduction.

[2]) See H. L. Strack, Introduction, p. 18 ff and Lieberman, Hellenism, on the publication of the Mishna and, especially, Appendix III.

[3]) See T. Ed. 1. 1 (454. 22) and refer to Epstein, Meb. Les. Hat., in the Introduction. On the activities of R. Jochanan see Allon, Toledoth Hayehudim, I. 3.

[4]) As found in Mishnah Eduyyoth.

[5]) b. Yom. 14b and J. ib. 39d (see Epstein, Meb. Les. Hat., pp. 28, 37).

[6]) b. Yom. 16a and see Epstein, Meb. Les. Hat., p. 31.

[7]) See Epstein, Meb. Les. Hat., p. 25 ff and H. L. Strack, Introduction, ch. II § 3.

[8]) See T. Ara. 5. 15 (550. 30) and T. Zab. 1. 5, 6 (676. 33-677. 1) and I. Kanowitz, Rabbi Akiba (Jerusalem, 1956). The former compilation of halachoth was known as Mishnah Rishonah.

other schools were established in the South. There the disciples
of Rabbi Aqiba continued the work of their master [1]). Rabbi Jehuda
ben Elai laid the foundation for the Midrashic treatise on Leviticus.
Rabbi Meir proceeded with the codification of the oral law producing
up to date and a better edition of the Mishnah. Rabbi Shimeon ben
Jochai's school produced a Midrashic work on the Pentateuch.
Rabbi Nehemiah edited a supplement to the Mishnah, and Rabbi Jose
ben Halaftah edited the rabbinical interpretation and presentation of
history, Seder Olam [The Order of the World]. The disciples of
Rabbi Ishmael, a colleague of Rabbi Aqiba, composed a Midrashic
work on the last four books of the Pentateuch [2]).

The emergence of different Midrashic works and codes of law
during Rabbi Aqiba's and his disciples' times (90-200 A.D.) led to
culmination of a supreme perfected code of six orders [3]) (laws concerning seeds, seasons, women, torts, sanctities and purities) at the
seminary of Rabbi Juda the Prince at Tiberius [170-217 A.D.]. This
work too underwent a final revision and became the authoritative
code of Jewish law, based on the oral tradition, along side the Mosaic
code (the written tradition).

We have noted that the Jewish scholars at Jamnia in later generations were motivated to compile and edit the oral tradition as a
result of the destruction of the Temple and the persecutions. The
awareness that the oral tradition of the past might be forgotten contributed to the Rabbis' motivation. In the same manner F. C. Grant [4])
enumerates the reasons that motivated the members of the early
Christian community to record the sayings and the description of the
events during the life and death of their master as the delay of the
parousia, the awareness that preservation of the material is useful
for the sake of memorization and for the purpose of conversion. We
have also observed that two distinct paths guided the Jewish scholars
in codifying and compiling the oral tradition: a) Testimony was
given by different students to the validity of the statements and the
events. b) Notebooks of different scholars were used in composing

---

[1]) b. Sanh. 86a, See A. Guttmann, H.U.C.A., XVII, p. 395 ff.

[2]) On the different works of the two schools, that of R. Aqiba and the one of
R. Ismael, their students, terminology, manner of interpretation, see Epstein,
Meb. Les. Hat., part. III.

[3]) See H. L. Strack, Introduction, ch. III; The orders follow the Midrash-
halachah on Ex. 21-23. 9 (i.e. Damages) and on Leviticus i.e. Sanctities, Purities
and Women (cf. Ant. III. 9-12. 2) Seeds and Festivals.

[4]) The Gospels: their origin and their Growth, London, 1957, p. 31ff.

the different codes. The same can be said for the composition of the three Gospels. They drew from a common source, the Marcan recension as attested and related by the head of the apostles, Peter. The Gospels according to Luke and Matthew have also drawn from another common source (the Logia) in addition to other materials. The explanation can be attributed to several note-books kept by various disciples which were employed by the authors. Other events that occurred during the life and after the death of the master were included in the Gospels only on the basis of the disciples' testimony to their validity. The preface to Luke states: "Forasmuch as many have taken in hand to set forth in order a declaration of those things which are most surely believed among us. Even as they delivered them unto us which from the beginning were eyewitnesses and minis-ters of the words".

The early church fathers shed light on the language in which the logia were composed. They maintained that it was the Judean dialect, Aramaic-Hebrew, and the sayings found in the Gospels do point to Aramaism. Linguistic criticism find support in Ch. C. Torrey "Our Translated Gospels" (New York, 1936) and in M. Black "An Aramaic Approach to the Gospels and Acts" (Oxford, 1946). The Talmud (b. Shab. 116 a, b) records that in the days following the destruction of the Temple, a Christian scholar [1] was confronted by the wife of Rabbi Eliezer and her brother, Rabban Gamliel II. The scholar quoted two passages from the sect's books, both in Aramaic. One is said to be found at the end of the book, whereas in Matthew it appears in the Sermon of the Mount, a collection of sayings (see p. 162) [2].

On Books of Historical Nature

An important part of the Holy Scriptures is occupied with histori-cal material composed of diversed elements: genealogical accounts, heroic tales described in sagas and epics, records such as documents and diaries, compilation of historical events as recorded by the scribes of the king's court, and a historical novel with a religious purpose. The same type of material appears during the Maccabean and Herodian periods. Some historical novels with a religious purpose are the Story

---

[1] פִּילוֹסְבָא, an elder-friend, cf. the third epistle of John, 1, 15. (πρεσβύτερος, φίλοι).   [2] The other passage concerns the law of inheritance in regard to the Mother's properties. Jesus' teaching that "the son and the daughter shall inherit alike" is in accordance with the teaching of Zachariah ben Haqaṣab (c. 50 A.D.), see b.B.B. 111ᵃ.

of Sussana (upholding the Pharisaic stand on the issue of false witnesses), possibly the Book of Judith (a polemic writing against the Samaritans) and the pre-Destruction work of the zealous Pharisees, Megillath Taanith (a list of important historical events during the Hasmonaean and Herodian periods commemorated as semi-holidays). An account of historical happenings is recorded by Jason of Cyrene (the source for the second book of Maccabees), the author of Maccabees I, Nicholas of Damascus at the Herodian court and Josephus, a Jewish historian employing earlier material in his works, Antiquities and the Jewish War. Letters, too, served as a source for historical information, such as the letter of Aristeas, the letters of Judas Maccabeus to Alexandrian Jewry and the letters of the Pharisaic leader, Gamliel I, and his son Shimeon I. Documents are preserved in the Books of Maccabees and in Josephus' works. Even the Ketubah (a marriage document) was studied by the early masters, Hillel and Shammai, for halachic conclusions. Biblical narratives were freely reproduced with extensive emendations, such as the additions to Daniel and the Book of Esther, the Prayer of Menasses, the exegetic material in the book of Jubilees, and the legends found in Josephus' works. The story of Tobit shows also foreign elements integrated with the personality of Tobit. Legends about the activities of the great men of the past were widely circulated and in the oriental manner orally recounted allowing exaggeration and reinterpretation. Such are the miraculous deeds attributed to Shimeon I the pious [1]) in the days of Alexander, and to the successive high priests with the same name [2]). Oniaus, the rain maker and his grandson Abba Hilkiyah became personalities woven in beautiful legends [3]), even though harsh words were spoken to Oniaus by the contemporary Pharisaic leader, Shimeon ben Shetach.

Beautiful tales and exegetic portrayal of the great biblical personalities were introduced by scholars of the period. For some groups the assumptions of Enoch and Moses [4]) served as a basis for further contemplation on the mysteries of the heavens. For the masses Moses represented the redeemer par-excellence [5]), Samuel and Ezra the teachers par-excellence and Elijah the prophet par-excellence [6]).

---

[1]) M.T. scholion 9 (14). Cf. Ant. XI. 8. 5.
[2]) T. Sot. 13. 6, 7 (319. 9-20) compare II Macc. 1. 18-24.
[3]) b. Tann. 23a, b, M.T. scholion 12 (21). Cf. Ant. XIV. 2. 1 § 22.
[4]) See the Book of Enoch and the preface to Jubilees.
[5]) See Ecc. R. on 1. 9 (p. 33) for the comparison of the coming Messiah and Moses.
[6]) See L. Ginzberg, The Legends of the Jews, vols. III, IV (1954) on Moses Elijah and Samuel, and see Jer. 15. 1. On Ezra see above p. 13.

In the period before and after the Destruction a portrayal of the activities of the teachers assumed unconsciously the image of the heroic prophets of the past. P. Fiebig in Jüdische Wundergeschichten des N.T. Zeitalters, p. 69 ff (Tübingen, 1911), shows that the miraculous acts of the Jewish masters were described along the lines of the stories related of Moses, Elijah and Elisha. In the same manner the life of Jesus was reproduced along the lines [1]) of known aggadic folklore, and the biography of the master was dressed in the mantle of the recognized ancient miracle-workers.

The synoptic Gospels can be divided into the following sections: a) Prelude (from the birth until the appearance of Jesus at the Jordan river)—Matt. I-II. 23, Luk. I. 1-II. 52, which is lacking in Mark. b) The appearance of Jesus at the Jordan river and the ministry in Galilee and in the bordering southern and northern countries—Matt. III. 1-XX. 34, Luk. III. 1-XIX. 27, and Mark. I. 1-X. 52, c) In Jerusalem—Matt. XXI. 1-XXVII. 66, Luk. XIX. 28-XXIII. 56 and Mark. XI. 1-XV. 47, d) The aftermath-Matt. XXVIII. 1-20, Luk. XXIV. 1-53 and Mark. XVI. 1-20. Section c is common to all four Gospels while section d is found in variants as to the order of events, the localities where Jesus reappeared and the nature of the experience; yet it was the common knowledge and incontrovertible conviction of the early Christians. Our examination of the typification of Jesus' life relates only to sections a and b.

Section a which is found only in Luke and Matthew, presents narratives of the birth and the early life of Jesus. They differ in the presentation of the accounts. Matthew reproduces the account according to the tales woven about birth and early youth of Moses the Redeemer, since the author stresses the Messianic attribute of the master—already noted in the genealogical record prefixed to the account. Luke on the other hand, presents the account analogous to the birth and the early life of Samuel, the great prophetic teacher; since he stresses the ministerial aspect of the master. The author [2])

---

[1]) In the same manner Josephus and the Rabbis interpret the events at the time of the destruction of the Second Temple with the written account of the events during the destruction of the First Temple, see Pesiqta Rabbati, Asser Teasser, and Bell. 5. 10. 3, 12. 3 and compare II Kin. 24, 25 (see further A. Shalit introduction to Qadmoniyoth 2 ed., Israel, 1955).

[2]) The author of the Gospel according to Luke also introduces the tale of the shepherds and the birth of the redeemer in Bethlehem. A parallel is found on the expected Jewish Messiah in J. Ber. 5a—since the author, as does the author of Matthew, also stresses the messiahship of Jesus (as will be shown below).

describes Jesus, already as a youth in the Temple, "causes astonishment at his understanding and answers". However both Gospels reproduce the account of Jesus' birth caused by heavenly power, a description found of the birth of Noah (Gen. Apoc. col. II, Eth. En. 106, 1-12) and that of Malki-Ṣedeq (Sl. En. 23. 1-26).[1]) The following chart correlates the exegetic and biblical description of the personalities of Moses and Samuel with that of Jesus as found in the Gospels according to Matthew and Luke.

Jesus	*Matt.*	*Moses*	*Sources*
Jesus from Abraham is 3 times 14 (2 times 7) generations removed	I. 17	Moses from Abraham is 7 generations removed	Lev. R. on 23. 24 (p. 378)
Joseph was minded to put away 'his wife', Mary, and was restrained by an angel	I. 19. 24	Amram was minded to put away his wife, Yochebed, and was restrained by his daughter	Ex. R. on 1. 15 (p. 18), see Mid. Hag. Ex. 2. 1
The naming of the child by the angel	I. 21	The naming of the child by the daughter of Pharaoh	Ex. 2. 10
Herod and the Magi	II. 1-3	Pharaoh and the Estralogin (Ant. II. 9. 2)	Ex. R. on 1. 22 (p. 25) see Mid. Hag. Ex. 1. 22
The flight: away from the native country caused by Herod's persecution	II. 14	The flight: away from the place of birth caused by Pharaoh's persecution	Ex. 2. 15
The extermination of the innocent babes	II. 16	The extermination of the innocent babes	Ex. 1. 22
The return: "For those who sought the child's life are dead"	II. 20, 21	The return: "All the men are dead which sought thy life".	Ex. 4. 19
The death of Herod	II. 19	The death of Pharaoh	Ex. 2. 23

Jesus	*Luk.*	*Samuel*	*Sources*
The angel blessed Mary saying "For thou hast found favour with God"	I. 30	Eli blessed Hannah saying "God of Israel will grant thy petition".	I Sam. 1. 17
The prayer of Mary in the priest's house, that of Zecharia's	I. 46	The prayer of the mother in the priest's house, that of Eli's	I Sam. 2. 1

---

[1]) The above names are connected with the personalities of the Messiah. Noah as Menachem, Yalqut Shime'oni I § 42, cf. J. Ber. 5a, and Malki Ṣedeq as the priestly Messiah, b. Suk. 52b and Cant, R. 2. 12.

The prayer: I. 46-55
"My soul doth magnify
the Lord, And my spirit
hath rejoiced in God my
Saviour. For He hath
regarded the low estate
of handsmaiden . . . For
He that is mighty . . .
and holy is His name . . .
He hath showed strength
with His arm, He hath
scattered the proud in
the imagination of their
hearts. He hath put the
mighty from their seats
and exalted them of low
degree. He hath filled
the hungry with good
things and the rich He
hath sent empty away".

The naming of the child I. 60
by the mother
The prayer of Zecharia: I. 69
"And hath raised up a
horn of salvation".

After the period of puri- II. 22
ty, a visit to the Temple

Bringing of the sacrifi- II. 24
cial offering
Simeon receives the child II. 25, 28

And the parents went II. 41
up every year to the
Temple
The child sits and tea- II. 46
ches in the Temple
"And Jesus increased in II. 52
wisdom and stature and
in favour with God and
man".

The prayer: I Sam. 2.
"My heart exulteth in 1-10
the Lord, my horn is
exalted in the Lord . . .
Because I rejoice in Thy
salvation. There is none
holy as the Lord neither
is there any rock like our
God . . . The bows of
the mighty men are
broken . . . and they
that were hungry ceased
while the barren hath
born seven . . . The
Lord maketh rich. He
bringeth low. He also
lifteth up. He raiseth
the poor out of the dust
. . . for by strength shall
no man prevail".

The naming of the child I Sam.
by the mother   1. 20
The prayer of Hannah: I Sam
"And hath raised up a 2. 10.
horn of his anointed".

After the period of I Sam.
nursing a visit to the 1. 24
Tabernacle

Bringing of the sacrifi- I Sam.
cial offering   1. 24
Eli receives the child   I Sam.
                        1. 23

And the parents went up I Sam.
every year to the Taber- 1. 3
nacle
The child sits and serves I Sam..
in the Tabernacle   3. 1
"And the child Samuel I Sam.
grew on and increased in 2. 26
favour both with the
Lord and also with
men".

The three synoptic Gospels relate that at the time of the trans-
figuration of Jesus, Moses and Elijah appeared talking with him.
The disciples accepted and recognized their master as the Messiah
and a great prophet. Thus, the early Christian writers consciously
portray Jesus in the period of his ministry (section b) along the

lines describing the ministry of Moses, the first redeemer, and Elijah, the great prophet (including Elisha, his disciple). This type of typology [1]) is presented in the following chart:

Jesus	Moses	Elijah (Elisha)
A meeting with John the Baptist (a priest and a relative): "For so it becomes us to fulfil all the justice" (Matt. III. 13-15, Mk. I. 9, Luk. III. 21)	A meeting with Aaron (a priest and a brother): "For he will be thy spokesman though you shall be to him a master" (Ex. 4. 14-16; 5. 27-28)	
Forty days and nights as a period of examination and temptation in the desert. "And the angels ministered unto him" (Matt. IV. 2, 11, Mk. I. 13, Luk. IV. 2)	The desert as a place for preparation and a test of leadership (Ex. R. on 3. 1 (p. 48-50)). Moses on the Mount for 40 days and nights (Ex. 24. 18)	A period of examination in the desert for 40 days and nights "And the ravens brought him bread and flesh" (I Kin. 17. 6 and 19. 8)
A call for the disciples: the disciples forsake the fish-net and home (Matt. IV. 18-22 so IX. 9, Mk. I. 18-20 so II. 14, Luk. V. 10, 11 so V. 27, 28)		A call for the disciple. The disciple forsakes the oxen and home (I Kin. 19. 19-21)
The mission: A call for repentance and healing the sick (Matt. IV. 23-24, Mk. I. 39, Luk. IV. 44)		The mission: A call for repentance (I Kin. 18. 20-40) and healing (ib. 17. 17-24)
The demonic says: "I know thee who thou art, the holy one of God". Compare the centurian statement, Matt. XXVII. 54, (Mk. I. 24, Luk. IV. 34).		The woman whose child was raised from the dead says: "Thou art a man of God" (I Kin. 17. 24, see also II Kin. 4. 9)
Cleansing of the leper (Matt. VIII. 2, 3, Mk. I. 41, Luk. V. 13)	Cleansing of the leprosy of Miriam as a result of Moses' prayer (Num. 12. 10-13)	Cleansing of the leprosy of Naaman (II Kin. ch. 5)

---

[1]) On typology see D. Daube, The New Testament and Rabbinic Judaism, 1956, part. I.

Jesus	*Moses*	*Elijah* (Elisha)
The messengers sent by Jesus are not received: "Master, wilt thou that we command fire to come down from heaven and consume them". (Luk. IX. 52-54).		The messengers sent by King Ahaziah: "If I be a man of God, let fire come down from heaven and consume thee" (II Kin. 1. 12)
The Pharisees say: "This one doth not cast out devils but by Beelzebub" Jesus reply: "I cast out devils by the spirit[1]) of God" (Matt. XII. 24, 28, Mk. III. 22, Luk. XI. 15, 20)		The reply of Elijah: "Is it because there is no God in Israel that thou sendest to inquire of Baal-Zebub" (II Kin. 1. 6)
The healing of the centurion's servant (Matt. VIII. 5-13, Luk. VII. 2-10)		The healing of a centurion (II Kin. 5. 1-14)
The meeting with the possessed with the devil crying to Jesus, and the appearance of a herd of pigs with whom the possessed were drowned (Matt. VIII. 28-32, Mk. V. 1-13, Luk. VIII. 27-33)		The meeting with the youths crying at Elisha, and the appearance of a herd of bears who devoured the youths. (II Kin. 2. 23, 25)
The raising of a widow's son: "And he delivered him to his mother". (Luk. VII. 12-15)		The raising of a widow's son: "And he delivered him to his mother". (I Kin. 17. 17-23)
The ruler's daughter is raised: "And when Jesus came into the ruler's house and saw the minstrels . . . He went in" (Matt. IX. 23-25, Mk. V. 35-42, Luk. VIII. 41-55)		The distinguished woman's son is raised: "And when Elisha came into the house behold the child was dead . . He went in" (II Kin. 4. 32-37)

---

[1]) Luk. reads finger (באצבע) instead of Matt. באצבטע.

Jesus	Moses	Elijah (Elisha)
The sedition of the Pharisees (Matt. XII. 14, Mk. III. 6 [with their associates], Luk. VI. 7, 11)	The sedition of Korah and his associates (Num. ch. 16)	
The twelve apostles, "who will judge the twelve tribes of Israel" [Matt. XIX. 28] (Matt. X. 1-4, Mk. III. 14-19, Luk. VI. 13-16)	The twelve messengers, "of each tribe" (Num. 13. 2-15)	
Surnaming of Simon [and James and John] (Mk. III. 16, 17, Luk. VI. 14)	Surnaming of Hoshea (Num. 13. 16)	
The appointment of the seventy (Luk. X. 1)	The appointment of the seventy (Num. 11. 24)	
The renouncement of his brothers and mother (Matt. XII. 46-50, Mk. III. 31-35, Luk. VIII. 19-21)	The renouncement of his wife (Sifre Num. 99 (27a))	
A cure can result from a contact with the master's cloth (Matt. XIV. 36 [IX. 21], Mk. VI. 56 [V. 27], Luk. VIII. 44)		A cure can result from a contact with the master's cane (II Kin. 4. 29)
"From whence hath this man this wisdom? ... Is not this the carpenter the son of Mary?" (Matt. XIII. 54, 55, Mk. VI. 2, 3).	"Are you not the son of Yochebed? You seek to become a ruler and a judge over us" (Ex. R. on 2. 14 (p. 38))	
Hearing the death of John (Matt. XIV. 13, Mk. VI. 29. 30, Luk. IX. 10)		Hearing the death of the true prophets (I Kin. 18. 13)
"And he began to teach them ... And when it was evening, his disciples came to him saying ... send the multitudes away" (Matt. XIV. 15, Mk.	"Moses sat to judge the people, and the people stood before Moses from morning till evening" (Ex. 18. 13, 14)	

Jesus	*Moses*	*Elijah* (Elisha)
VI, 34, 35, Luk. IX. 11, 12)		
The miracle of the 5000 and the 4000 "And they did all eat and were filled and ... remained" (Matt. XIV. 20, 21, XV. 37, 38, Mk. VI. 42, 43, VIII. 8, 9, Luk. IX. 17)	The miracle of the manna and of the quails (Ex. 16. 14, Num. 11. 31)	The miracles of the oil and the bread. (I Kin. 17. 16, II Kin. 4. 44 "And they did eat and left thereof"
A mount: a place for beatitudes and instructions [on the commandments] (Matt. V. 1 ff, Mk. III. 13 a calling for disciples, Luk. VI. 12 a place for prayer)	A mount: a place for blessings and ten commandments. (Ex. 19. 20, Deut. 6. 5ff)	A mount: a place for instruction (I Kin. 18. 19)
The walking on the sea (Matt. XIV. 25, Mk. VI. 49)	The splitting of the sea (Ex. 14. 15-22)	The splitting of the river (II Kin. 2. 8)
Jesus in the company of Peter, James and John ascend the high mountain (Matt. XVII. 1, Mk. IX. 2, Luk. IX. 28)	Moses in the company of Aaron and Eleazer ascend the high mountain (Num. 20. 25-27, see also Mech. 12. 3 (4a))	
"A cloud overshadows them and behold [1]) a voice out of the cloud" [erecting tabernacles] (Matt. XVII. 5, Mk. IX. 7, Luk. IX. 34, 35)	"A cloud overshadows them and a voice is heard" (Num. 12.5, on tabernacles = clouds of Glory see Mech. on 13. 20 (29b))	
The moon-struck lad and the failure of his disciples (Matt. XVII. 14-17, Mk. IX. 17-19, Luk. IX. 38-41)		The sun-struck lad and the failure of his disciple (II Kin. 4. 18-37)
"His looks(πρόσωπον) did shine ... they were afraid" (Matt. XVII. 2, 6, Mk. IX. 2, 6, Luk. IX. 29, 34)	"The skin of his face(πρόσωπον) shone and they were afraid to come nigh" (Ex. 34. 30, see b.B.B. 75a)	

---

[1]) Matt. reads וארי, whereas Mk. and Luk. ואתי.

The above typology, which compares Jesus with Moses, the first redeemer and Elijah (on the association of the last two see Deut. R. on 10. 1 (p. 87) in the name of R. Jochanan ben Zakkai) is based on the tradition: "As the first redeemer was, so shall the last redeemer be" (see p. 95 n. 5 and J. Mann, The Bible as Read and Preached in the Old Synagogue, Hebrew section, p. 219). Thus Matt. 17.4, Luk. 9.33, and Mk. 9. 5 relate that Peter wanted to erect three tabernacles for Moses, Elijah and Jesus (see further I. Abrahams, Studies II, p. 50 ff).

In the same manner a parallel can be drawn in section c and in the story told of the last day of Elijah on earth. The disciples are told on the road of the forthcoming death of their master [Matt. 20. 17-19, Mk. 10. 32-34, Luk. 18. 31-33] and the disciple of Elijah is told on the road: "Knowest thou that today Yahweh will take away thy master" [II Kin. 2. 3]. Peter assures his master that "I will never be offended (because of thee)" [Matt. 26. 33, Mk. 14. 29] or as Luk. 22. 33 reads: "I am ready to go with thee both into prison and to death" and he betrays his master thrice. Elisha assures his master thrice: "I will not leave thee" [II Kin. 2. 2, 4, 6]. "Elijah went up by a whirlwind into heaven" [ib. 2. 11], and at the time of Jesus' death "the earth did quake and the rocks rent" [Matt. 27. 51] or "the sun was darkened" [Luk. 23. 45]. Fifty men were looking for the body of Elijah for three days and it was not found [II Kin. 2. 17] At the end of three days Jesus' body was not found in his grave [Matt. 28. 1, 7; Mk. 16. 2, 6; Luk. 24. 1, 3].

Another feature of the Holy Scriptures is the genealogical records. Great stress was placed on family lineages and especially those of the priests. Archives were designated for keeping family records for registration purposes. Rabbi Levi (c. 250 A.D.) [1] informs us that a family record was found in Jerusalem indicating that Hillel was of Davidic descent—an important factor in establishing the patriarchy from Hillel's line. The appointment of Rabbi Eleazer ben Azariah as the head of Jamnia's academy (c. 100 A.D.) in preference to Rabbi Aqiba, a greater scholar, was attributed to his lineage from Ezra. The work of Seder Olam Rabba was reedited to establish the link of the Babylonian exiliarch with the Davidic line.

A striking feature in the two Gospels, the ones according to Luke and Matthew, is the genealogical records establishing Jesus descent from David, whose shoot will bear the expected Messiah [Hos. 3. 4-5, Jer. 30. 9]. A more striking feature is the enumeration of the genera-

[1] See above p. 48 n. 13 and p. 49 n. 1.

tions in groups of fourteen as found at the beginning of Matthew. Since the author intentionally omits two important kings, Jeoash and Amaṣiah, to produce a succession of fourteen kings, G. H. Box [Interpreter, Jan. 1906 p. 199] explains "By this means the genealogy was invested with the character of a sort of numerical acrostic on the name of David (D'W'D'=14)". A more definite reason was in the mind of the author for producing such a record in the beginning of the Gospel.

Exodus Rabbah on 12. 2 (p. 196 f) [1]) renders the following exegesis on the verse [Ps. 72. 7]: " 'In his days let the righteous flourish and abundance of peace till the moon be no more'. Even before God brought Israel out of Egypt, He intimated to them that royalty would last for them only until the end of thirty generations—The moon begins to shine on the first ... and goes on shining till the fifteenth day when her disc becomes full. From the fifteenth till the thirtieth day her light wanes; till on the thirtieth it is not seen at all. With Israel too there were fifteen generations from Abraham to Solomon ... so did Solomon reign over the whole earth [2]). Thus the disc of the moon was at its fullest. Henceforth the kings began to diminish in power ... that is till nothing remained of the thirty generations during which Israel enjoyed a kingdom". In this way the author of Matthew shows that the fourteen generations until David's rise to power ushered in the golden Jewish age at the time of Solomon. This is to be compared to the fullness of the moon. The succeeding fourteen generations of the Judean kings until the destruction of the Temple are the reducing phase of the moon which culminates in complete darkness. With the following fourteen generations the moon reaches its fullness again, for the author, with the appearance of Jesus. Compare the reading in J. Mann, op. cit., Hebrew section, p. 200: "This is the Messiah with whom God will make the moon full".

The genealogy of Jesus according to Luke differs from Matthew's account in two respects: a) It retraces the lineage from Adam the son of God [3]), b) It differs in the enumeration from David both in number and name. Yet it produces the following similarities: a) The lineage from Abraham until David is in the same succession of fourteen names, b) the appearance of Shaltiel and his son Zerubabel in the latter part of

[1]) Already recognized by N. Krochmal, More, p. 48, at the end, compare also Num. R. on 7. 17 (p. 531) and Gen. R. on 49. 9, 10 (p. 1258).
[2]) See b. Meg. 11b.
[3]) So according to rabbinic tradition Adam was the creation of God, see b. Sanh. 38 b.

the account. The intention of the author in producing a genealogy from Adam through David and Zerubabel can be, thus, explained: Adam appears at the beginning of the record due to the existing aggadic tradition. It states [1]): "While Adam lay a shapeless mass before Him at whose decree the world came into existence He showed him every generation and its sages, every generation and its judges, scribes, interpreters and leaders". The theory further states [2]): "The royal Messiah will not come until all the souls which [God] contemplated creating have been created". David, the true Messiah of Israel was conceived in the creation of Adam. Thus another aggadic tradition links the lives of Adam and David saying [3]): "Adam contributed seventy years of his life so that David may live". Zerubabel, a descendant of David was declared by the contemporary prophets [4]) the branch of David, the Messiah after the destruction of the First Temple. For the Christian sect Jesus was the son of David, the true Messiah—a final link with Zerubabel, David and Adam as contemplated in the creation of the latter.

On Prophecy [5])

The prophets of the First Jewish Commonwealth, the years of Babylonian exile, and the period of Return were also teachers, statesmen and interpreters of events. Stirred by a heavenly spirit [6]) or in a state of ecstasy, they heard the voice of God [7]) or witnessed a vision [8]) which they related in an oracle—and on occasion they instructed their disciples to put it in writing. These revelations—as shown by W.O.E. Oesterley and T. H. Robinson in "Hebrew Religion", London, 1931, ch. VIII—touch on five aspects of Yahweh as a law maker, the Lord of nature, the Lord of history, the Lord of end of things, the Lord of universal morality and the Lord who makes no ritual demand. The prophets [8]) called for repentance, to purge the sins and evil doings of the nation and the individual—a step

---

[1]) Gen. R. on 5. 1 (p. 231) compare I A.D.N. 31 (p. 46a) Midrash on Psalms 139 (p. 265b), b. Sanh. 38b and b. A.Z. 5a.
[2]) Gen. R. 5.1 (p. 233); cf. b. A.Z. 5a (in the name of R. Jose).
[3]) Yalqut Shime'oni § 41 on Gen. 5. 1. For a different reason see Jub. 4. 30.
[4]) Zech. 6. 12 and Hag. 2. 23.
[5]) On Bath-Qol see Lieberman, Hellenism, p. 194 ff, and A. Marmorstein, Studies in Jewish Theology, p. 122 ff.
[6]) See Ez. 2. 2; 11. 5, I Sam. 10. 10; 16. 13, Is. 61. 1.
[7]) See Ez. 1. 25; 37. 7, Mic. 6. 9, Is. 6. 8; 40. 3.
[8]) See Ez. chs. 1, 8, 37 and Is. ch. 6.
[9]) See J. Klausner, The Messianic Idea in Israel, part A.

which according to the prophet could lead to redemption, an age of peace and prosperity. The events during the lifetime of the prophets stirred these men to react with oracles of admonition and on retribution on the 'Day of Yahweh'—the day of the Great Judgement. They were capable of interpreting the change of events, and of seeing in the rise of a new ruler a messianic hope or, on the other hand, a period of disaster.

The words or works of the prophets which were recorded for posterity were considered—as shown in Part A—by later generations as divinely inspired. With termination of the era of prophecy the teachers and scribes of the succeeding periods were responsible for the interpretation of the divine Law and the words of the prophets. Revelation now assumed another character: the conservation of the inspired words through tradition and interpretation. The introduction of new norms to guide the daily life of the people was considered by the Pharisees a link with the true law, the law of Moses on Sinai. The examination of the Scriptures in the form of midrash (exposition) or pesher (uncovering the meaning of the text) was the revelation of the teachers. Disclosed knowledge—on eschatology, on the interpretation of history, on man, nature and God—a revelation which also edifies, comforts and admonishes, had created apocalyptic, apocryphal and aggadic (interpretations of the story of creation and the divine chariot [Ez. I]) literature. Knowledge of the end of days was revealed in visions [חָזוֹן so Dan. 8. 1] and recorded in symbolic and mythological pictures.

The oracles and statements of the prophets of old were reinterpreted or projected to present events or personalities. This is known as pesher-interpretation (see further p. 151). Thus, revelation of the past became the revelation in the present. A form of revelation was recorded in the Book of Daniel [9. 2]: "I, Daniel, meditated on the books over the number of years concerning the word of Yahweh which came to Jeremiah the prophet (Jer. 25. 12): 'And it shall come to pass when seventy years are accomplished [that I will punish the king of Babylon and that nation, saith Yahweh]'". This was interpreted by Daniel through a vision [בֶּחָזוֹן Dan. 9. 21] to denote (ib. '9. 24-27): "Seventy hebdomads (490 years) are decreed upon thy people and thy Holy City", of which (ib. 9. 25) "from the going forth of the word (the prophecy of Jeremiah) to restore and to build Jerusalem unto one anointed a prince (probably Zerubabel or Jehoshua (Zech. 4. 12)) shall be seven hebdomads" (from 588/89 B.C., the time of the destruction of the First Temple to 538 B.C., the year of the declaration of Cyrus and the Return) "and for threescore and two hebdomads, it (Jerusalem) shall be built again with a broad-way (רְחוֹב see Neh. 8. 1), and after

threescore and two hebdomads shall the anointed (the High Priest Onias III) be cut off (from 515 B.C., the year when the Second Temple was completed, to 171 B.C., the year Onias III was murdered at the court of Antioch, II Macc. 4. 34) and the people of the ruler (Antiochus IV Epiphanes) who come shall destroy the city and the sanctuary ... and he shall impose a covenant with many (the Hellenistic Judaic groups) for one hebdomad (171-164 B.C.) and for a half a hebdomad he shall cause the sacrifice and the meal-offering to cease" (3 1/2 years of profaning the Temple, the placing of an "abomination" (Dan. 9. 27, 8. 13, 12. 11), a heathen altar (see I Macc. 1. 54)). This type of revelation in the form of interpretation of the events attributed to the author of Daniel was again reinterpreted by later apocalyptic writers such as the author of E. Enoch (89. 59; 93) and the author of Test. L. (16. 1).

The mode of interpretation or revelation described above was adopted by the Teacher of Righteousness, by Jesus, by the Gospel writers and the Rabbis. The Teacher of Righteousness interprets the statement in Nah. 2. 12, 13 [1]: "Where a lion and the lioness [1] walked, and the lion's whelp, and did not cause fear" to denote Demetrius III Eukairas and "the lion did tear in pieces enough for his whelps and strangled for his lioness" to denote "a lion of wrath", which undoubtedly refers to Alexander I Jannaeus. Jesus [2] interprets Mal. 3. 1, "Behold I send My messenger [before thy face] and he shall clear the way before Me (Snyoptics read "thee")", to imply John the Baptist, the expected Elijah before the arrival of the Messiah. In the same manner he interprets [3] "the stone" in Ps. 118. 22 to denote himself (a play on the words; stone (אֶבֶן) and son (בֵּן)) and "the builders" [4], the Pharisees. Luke 18. 31 [5] attributes the following statements to Jesus: "Behold we go up to Jerusalem and all that is written by the

---

[1] So Masorah לביא, but the Pesher and LXX read לבוא.

[2] Luk. 7. 27, 28, Matt. 11. 10, 11 (note the pesher expression οὗτός ἐστιν = דִין הוּא) and so Mk. 1. 2 (introduced by the author). Clear the way of God (Is. 40. 3) was John's message.

[3] Compare b. Ber. 64a, the builders are the students of the Law.

[4] Luk. 20. 17, 18, Matt. 21. 42-44, Mk. 12. 10, 11, and see p. 154.

[5] See also Luk. 4. 21; 22. 37; 24. 44.

prophets concerning the Son of Man shall be fulfilled". The preaching
of the early Christians followed the same mode of interpretation to
show that the promises made by the prophets were fulfilled with the
arrival of their master. Thus, the Gospel writers describing the life
and death of Jesus introduced the remark: "that it might be fulfilled
which was spoken by the prophet" with a quotation from the Bible [1].
The Rabbis, too, in interpreting the events of their times, state [2]:
"This is to fulfil what was said" followed with a quotation from the
Scriptures.

A rabbinic tradition states [3]: "Since the death of the last prophets,
Haggai, Zechariah and Malachi, the Holy Spirit departed from Israel;
yet they (the teachers) made use of the Bath-Qol (a daughter of voice)"
or as a variant in T. Sot. 13. 2 (318. 23) reads: "they would make it
known to them through a Bath-Qol". The Rabbis noted that in a time
lacking men inspired by the Holy Spirit (prophets) prophecy and
revelation were determined through the medium of a Bath-Qol. Bath-
Qol is found in rabbinic literature to denote three types of revelation:
a) It is introduced to a message of the Scriptures, which is interpreted to designate important events. b) It signifies an echo, a sign or
a statement made by a teacher, a child and even a lunatic which was
interpreted as a prophetic message. c) It, also, signifies a decision of
the academy or an indication of individual mental productivity,
which was interpreted as divinely guided.

The first designation of Bath-Qol was described above and the
following examples drawn from the rabbinic literature illustrate
this point. The story (II Macc. 7 and IV Macc. 8 ff) relating the
martyrdom of Hanna and her seven sons, in the early days of the
Hasmonaean period, is reproduced by the Rabbis [4] with the concluding remarks: "A Bath-Qol went forth and said (Ps. 113. 9): 'The
mother of childern is happy' and the Holy Spirit cried out (Lam. 1. 16):
'For these things I weep' ". Other examples of interpretation of events
concluding with the remark: "and the Holy Spirit cried out" (with a
quotation from the Scriptures) are found in the Midrash on Lamentations. In this manner the Rabbis saw in the words of the Scriptures
the utterance of the Holy Spirit (or of the heavenly voice) which foretold the present event. In the same mode of interpretation, Rabban

---

[1] See for example Matt. 1. 22 and John 12. 38.
[2] For example Lam. R.on 1.1 (p. 69 ff). The Hebrew phrase is לְקַיֵּם מַה שֶּׁנֶּאֱמַר
[3] T. Sot. 13. 2 (318. 22) and compare b. ib. 48b, b. Yom. 9b and b. Sanh. 11a.
[4] b. Git. 57b and Lam. R. on 1. 16 (p. 130 ff).

Jochanan ben Zakkai (c. 70 A.D.) said [1]): "What answer did the Bath-Qol give to that wicked one (Nebuchadnezzar, the king of Babylon, who in Rabban Jochanan's time possibly suggested Titus) when he said (Is. 14. 14): 'I will ascend above the heights of the clouds; I will be like the Most High'. A Bath-Qol went forth and said to him: O wicked man, son of a wicked man ... who stirred the whole world to rebellion against Me, How many are the years of man? seventy or even by reason of strength fourscore years, so it is stated in Ps. 90. 10. Is not the distance from the earth to the firmament a journey of 500 years, and the thickness of the firmament is a journey of 500 years and likewise the distance between one firmament and the other (for there are seven heavens in Jewish tradition, Sl. En. 3-9, b. Hag. 12 b) and you have said: 'I will ascend above the heights of the clouds, I will be like the Most High' Nay, thou shalt be brought down to the nether-world, to the uttermost part of the pit". Rabban Jochanan interpreted the words of the prophet as a statement made by Nebuchadnezzar (Is. 14. 14) and a reply given by the Bath-Qol (Is. 14. 15). For a further illustration [2]) of this type of interpretation see Part D. pp. 151, 152.

The second designation of a Bath-Qol is noted in the explanations of Rabbi Jochanan ben Naphcha (c. 250 A.D.). Rabbi Jochanan states (b. Meg. 32a): "Whence do we know that we may make the use of a Bat-Kol, for it is said (Is. 30. 21) 'and thine ears shall hear a word behind thee saying' ". The type of a Bath-Qol is explained [passim]: in case one hears the voice of a man in town and a voice of a woman in the country and it says "yes, yes" or "no, no". An echo is heard after a decision, thereby, affirming the decision as heavenly approved. An echo was also regarded as valid testimony to a corroboration of the death of a husband, which would permit the wife to remarry. The decision of the academy of Hillel [3]) was incorporated in the Jewish code [M. Yeb. 16. 6]: "A woman may be given permission to marry again on the evidence of a Bath-Qol". The following case was recorded [passim]: "It once happened that someone was

---

[1]) b. Hag. 13a and b. Pes. 94a.

[2]) Where the Babylonian rendition reads "Bath-Qol", the Palestinian reads Ruah Haqodesh, e. g. b. Sot. 10b compare Gen. R. 85 (p. 1045), b. Ker. 5b compare Lev. R. on 2. 3 (p. 43) and Sifra on 10. 4 (46a)—as noted also by Bacher, Terminologie, רוח הקדש. On the concept of Ruah-Haqodesh see L. Heinemann, Die Lehre vom Heiligen Geist im Judentum und in den Evangelien, M.G.W.J. 66 (1922) and 67 (1923) and A. Marmorstein, Studies in Jewish Theology.

[3]) b. Yeb. 122a.

standing on the top of a hill and said: 'so-and-so son of so-and-so
of such-and-such a place is dead'. But when they (the Rabbis) went
(to the top of the hill) they found no one there; his wife, however,
was permitted to remarry"—their decision was based on an echo or
rumour. Rabbi Jochanan also states (b.B.B. 12 b)[1]): "Since the Temple
was destroyed, prophecy has been taken from the prophets and given
to lunatics and children". The Talmud [passim] illustrates how the
words of a lunatic were taken as prophecy with the following case:
"Mar (master) Tabiumi, the son of R. Ashi, (c. 450 A.D.) was one day
standing in the manor of Mahuza (a town on the Tigris) when he
heard a certain lunatic exclaim: 'The man who is to be elected head of
the academy in Matha Meḥasia (a suburb of the Babylonian town Sura
—a center of learning headed by his father) signs his name Tabiumi'.
He said to himself: 'Who among the Rabbis signs his name Tabiumi?
I do. This seems to show that my lucky time has come' ". A verse
quoted by a child was regarded by Rabbi Jochanan as a sign of prophecy. It is told [b. Hul. 95 b] that R. Jochanan wished to meet
Samuel, the head of the Babylonian academy at Neharda. So he said to
a child: "Tell me the (last) verse you have learned". He answered
(I Sam. 28. 3): "Now Samuel is dead". Said R. Jochanan: "This means
that Samuel has died". A Bath-Qol was designated for a sign resulting
from a verse quoted by a child in the following tale. Rabbi Elisha ben
Abuyah (c. 100 A.D.) who in later days became a heretic was encouraged by his pupil, Rabbi Meir, to repent. He heard [2]) a Bath-Qol
coming forth and saying (Jer. 3. 14): "Return ye backsliding children"
except 'the other' (a name given to Elisha by the Rabbis upon his
apostasy). In another tale [3]) it is told: "R. Meir took his teacher Elisha
to a schoolhouse—Elisha said to a child: Recite for me thy verse. He
answered (Ps. 50. 16) 'But unto the wicked (וְלָרָשָׁע) God saith: 'What

hast thou to do to declare My statutes?'. The child was a stutterer so it
sounded as though he answered. 'But to Elisha (וּלֶאֱלִישָׁע) God saith

etc.' ". In the same manner, Jesus [4]), who was proclaimed by the
shouts of the children in the Temple (Ps. 118. 25, 26): "Save now
(Hosanna) ... Blessed be he that cometh (referring to Jesus)", replied

---

[1]) See also the statement of R. Jochanan in b. Ber. 57b: "If at the moment of
rising a text occurs to one, this is a minor prophecy".
[2]) b. Hag. 15a compare J. ib. 77b.
[3]) b. Hag. 15b.
[4]) Matt. 21. 15, 16, Mk. 11. 9, 10 and Luk. 19. 38, 39, 40. The verses (Ps. 118. 25,
26) form a passage from Hallel recited by the students see, T. Sot. 6. 2 (303. 17).

to the angry priests and scribes (Ps. 8. 3) "Out of the mouth of babes and sucklings Thou (God) hast established might". Jesus' reply connotes that the verse spoken by the children is a sign of prophecy.

A heavenly sign such as the appearance of a bird was taken by the Rabbis as a sign of prophecy, the equivalent of a heavenly voice (Bath-Qol). A story is told (Gen. R. 79. 6 (p. 941)): "Rabbi Simeon ben Yochai and his son R. Eleazer (c. 140 A.D.) were hiding in a cave for thirteen years during the Hadrianic persecution. At the end of thirteen years, R. Simeon went out and sat at the entrance of the cave. He saw a hunter engaged in snaring birds and heard a Bath-Qol exclaim from heaven "Dimissio"' (amnesty!) and the bird escaped. He then heard a Bath-Qol a second time proclaim "σπέχουλα" (death!) and the bird was caught. He remarked: 'Even a bird cannot escape without a decree of Heaven, how much more then the life of a human being!'. Thereupon he went forth and found that the trouble had subsided".

At the time of Jesus' baptism it is recorded [Matt. 3. 16, Mk. 1. 10]: "And, lo, the heavens were opened unto him and he saw the Spirit of God (Luk. 3. 22 reads Holy One)[1]) descending like a dove". A dove has represented for the Jewish teachers the chosen ekklesia of Israel and a prophetic sign[2]). Thus, the heavenly sign at the baptism of Jesus[3]) in the picture of a dove was accompanied with a Bath-Qol saying "This is My beloved [son], in whom I am well pleased" (Is. 42. 1)—the sign suggested for the Christians that Jesus was the chosen son of God.

A Bath-Qol also represents a statement foretelling the future made by a teacher, or a revelation to a priest at the time he administered the incense-offering. Josephus relates (Ant. 15. 10. 5) that Menahem, an Essene teacher, foretold the future concerning the youth Herod, saying: "You will surely become a king, and because God considers you worthy of it, you will have a successful reign". The Talmud reproduces the account as follows (b. B.B. 3b): "Herod, a governor (עַבְדָּא) appointed by the Hasmonaean family, set his eyes on a certain young maiden (Mariamni, to secure kingship over the Judaic state). One day he heard a Bath-Qol saying: 'Any governor that rebels now

---

[1]) "Αγιος = קוּדְשָׁא, an appellation of God see Marmorstein, The Old Rabbinic Doctrine of God, p. 97.

[2]) b. Ber. 53b about Rabba bar bar Channah (c. 300 A.D.), b. Shab. 49a about Elisha at the time of Roman persecution, b. Git. 45a about R. Nahman (c. 325 A. D.) and b. Sanh. 95a. See also Targum Cant. 5. 2.

[3]) Matt. 3. 16, 17, Mk. 1. 10, 11, Luk. 3. 21, 22.

will succeed'". Josephus [Ant. 13. 10. 7 § 300] also states that Yocha
nan I Hyrcanus "was accounted by God worthy of three of the greatest
privileges; the rule of nation, the office of the high priest and the gift
of prophecy". Concerning the gift of prophecy, Josephus [Ant. 13. 10.
3 § 282] and a rabbinic tradition [T. Sot. 13. 5 (319. 8, 9)] relate
"that on the very day on which his sons fought with Cyzicenus, Hyrcanus who was alone in the Temple burning incense as High Priest
heard a Bath-Qol saying: 'the youths were victorious in the battle at
Antioch' ". In a similar manner Luke (1. 8-23) relates: "And it came
to pass that while he (Zechariah, the father of John the Baptist)
executed the priest's duties ... to burn incense [1]) ...there appeared
unto him an angel. ... The angel said unto him: "Fear not Zechariah,
for thy prayer is heard; and thy wife Elisabeth shall bear thee a son
and thou shalt call his name Yochanan".

The third designation of a Bath-Qol is to be explained with the
statement made by R. Abdimi of Haifa [1]) (c. 300 A.D.): "Since the
Temple was destroyed, prophecy has been taken from the prophets
and given to the Hakhamim (the teachers of the academy)". This
statement corresponds to the rabbinic tradition [S.O.R. 30 (p. 65)]:
"Until then (rise of Alexander) the prophets prophesy by the Holy
Spirit from then and on (Pr. 22. 17): 'Incline thine ear and hear the
words of the Hakhamim' ". Thus, a decision reached in Jamnia's
academy accepting the opinion of Hillelites [1]) as authoritative is designated by a Bath-Qol—to be heavenly guided. The sessions held [1])
in various times to declare the worthiness of the individual teacher
(described as a person deserving the presence (Shekhinah) of God)—
as in our days the ceremony of bestowing an honorary degree—was
indicated by a Bath-Qol. A Bath-Qol is also introduced to show the
argumentative capabilities and the mental productivity of the teacher
in a debate. A rabbinic tradition (b.B.M. 59 b) relates that Rabbi
Eliezer ben Hyrcanus (c. 90 A.D.) in a dispute over a halachic question
demonstrates a proof from a Bath-Qol (i.e. general recognition) which
declared: "Why argue with R. Eliezer, seeing that in all matters the
halachah agrees with him!"

---

[1]) On the drawing of lots for burning incense see M. Tam. 5. 2; 6. 3.

[2]) b. B.B. 12a·

[3]) b. Erub. 13b and see J. Ber. 3b (R. Jochanan states that the Bath-Qol was
declared in Jamnia).

[4]) b. Sot. 48b, conferring an honour on Hillel at Jericho, on Samuel the minor
in Jamnia. See also T. ib. 13. 3, 4 (318.23-319. 5).

The Synoptics indicate [Matt. 7. 28, 29, Mk. 1. 22, Luk. 4. 32] that the teachings of Jesus caused astonishment and bewilderment among the people, to which they add: "For he taught them like being possessed with Power[1]) and not as the scribes". Thus, John (12. 28) describes that Jesus also was recognized and glorified in the Temple through a Bath-Qol. "Then came forth a Bath-Qol from heaven saying: 'I have glorified and will glorify again' (cf. LXX of I Sam. 2. 30). A Messiah—according to the prophet (Is. 11. 2)—is an individual on whom "the spirit of Yahweh (the Targum renders: the spirit of prophecy), the spirit of wisdom and understanding, the spirit of counsel and might rest". A claim to messiahship was tested by the capabilities of the claimant (ib. 11. 3): "to be stirred with the fear of Yahweh" or as explained by the Rabbis: to judge though detection [√ריח to smell]) "and not to judge after the sight of the eyes". In this manner a rabbinic tradition claims [2]) that Bar-Kosiba, a claimant to messiahship, was tested by the Rabbis. In the days of the Hasmonaean period, the spirit of prophecy which rests on the Messiah was explained [Test. L. 18. 6]: "The heavens shall be opened, and from the temple of glory shall come upon him sanctification with the Father's voice (φωνῇ=Bath-Qol) as from Abraham to Isaac". Thus, according to the early Christians, prophecy reappeared with the arrival of Jesus, the Messiah. As stated in ib. 18. 11: "And he shall give to the saints to eat from the tree of life (cf. John 6. 51, bread of life) and the spirit of holiness (Ruah Haqodesh, cf. Acts 2. 4) on them".

On Liturgy

The exiles in Babylon adapted themselves to the new country following the advice of Jeremiah [3]), the prophet at the time of the destruction of the First Temple. Living in ghetto-type communities, and having been deprived of their country and their national sanctuary— a house of worship in which the presentation of sacrifices was the strongest religious expression—the Jews developed an important institution, the synagogue [4]). It was a place where "ye shall call upon Me and go and pray unto Me, whereupon I shall hearken unto you; and ye shall

---

[1]) Ἐξουσία=תוקפא (Targum Deut. 32. 15) an appellation of God. Cf. Matt. 21. 23 "With what power do you do these?" and Jesus reply: "From Heaven (an appellation of God)".

[2]) b. Sanh. 93b.

[3]) Jer. 29. 4-20.

[4]) See L. Rabinowitz on Synagogue in Manson's Companion to the Bible, Edinburgh, 1945 and I. Abrahams, Studies in Pharisaism, I ch. 1.

seek Me and you will find Me", a house of religious activities and prayers as described in the address sent to the Babylonian Jewish communities by Jeremiah [Jer. 29. 12. 13]. Ezekiel [1]), the prophet of Exile, addressing the communities at Tel-Abib, Tel-Melah, Tel-Harsha, Cherub and Addan says: "Thus saith the Lord Yahweh: Although I have removed them (the Jews) far off among the nations, and although I have scattered them among the countries, yet have I been to them a little sanctuary in the countries where they come". The Rabbis maintained [2]) that the "little sanctuary" refers to the synagogue erected by the exiles and tradition points to such a synagogue founded in that time.

The prophetic aspirations during the years when the Second Temple was built express a desire for a house of worship and prayer. Prayer —as shown in Part A, p. 21—was the medium of expression of the Scribes. The Levites occupied an important position as singers at the Temple services. They were present in the epoch-making month in the days of Ezra, assisting with the reading and translation of the Law— a practice later adopted and integrated into the Temple and the synagogue services. They offered a prayer [3]) reviewing the past events and petitioning for guidance in present and future undertakings—a form also found in the Psalms. Psalms were written by the Levites and were designated to be chanted during the daily services of the Temple. The Thanksgiving-Hymn of Ben-Sira echoes the words of the Eighteen Benedictions, which with the destruction of the Temple became the standard liturgy for the daily synagogical services. The composition, which was attributed to the Men of the Great Synagogue [4]), the Hasidean Scribes, was rearranged and accepted as a standard liturgy at Jamnia's academy [5]).

During the Maccabean and Herodian times, the teachers of different circles coined and produced liturgical pieces, benedictions and songs of praise. They adopted the style of the authors of old and included phrases from the inspired words of the Holy Scriptures. The accepted rule that teachers of different circles transmitted to their pupils their

[1]) Ez. 11. 16.
[2]) b. Meg. 29a. Tradition mentions the Synagogue of Shaf We-Yathiv at Neharda see Rashi ad loc., compare Levin, Oṣar Hageonim, Megilla, p. 53.
[3]) Neh. 9. 4-37, compare Ps. 105, 106.
[4]) J. Ber. 4d and b. Meg. 17b.
[5]) b. Ber. 28b, J. ib. 8a. See also I Elbogen, Geschichte des Achtzehngebets, M.G.W.J. 46 (1902) and K. Kohler, The Origin and Composition of the Eighteen Benedictions, H.U.C.A. I.

form of liturgy prevailed as late as Amoraic times [1] (after 220 A.D.).
Luke (11. 1-4) relates that the disciples requested of Jesus: "Teach
us to pray as John (the Baptist) also taught his disciples". Only after
the destruction of the Temple were the first efforts made to standarize
daily prayer—as shown above with the Eighteen Benedictions—
owing to their early origin as the case was with the Psalms in both
the Jewish and Christian houses of prayer.

The early Christians adopted a form of prayer attributed to Jesus,
known as the Lord's Prayer. The prayer follows the rabbinic prescription on liturgy. Rabbi Hanina (c. 200 A.D.) observed in the Eighteen Benedictions the following pattern [2]: "In the first ones (see I.
Baer's Abodath Israel, pp. 87, 89) he (the one who prays) resembles
a servant who is addressing a eulogy to his Master, in the middle
ones [3] (ib., pp. 90-99) he resembles a servant who is requesting a
largess from his master". Thus, the Lord's Prayer begins with a
eulogy "Our Father who art in heaven, hallowed be Thy name" and
ends with a petition "Thy kingdom come [4], Thy will be done as in
heaven so on earth. Give us this day tomorrow's bread and forgive us
our debts as we forgive our debtors and lead us not into temptation but
delive us from Evil". The liturgical formula which begins the Lord's
Prayer is similar to the form found in S.E.R. (pp. 51, 83, 100): "My
Father who art in heaven blessed be Thy great name". The petition
found in the Lord's Prayer is found in a similar prayer known as
Tefillah Qeṣarah (a condensed form as compared to the lengthy
Eighteen Benedictions) to be said in an emergency. The prayer was
transmitted by R. Eliezer (c. 90 A.D.), who was also approached by
his disciples to demonstrate a brief prayer, as follows [5]: "Do Thy
will in heaven and give rest of spirit to them that fear Thee on earth,
Do as it seems right in Thy eyes". In the Benedictions recited by the
Jew in the morning [6], the following is to be said: "Bring us not into

---

[1]) For Example J. Ber. 7d, M. ib. 4. 2 and T. ib. 3. 7 (6. 16-25).

[2]) b. Ber. 34a compare J. ib. 8b.

[3]) The last three are not discussed since their origin was in the Temple. Whereas
the first three and the middle ones had their origin with the Hasideans, the coined
prayers of the individuals (see K. Kohler, op. cit.).

[4]) "To accept the yoke of the Kingdom of Heaven" is related in rabbinic
literature to "reciting the Shema", see Deut. R. Va-Etchanan (p. 60) וְאֵי זֶהוּ
מַלְכוּת שָׁמַיִם:יְ אֱלֹהֵינוּ יְ אֶחָד and see also Sifre Num. § 114 (34b).

[5]) See T. Ber. 3. 7 (6. 17) and Sifre Num. § 105 (28b). Compare the petition for
sustenance in Jesus' prayer with the prayer of Others, J. Ber. 8a.

[6]) b. Ber. 60b; a form included in the Didache.

sin ... nor lead us into temptation ... but keep us from evil men".
Whereas petition for bread, proclaiming God the sole provider, was
the reason for introducing Ps. 145 three times a day in synagogical
services (b. Ber. 4 b).

The Oral Tradition as Expanded during The Hasmonaean-Herodian Period

The epilogue to Koheleth [Ecc. 12. 11] states: "The words (or
works) [1]) of the wise-men (דִּבְרֵי חֲכָמִים) are as goads and as nails well
fastened are [the works] of the masters of assemblies (בַּעֲלֵי אֲסֻפּוֹת) ;
they were given from one shepherd (i.e. Moses)". The epilogue
sheds light on the structure of the oral tradition as verified by rabbinic
sources [2]). "The works of the wise men" (דִּבְרֵי חֲכָמִים) is interchangeable with the Tannaitic expression "the works of the Scribes" (דִּבְרֵי
סוֹפְרִים) [3]),and the "assemblies" synonymous with "Batey Hawa ʿad" [4])
or "Kenishta" [5]). The works, enactments and decisions introduced
by the Hakamim-Soferim during the Maccabean and Herodian period
were created in the assembly house—more commonly known as the
Beth-Din [6]) (the court), whose members were known as Zeqenim (elders) [7]). Thus, their decisions were entitled "Maʿaseh-Zeqenim" (the
works of the elders) [8]), "Dibrey Zeqenim" or "Dibrey Soferim". In the
Gospels [9]), their words are known as "ἡ παράδοσις τῶν πρεσβυτέρων".
These terms refer to the rulings emanating from different schools.

---

[1]) Dibrey meaning words see Is. 1.1, meaning works see I Chr. 29. 29; ʾasephah
denoting synagoge, see Part A, p. 15 n. 1.

[2]) See Ecc. R. on 12. 11 (p. 313), Num. R. on 11. 16 (p. 668), J. Sanh. 28a and
T. Sot. 7. 11 (307. 13), b. Hag. 3b.

[3]) M. Sanh. 11. 3 (Dibrey Soferim), J. ib. 30b (Dibrey Zeqenim); On Dibrey
Hakhamim see e.g. b. Shab 12b.

[4]) M. Sot. 9. 15, Ab. 1. 4, b. Ber. 24b and T. Meg. 4 (3). 5 (225. 14).

[5]) M. T. 10 (p. 16), see further H. Lichtenstein, Die Fastenrolle, H.U.C.A.
VIII-IX (1931-32).

[6]) Beth-Din of Jamnia (Sifre Deut. § 153, 154 (104b, 105a) is interchangeable
with Beth-Hamidrash (T. Yad. 2. 16 (683. 20) and Beth-Hamidrash of R. Jochanan
ben Zakkai (Lam. R., Pethichta, (p. 18). Beth-Din of Juda the prince (b. A.Z. 36a)
is interchangeable with Beth-Hawaʿad (J. Shab. 12c).

[7]) See M. Yom. 1. 3 (pre-Destruction) and T. Kel. B.B. 2. 4 (392. 7)—at Jamnia,
M. Suk. 2. 7 and T. Yad. 2. 16 (683. 19).

[8]) M. Yad. 4. 3. Cf. T. Sheb. 8. 7 (73. 5).

[9]) Mk. 7. 3. Cf. Ant. XIII. 16. 2 § 408 (τὴν πατρῴαν παράδοσιν).

"Dibrey Soferim" [1]) is applied to the rule enacted by the academy of Hillel on the recitation of the Shema (Deut. 6. 4-9, 11. 13-21 and Num. 15. 37-41). "Ma'aseh Zeqenim" [2]) is applied to the enactment of the Jamnia court based on a prior decision. "ἡ παράδοσις τῶν πρεσβυτέρων is associated with the ruling concerning the defilement of the hands enacted by Hillel and Shammai [3]).

A decision at the academy was reached in the presence of the doctors of the law by a majority consent [4]). Prior to the time of Hillel and Shammai the enactments were, in fact, the decisions of the legislative and judicial body since it was under Pharisaic auspices. With the creation of the two academies, the decision proclaimed by one house did not affect the members of the other school, and although in some cases it even produced bitter strife [5]) it did not evolve in a true split [6]). The house of Hillel followed the path paved by their master, a man with a liberal approach producing enactments for the betterment of society [7])—the Taqqanoth. This scholar refained from enforcing his decision [8]) and tales were told of his humbleness [9]). Upon his death, he was eulogized [10]): "Alas the pious, alas the humble, the disciple of Ezra". His disciples adopted the same liberal stand and enacted [11]) measures for the protection of the individual. The later school accepted the decisions reached by the academy of Hillel due to the disciples' meekness and humbleness [12]). The members of Shammai's academy, the opposing school, were associated with the haughty ones [13]) and the zealots [14]). Their master was strict in his teachings [15]) and hasty in

[1]) J. Ber. 3b; See further b. Sanh. 88b on Phylacteries and Fringes.

[2]) M. Yad. 4. 3.

[3]) J. Shab. 3c., b ib. 14b.

[4]) See T. Shab. 1. 16 (111. 3), T. Toh. 9. 14 (671. 1)—at the academy of Juda, T. Yad. 2. 16 (683. 24)—at the academy of Jamnia

[5]) T. Hag. 2. 11, 12 (236. 3-10). One can accept the decision of either academy, see T. Ed. 2. 3 (457. 19).

[6]) T. Yeb. 1. 10 (241. 30).

[7]) For example the enactment of Prosbol (a document issued by the court to secure exemption from the Sabbathical laws (Deut. 15. 2)), see M. Sheb. 10. 3; the enactment on the sale of houses in a walled city, see M. Ara. 9. 4.

[8]) b. Shab. 17a.

[9]) See I A.D.N. 15. 2 (p. 30b) and b. Shab. 31a.

[10]) T. Sot. 13. 3 (319. 2) and see Lev. R. on 1. 1 (p. 9)—the statement by Hillel.

[11]) See T.B.K. 10.5 (367. 4, 5) and b. Git. 55a—known as the enactment of those who return the stolen goods.

[12]) b. Erub. 13b.

[13]) T. Sot. 14. 9 (321. 1).

[14]) See further H. Grätz, G.d.J., III, n. 23, p. 485; and see J. N. Epstein, Meb. Les. Hat., p. 746.

[15]) b. Hul. 107b, M. Suk. 2. 8.

his decisions [1]). Stories [2]) were circulated about the master describing him as a qapdan (pedant). His disciples, too, were men of temper and zealous nature. During the lifetime of their teacher, with a show of arms [3]), they forced Hillel and his followers to abide by Shammai's decision. In the years prior to the destruction of the Temple, they also compelled [4]) the members of Hillel's academy to issue the Eighteen Measures against the heathens. I. H. Weiss [D. D. Wed. I, pp. 174, 175] concluded that the members of Shammai's academy were in sympathy with the Zealot's cause. They maintained, in opposition to Hillel's school, that under no circumstances should one swear allegiance to the monarchy [5]). In their refusal to swear allegiance to the Roman emperor, Josephus [Ant. 17. 2. 4] relates that over 6000 zealous Pharisees who claimed allegiance only to God were fined by Herod for their action.

In the same spirit Juda the Galilean and Zadok the Pharisee [6]) of Shammai's academy were responsible for the formation of a fourth sect known as Zealots. The Zealots, following in the main the Pharisaic doctrines, added that they did not recognize any earthly king as their master except God [ib. 18. 1. 1, 6]. The friction that existed between the Zealots and the liberal Pharisees is recorded in M. Yad. 4.8 as follows: "Zadok the Galilean [7]) said: I complain against you o Pharisees that you write the name of the ruler and the name of Moses together on a bill of divorcement (The document begins with a date which stated the year of the rule of the reigning king and ends with "in accordance with the religion of Moses and Israel"). The Pharisees replied: We complain against you, o Zadok the Galilean, that you write the name of a ruler together with the divine name on a single page (of the biblical scroll) and furthermore that you write the name of a ruler above and the divine name below as it is written (Ex. 5. 2): 'And Pharaoh (the ruler) said who is Yahweh (the Divine Name) that I should hearken unto His voice to let Israel go' ". In the days of the Jewish war with the Romans, Jochanan ben Zakkai, a disciple of Hillel, did not sympathize with the Zealots'

---

[1]) T. Sheb. 3. 10. (64. 27)
[2]) I A.D.N. 15 (p. 31), b. Shab. 31a.
[3]) b. Shab. 17a. See further p. 142.
[4]) T. Shab. 1. 16, 17 (111. 4-6) and M. T. (p. 24). Cf. J. Shab. 3c.
[5]) M. Ned. 3. 2.
[6]) Ant. 18. 1. 1. On Zadok see Hyman, Toledoth Hatannaim.
[7]) See J. Wellhausen, Die Pharisäer und die Sadducäer, 2 ed. Hannover, 1924, p. 63 n. 1.

cause. He [1]) cunningly left the besieged city and met Vespasian to appeal for the liberal Pharisaic cause of truce. On the other hand, the zealous Pharisees (of Shammai's academy) issued measures against any association with the heathens [2]), especially the Syrians and Romans who were living in Galilee, the area of the Zealotic activities. Thus, in the event [3]) a Jew was found to have had intercourse with a Syrian woman, he was maimed by the Zealots.

An analysis of the religious productivity during the Maccabean and Herodian periods—acts of reform, decisions, teachings, interpretations, edicts and enactments—indicates a general change of three consecutive periods of development. The first phase (166-130 B.C.) covers the period of Judas, Jonathan, Simeaon and his son John Hyrcanus I reign. This period, which witnessed the closing stages of the Great Assembly and the Gerousia, served as a background for the emergence of the two fronts, the Pharisees and the Sadducees, and the appearance of Essene communities. At the beginning of the period the zealous Hasideans and Hasmonaeans eliminated the Hellenized groups, destroyed the abominations, rededicated the Temple and restored a Mosaic rule. The first act of the Hasmonaeans was to circumcise the children who were denied by the Greek edicts this religious rite [4]). The above demonstration of zealotry for the Jewish law was followed by a day of fast, prayers and decision making at Mizpeh. There the assembly collected the Holy Scriptures of the preceding period, reinstated the Pentateuch as the constitution and restored the priestly institutions. The years following the decisive days of Judas Maccabaeus were years of restoration, expansion and preservation of the Judean state. The Hasmonaean court —mentioned in rabbinic source [5])—and the first two Duumvirates, the early Pharisaic leaders, were in the main concerned with the restoration of the Jewish religion as prescribed in the Mosaic law; the preservation of the Temple rituals; and the issuance of measures to protect the Judaic population from foreign imports and to prevent intermarriage and migration to other lands.

The second phase (130-67 B.C.) begins with the last years of John Hyrcanus I reign, the years in which the Sadducees rose to power,

---

[1]) b. Git. 56a, b.
[2]) See Grätz, G.d. J. III, n. 26.
[3]) M. Sanh. 9. 6 and b. A.Z. 36b.
[4]) I Macc. 1. 60; 2. 46.
[5]) b. A.Z. 36b, b. Sanh. 82a and b. Shab. 21b.

and ends with the reign of Salom Zion, the days in which the Pharisees were in control over the legislative and judicial body. The Duumvirates of the Pharisaic court were concerned in the main with the
establishment of judiciary system and jurisprudence.

The third phase (63 B.C.-70 A.D.) encompasses the Herodian
and procurators rule, the period of the academies of the last two
Duumvirates—Shemaiah and Abtalion, and Hillel and Shammai.
The academies of the latter extended the study of the Jewish religion
and its laws in three important areas: a) the Pharisaic code of separation
and purity (priestly and non-priestly laws), b) the assigment of definite
quantitative and qualitative measures or modes of applications to the
religious precepts recorded in the Pentateuch (where the law itself
does not always define the necessary measure or mode of application),
c) the festivals (rites, the form of liturgy and the manner of observance).

When the great period of intellectual activity of the Soferim ended,
it left for the succeeding generations two areas of achievement,
the written and the oral tradition. The two parties, the Sadducees
and the Pharisees, accepted and adopted the written tradition (the
(Holy Scriptures) as a source for law and Jewish wisdom. Yet the
Pharisaic teachers were the ones who stressed the further development
of the oral tradition. They [1]) maintained that the work of the students
of the law in every generation is a continuation in the chain of tradition, and their conclusions are as authoritative as the written Mosaic
law; since the interpretation and the Law emanate from the same
source—Moses at Mount Sinai. Josephus confirms this Pharisaic
stand saying [2]): "The Pharisees had passed on to the people certain
halachoth (νόμιμάτινα) handed down by former generations and
not recorded in the laws of Moses, for which they are rejected by
the Sadducean camp". He further states: "The Pharisees are the men
who have the reputation as the most accurate interpreters of the laws
(νόμιμα)". The controversies, which resulted over the written Law
between the two parties, point to interpretations on behalf of the
Pharisees which can not be concluded from the literal meaning of the
words of the Mosaic law. The Pharisees resorted to explanations
which must have existed orally and which were employed to lend
authority to their decisions and teachings.

The following examples taken from the noted controversies al-

---

[1]) J. Pea. 15a, 17a.
[2]) Ant. XIII. 10. 6 § 297. Cf. ib. 16. 2 and see Bell. II. 8. 14 § 162.

ready demonstrated in Part B illustrate this point: 1) The controversy dealing [1]) with the date of the Feast of Weeks involves the meaning of the word "Sabbath" in the verse prescribing the date of the Feast of Weeks. Lev. 23. 15 states: "And ye shall count unto you from the morrow after the Sabbath ... seven weeks". The Sadducees maintained that Sabbath refers to the seventh day of the week— as mentioned in the same law [ib. 23. 3]. The Pharisees, however, explained the Sabbath as a day of rest, a holiday—as found in ib. 23. 24, 32—and therefore it can fall on every day of the week which happens to be the first day of Passover. To lend authority to their interpretation of the law, the Pharisees prescribed their own calendar based on monthly reckoning, they established the following day an important religious holiday, the day of the wave-offering, underlining it with a pompous ceremony. Their successors employed a religious norm requiring a numerical count of 49 days following the first day of Passover [2]). 2) The controversy [3]) about the ceremony of incense-offering on the Day of Atonement touches the meaning of "cloud" in Lev. 16. 2—the Mosaic prescription of the ceremony—"For with a cloud I shall be seen upon the ark-cover". The Sadducees maintained the cloud denotes the cloud of smoke produced by the incense offering before the High Priest's entry into the Holy Chamber. The Pharisees defined the cloud figuratively as presence of God upon the Ark. To safeguard their interpretation, the High Priest was kept under Pharisaic supervision a week prior to the services. 3) The controversy [4]) dealing with the allotment of the Tamid sacrifice pertains to the rule enumerated in the list of the sacrifices [Num. 28. 4]: "The one lamb shalt thou offer in the morning and the other lamb shalt thou offer at dusk". The Sadducees insisted that the prescription "shalt thou" denotes the high priest who was also responsible for the purchase of the lamb—as affirmed in the priestly code of Ezekiel [Ez. 46. 13]: "And he (so LXX, Syr., Vulg.) shall prepare a lamb of the first year ... for a burnt-offering unto Yahweh daily". The Pharisees, on the other hand, maintained that the law refers only to the services administered by the priest whereas the purchase of the sacrifices are made by the commoners—since the Law [Num. 28. 2 ff] is addressed to the

---

[1]) M. T. scholion 1 (pp. 3, 4), b. Men. 65a.
[2]) b. Men. 66a.
[3]) T. Yom. 1. 8 (181. 1-9), b. ib. 19b, J. ib. 39a, b.
[4]) M.T. scholion 1 (p. 3), b. Men. 65a.

community. 4) On the ritual of the red heifer [1]) the Sadducees maintained that the law as prescribed in Num. 19. 9: "A man that is clean (אִישׁ טָהוֹר) shall gather the ashes of the heifer" refers to a state of purity described in Lev. 22. 7: "And when the sun is down, he shall be clean". The Pharisees [2]), on the other hand, maintained that the Mosaic law, "A man that is clean", refers to "And he shall immerse in water, a man that is clean", the reading in Num. 19. 18, to be understood as "a man is clean through immersion". 5) On the question of false witnesses [3]), the Pharisees prescribed a death sentence for false testimony when death sentence was not carried out on the accused —abiding by the interpretation of the law Deut. 19. 19: "And ye shall do unto it (the pair of witnesses) as it has purposed to do unto his brother"; a testimony with intention to cause death to a brother is also punishable by death. The Sadducees disagreed, since the Mosaic rule in the same law states [ib. 19. 21]: "And thine eye shall not pity; life for life" only upon the execution of the accused can the schemers be brought to justice. 6) In the same respect the Pharisees [4]) reinterpreted the rule of lex-talionis to denote payment and not bodily harm. 7) The Pharisees also interpreted metaphorically [5]) the words [Deut. 22. 17]: "And they shall spread the garment before the elders of the city" to mean a presentation of proof and not literally a garment. 8) In the same respect the Pharisees explained the words [6]) [Deut. 25. 9]: "And spit in his face" as part of the ceremony, in case a levirate marriage does not take place, to denote noticeable spit and not spit literally ejected on the face of the dead husband's brother.

Josephus' statement [7]): "The Pharisees had passed on to the people certain halachoth handed down by former generations and not recorded in the laws of Moses" includes halachoth based on oral interpretations as well as halachoth handed down by former generations. An example of the latter is found in T. Yad. 2. 16 (683. 24):

---

[1]) M. Par. 3, 7. T. ib. 3. 8 (632. 6-13). Note: a Qal-Vahomer is employed by the Sadducean priest, T. ib. 3. 6.

[2]) Sifre Num. § 129 (p. 46).

[3]) M. Mak. 1. 7, b. ib. 5b, T. Sanh. 6. 6 (424, 26 ff) and Mech. on 23. 7 (p. 105b).

[4]) M.T. scholion 4 (p. 8). Compare the discussion in b. B.K. 83b, 84a.

[5]) M.T. scholion 4 (p. 9). See Sifre Deut. § 237 (118a)—the interpretation is attributed to R. Ismael as others are attributed to R. Jochanan ben Zakkai.

[6]) M.T. scholion 4 (p. 9). See Sifre Deut. § 291 (126a). L. Finkelstein, Pharisees II, p. 641, doubts the authenticity of the last three examples, yet they are demonstrations of many such passages which were literally interpreted by the Sadducees and loosely interpreted in the Pharisaic schools.

[7]) Ant. XIII 10. 6..

Rabbi Elazer the son of Azariah, a disciple of Rabban Jochanan ben Zakkai, and the head of Jamnia's academy states: "I have received from Rabban Jochanan ben Zakkai who has received from the Duumvirates (since he was a disciple of Hillel) who in turn received from the Prophets [1]) (namely the latter prophets in the days of Ezra) and the prophets from Moses a halachah attributed to Moses from Sinai (denoting the oldest form of halachah and at the same time pointing to the Pharisaic view that these oral halachoth are as authoritative as the Law on Sinai) that the tithes due the poor can be apportioned from the lands of Ammon and Moab on the sabbatical year". The Mosaic law [Lev. 25. 4, 5] states: "In the seventh year shall be a sabbath of rest unto the land ... thou shalt neither sow thy field, prune thy vineyard, that which groweth of its own accord of thy harvest thou shalt not reap and the grapes of thy undressed vine thou shalt not gather, it shall be a year of solemn rest for the land"—a prescription restated in the covenant of the Great Assembly [Neh. 10. 32]. Consequently the law denied the poor in this year the portion allotted to them. The Pharisees abiding by the oral tradition explained [2]) that since in the days of Ezra and Nehemiah the lands of Moab and Ammon were not under Jewish jurisdiction, the law of the sabbatical year could not affect these countries; even though in later times these countries were in Jewish hands (in the days of Jannai, Ant. XIII. 15. 4).

The Pharisaic schools, advocating a free interpretation of the text, also developed modes or rules governing interpretation. Seven hermeneutic rules were taught [3]) by the Pharisaic master Hillel. Four of these rules were used by Hillel in his teachings and of the other three, two were used by his predecessors, Shimeon ben Shetach, Shemaiah, and one by the elders of the academy. Enumeration and illustration of the rules in the manner they were used by the masters follows.

1) Syllogism—a minori ad maius (qal vaḥomer)—was employed by Hillel to explain a question raised by the inhabitants of Bathyra [4]): "Can the paschal lamb rites be administered on the Sabbath (a day which requires complete abstention from any laborious act)?" Hillel

---

[1]) Compare the chain of tradition in Ab. ch. I, Lev. R. on 1. 5 (p. 31) and Cant. R. on 7. 14 (p. 302). See also M. Pea. 2. 6.
[2]) b. Hag. 3b, b. B.B. 56a and M. Sheb. 6. 1.
[3]) T. Sanh. 7. 11 (427. 4). Sifra, Introduction (3a) and I A.D.N. 37 (p. 55b).
[4]) J. Pes. 33a, T. ib. 4. 1-2 (162. 21-163. 4) and b. ib. 66a. On Bathyra see Ant. 17 § 26.

said: "If the Tamid-offering, which does not entail a divine punishment
of Kareth (premature death) and is brought on the Sabbath (Num.
28. 10) the paschal lamb which entails a divine punishment of Kareth
(ib. 9. 13) surely can be brought on the Sabbath". The Sadducees,
too, employed syllogism in their argument with the Pharisees. The
Pharisees maintained that the son or his children take precedence
in the law of inheritance over the daughter of the deceased—basing
their argument on the double reading of Num. 27. 8: "In case a
man dies and to him is no son (וּבֵן אֵין לוֹ) then you shall pass his inheritance to his daughter"—the daughter receives the inheritance
only after an examination (עַיֵּין־לוֹ) of the son's progeny (including the
the son's daughter). The Sadducees argued [1]): "If the daughter of
his son, who succeeds to an inheritance by virtue of the son's right,
is heir to him, how much more his (the deceased) daughter who
derives her right from him himself". Jesus in his teachings employs
syllogism as illustrated in Part D, pp. 170, 171.

2) Analogy of words— δὶς λεγόμενα (Gezerah Shavah)—was
also employed by Hillel in response to the above question: "It is
written in the rules concerning the Second Passover (Num. 9. 2) 'in
its appointed time', and it is written in the rule concerning the Tamid
(ib. 28. 2) 'in its appointed time'. As it is stated of the Tamid 'in its
appointed time' and it can be brought on the Sabbath, so is the case
with the paschal lamb of which is stated 'in its appointed time' can
be brought on the Sabbath". Jesus, too, employs the analogy of
words in his teaching as illustrated Part D, p. 174.

3) Analogy of subjects and its deduction (Heyqesh)—was applied
by Hillel in the above case saying: "Since the Paschal lamb is a communal sacrifice (Ex. 12. 3, 4) and the Tamid is a communal sacrifice
(see above p. 74) therefore if Tamid, a communal sacrifice, is brought
on the Sabbath, the same applies to the paschal lamb, a communal
sacrifice, to be brought on the Sabbath".

4) "A subject that is to be comprehended from its context"—an
exploration of the text through a careful study of the contents (Dabar
Halamed Me'inyano)—was employed by Hillel [2]) in the question of
cleansing the plagued by the priest. The law states [Lev. 13. 37]:
"But if the scall stayed in its appearance and black hair grow up
therein, the scull is healed, he is clean and the priest shall pronounce

---

[1]) b. B.B. 115b and M.T. scholion 5 (p. 11).
[2]) J. Pes. 33a and Sifra on 13. 37 (66d). Friedmann in his Introduction to
Sifra explains it as Kelal uperaṭ.

him clean". Hillel explains " 'He is clean' would imply that he is at liberty to return to normal life, therefore it states 'and the priest shall pronounce him clean'. If it only would have stated 'and the priest shall pronounce him clean' then it would denote that a priest could pronounce even an unclean person clean. Therefore, the text must read 'he is clean and the priest shall pronounce him clean' ". This explanation resulted in the following rule [M. Neg. 3. 1]: "All are qualified to inspect signs for leprosy, but only a priest may declare them unclean or clean. He (the priest) is told 'say: unclean' and he repeats 'unclean' or 'say: clean' and he repeats 'clean' ".

5) Induction (Binyan 'Ab) was already introduced by Shimeon ben Shetach in the law of false witnesses. Shimeon admonished the action taken by his colleague Jehuda ben Tabbai who administered death penalty to one witness bearing false testimony. Shimeon [1]) explained: "The law on witnesses states [Deut. 19. 15]: 'one witness shall not rise up against a man for any iniquity or for any sin ... At the mouth of two witnesses or at the mouth of three witnesses shall a matter be established' ", thus the law establishes the rule: "Whenever the Mosaic law speaks of 'witness' (עֵד) it refers to two unless it specifies one (עֵד אֶחָד)". Such is the case in false testimony, the law reads עֵד (witness), denoting a pair.

6) "A comparison of subjects"—Kayoṣe' bo Bemaqom 'Aḥer ("as it is found in another place")—was introduced by the teacher Shemaiah in Aggadic matter. Shemaiah states [2]): "The complete trust that Abraham their (of the Israelites) forefather had in the Almighty was reason enough for the Almighty to cause the Red Sea to split as it is written [Gen. 15. 6]: 'And he believed in Yahweh and He counted it to him for righteousness' "—implying that the belief of Abraham at the "covenant of pieces" was credited to his children to save them for "they believed in Yahweh" [Ex. 14. 31]. Jesus, too, employs the above method; see Part D, p. 173.

7) Quantitative relation in the law (Kelal uperaṭ): when the law proceeds from the general to the particular, the general is defined by the particular—was employed by the early Elders (Zeqenim) [3]), the members of the academy. The Priestly law, pertaining to the sin-offering brought by a person in a state of impurity, states [Lev. 5. 2]:

[1]) b. Mak. 5b and see p. 121, n. 4.
[2]) Mech. on 14. 15 (p. 35b).
[3]) Sifra on 5.2 (22d).

"If any one touches any unclean thing"—a generality—"whether it be the carcass of an unclean beast, or the carcass of unclean cattle or the carcass of unclean swarming things"—the particular—"and be guilty ... he shall bring ... a sin-offering". The early Elders found the particular to be defining the general; that is, as the particulars are a source of impurity so in the case of all other sources of impurity one is guilty and has to bring a sin-offering.

From the above demonstration of the hermeneutic rules we can conclude that the period of exposition began with Shimeon ben Shetach who contributed to the elaboration of the law—so the Karaites [1]) maintained that with Shimeon the oral law of the Rabbinites was established—and has continued with the academies of his successors. The Houses of Shammai and Hillel employed the above hermeneutics in the study of the law [2]). As indicated above the quantitative relation in the law was adopted by the Elders of the academy. This rule was widened to include the following derivatives [3]): a) A generality and a specific in the law, the general follows the particular—as demonstrated in No. 7. b) A specific and then a generality—e.g. Ex. 22. 9: "In case a man delivers unto his neighbour an ass or an ox or a sheep (the particular) or any beast (the general) to watch" the general adds on the particular to denote any beast of value. c) A generality, a specific and a generality—e.g. Deut. 14. 26: "And thou shalt give the money (with which a farmer redeemed the tenth of his produce on the second or fifth year of the sabbatical cycle) for whatsoever thy soul desireth (the general) for oxen or for sheep or for wine or for strong drink (the particular) or for whatsoever thy soul asketh of thee (the general) and thou shalt eat there (in Jerusalem)"—the generalities follow the specific that one can purchase only things that are born or grown. d) A generality that requires elucidation by the specific and the particular by the general —e.g. Ex. 13. 2: "Sanctify unto Me all the firstborn"—the generality would denote even a female, therefore the law in Deut. 15. 19 specifies 'the male'. If the law specifies 'male' I would declare even if the female were born before a male, the male is still considered firstborn, therefore the law in Ex. 13. 2 specifies "first issue of

---

[1]) See A. Waxman, A History of Jewish Literature I, p. 400 (New York, 1930).
[2]) See A. Schwarz, Die Controversen der Schammaiten und der Hilleliten, Vienna, 1893.
[3]) In the Beraitha of R. Ismael found in the preface to Sifra, see H. L. Strack, Introduction, ch. XI § 3 and A. Schwarz, Quantitätsrelation.

the womb'—this particular would declare even if the male follows a miscarriage he is considered first-born. Therefore the general is stated before hand, "the first-born", i.e. any issue. e) A matter which was included in the general law and was detached therefrom to predicate concerning another rule—e.g. Lev. 7. 20: "And the person that eateth from the meat of the sacrifice of peace-offerings . . . having his uncleanliness upon him, that person shall be cut off from his people". This law concerning the peace-offering is detached from the general law mentioned in Lev. 22. 3. Thus the rule states: "the detached did not come to predicate that case only, but the whole of the general law". Namely, in this case all sacrifices intended for the altar are under penalty of death when offered in a state of impurity and not those sacrifices which are kept in the Temple treasury. f) A matter which was included in a general law and which is detached to elucidate something in harmony therewith—e.g. Lev. 13. 18-23 and ib. 13. 24-28 present two particular cases under the general headline of the cleansing of the plagued. In both cases the law introduces regulations which according to the rule "are to be derived for its laxity and not strictness"; namely in the cases of the plagued, the law requires only one week of detention. g) A matter which is included in a general law and which is detached to elucidate something different and not in harmony therewith—e.g. Lev. 13. 29-37 presents the case of the plagued in the head or the beard even though it ought to be included in the general law on the plagued of the body. In such a case the rule maintains "the detached is intended to be lax and not to be strict", i.e., the law points to a leniency that the plagued in the head or the beard need not be examined for white hair, and it comes to restrict that they are to be examined for yellow hair. h) A matter included in a general law and detached to determine someting new—e.g. Lev. 14. 13—concerning the leper's sacrifice—"And he (the priest) shall slay the lamb in the place where he slaughters the sin-offering . . . since it is as a sin-offering". The law introduces a prescription for the leper's sacrifice which requires the placing of the blood on the right ear and the great toe of the cleansed. In this case the rule maintains "the law can be restored to the general law only if the text does so", therefore the law introduces the statement "it is as a sin offering" denoting the application of the rite in accordance with the general practice, e.g. the sprinkling of the blood on the altar.

These derivatives of the rule on the quantitative relation in the

law were incorporated in the thirteen hermeneutics of Rabbi Ismael
found in the Introduction to Sifra, the expositional Midrash to Leviticus. During the Jamnia period the schools adopted the hermeneutics in the examination of the Law. The school of Rabbi Ismael [1])
was reserved in the examination of the text, applying the rule "the
Law speaks in the manner of the people", while the school of Rabbi
Aqiba [2]) adopted the methods of their master who examined every
word of the text.

---

[1]) See the analysis of Weiss, D.D. Wed. II chs. 6, 11.

[2]) Adopting the methods of his teacher, Nahum of Gimzu, see b. Hag. 12a and
b. Sheb. 26a, see further M. Mielziner, Introduction to the Talmud, 2ed. New
York, 1925. Thus there are two corpora of halachic Midrashim to the Pentateuch,
a corpus of R. Ismael's school and a corpus of R. Aqiba's school. On the difference
of the two see J. N. Epstein, Meb. Zes. Hat., p. 521 ff, and S. Horovitz in the
introduction to Sifre Num. The school of R. Ismael expanded the rule of Quantitative relation in the law in the form of a generality and a specific, whereas
the school of R. Aqiba introduced the rule of inclusion and exclusion.

THE MESSAGE OF JESUS IN THE LIGHT OF PHARISAIC TEACHINGS

THE JEWISHNESS OF JESUS

The Jewish inhabitants of Galilee, though separated from Judea and its center of learning, Jerusalem, were affected by the decisions and teachings rendered in the academies. Letters were issued by Gamliel I [1]), the head of Hillel's academy, and in later days by his son Shimeon II [2]) to the inhabitants of upper and lower Galilee on important religious questions such as the clearance of back payments to the Temple. The men who played the major role in the daily lives of the Galileans were the Essene teachers, the Pharisaic Shammaites, and their associates, the Zealots [3]). The Pharisaic Shammaite, Zadok, and Judah the Galilean founded a fanatic party known as Zealots who "acknowledge no leader or master but God". The enthusiastic members were committed to casting off the yoke of Roman authority and to restoring the independent religious Jewish state at any cost [4]). "It was light thing for them to go forth to meet death, nor did they regard the death of their companions and kinfolk, if only they might save themselves from the burden of a human rule". The Teacher of Righteousness was also dissatisfied with the Roman rule and prepared the members of his Essenic communities for future combat with the Romans [5]). Yet, he differed from the Zealots in the approach to the problem. While the Zealots insisted on an immediate solution through a show of force and following that the community could be purified to accept religious authority, the Teacher of Righteousness maintained that first the Jewish people must be

---

[1]) b. Sanh. 11b, T. ib. 2. 6 (416. 29), J. M. Sh. 56c.

[2]) Midrash Tannaim on Deut. 26. 13 (ed. Hoffmann, p. 176) and refer to A. Büchler, Studies, part II, p. 1-14.

[3]) Shammai was a Galilean (I. Abrahams, Studies, I p. 15) and one of the disciples of Jesus, Simon, was a Zealot (Matt. 10.4, Luk. 6. 15). John, who had Essenic tendecies (Abrahams, op. cit., p. 34), baptised at Aenon near Tiberias sea.

[4]) Ant. XVIII. 1. 6 and see Klausner, Jesus, p. 204 ff.

[5]) As described in "The Scroll of the War of the Sons of Light against the Sons of Darkness", ed. Y. Yadin, Jerusalem, 1957.

cleaned and prepared to accept a religious authority and then the arrival of a Kingdom of God could be fulfilled. In this atmosphere the teacher of Nazareth was raised. He absorbed the teachings expounded by the Pharisaic teachers on the Sabbath as the custom prevailed; and he was exposed to the preachings of the wandering Teachers of Righteousness, John who was one of them preached [1]): "Repent ye for the Kingdom of Heaven is at hand". Thus, Jesus included in his teachings the preachings of the Pharisaic members and those of the Teacher of Righteousness. He proclaimed [2]): "Repent: for the Kingdom of Heaven is at hand". He explained [3]) that the Mosaic law permits a divorce [Deut. 24. 1] only in case the wife has committed adultery (עֶרְוַת דָבָר); which coincides with the opinion of Shammai's academy [4]). He preached [5]) the golden rule as the cornerstone of the Mosaic and prophetic teachings which echoes the teaching of Hillel [6]). Jesus of Nazareth was true to his Jewish heritage throughout the period of his ministry [7]). He adhered to the principles of the Jewish faith; a belief in God, the Creator of the universe [8]) who presides over evil and good [9]); prayers to this God, the Father who is in heaven [10]); adherence to a national Jewish pride, the doctrine of the elected people [11]); acknowledgment of the Torah and the words of the prophets as the authoritative Divine truth [12]). Moreover on controversial issues concerning religious principles, he adopted the Pharisaic stand; an acceptance of the oral tradition as formulated in

---

[1]) Matt. 3. 2, verse 3 declares the same as in I Q.S. 8. 14. Compare Matt. 21. 32 (ὁδῷ δικαιοσύνης) with I Q.S. 4. 2 (דרך צדק), the lesson for the Teacher of Righteousness (Maskil).

[2]) Matt. 4. 17, Mk. 1. 15

[3]) Matt. 5. 32, 19. 9, but see pp. 161, 163.

[4]) M. Git. 9. 10 and Sifre Deut. § 269 (p. 122a).

[5]) Matt. 7. 12, Luk. 6. 31 and compare the teaching in Vat. Tob. 4. 15, 16, Test. Sh. 4. 7 and Test. G. 6. See Abrahams, Op. cit., p. 20 ff.

[6]) b. Shab. 31a. Ab. 1. 12: Hillel says: "Love the creatures".

[7]) See Klausner, Jesus, p. 363 ff and J. Wellhausen, Einleitung in die drei ersten Evangelien, Berlin 1905, p. 113.

[8]) Matt. 11. 25, Luk. 10. 21; compare Is. 42. 5.

[9]) Matt. 5. 45 compare Is. 45. 7.

[10]) Luk. 22. 41, 42 (prayer in time of need). Matt. 11. 25, 26 (prayer of thanks) and Matt. 6. 9—In rabbinic literature (b. Sanh. 42a): "to' receive the presence of Father who is in heaven" denotes prayer. On "Father", a synonym of God see Marmorstein, The Old Rabbinic Doctrine of God, p. 56 ff.

[11]) Matt. 10. 6, 7; 16. 24. Sheep represent Israel, see Jer. 50. 17 and Mech. on 19. 6 (71a).

[12]) Matt. 5. 18, 19, Luk. 16. 17 compare the words of R. Shimeon ben Yochai (c. 150 A.D.) Cant. R. on 5. 11 (p. 242).

the academies [1]); a belief in reward and punishment [2]); the belief in resurrection [3]) and in the doctrine that the whole creation is under Divine care [4]). He also observed the Judaic precepts. He wore a garment with the prescribed fringes (κράσπεδον = כְּרוּסְפְּדָא = צִיצַת) [5]).

At meal time, he followed the religious procedure: a blessing over the meal, the breaking of the loaves followed by the distribution of food [6]). He even insisted on seating in groups during the meal [7]) as the custom prevailed. He attended the synagogue services on the Sabbath and participated in the reading of the Scriptures [8]). He abided by the laws of the Sabbath, entering the city boundaries before sunset [9]) in order not to transgress the rule of Teḥum [10]) (a prohibition against trespassing the city limits, a distance of 2000 cubits) and awaiting the expiration of the holy day before proceeding with physical undertakings [11]). He observed the festivals of the liturgical year, joining the masses on the annual pilgrimages [12]). During the Passover night (so the Synoptics) he proceeded in accordance with the prescribed order of the Paschal meal. First, he prepared a place for the feast where he can be counted as the member of the group [13]). On the night of the feast he began with the sacramental wine [14])—this sign symbolizes the start of a holy day. Then he continued with the dipping in the dish [15]), the breaking of the bread and its distribution,

---

[1]) Matt. 23. 2, 3. Yet the opposition to the Pharisees' teachings (e.g. Mk. 7. 1 ff) will be described later as opposition to one school of the Pharisees.

[2]) Matt. 13. 24-43, compare Dan. 12. 2, 3.

[3]) Matt. 22. 29-32, Mk. 12. 24-27, see b. Sanh. 90a, b.

[4]) Matt. 6. 25-32, 10. 29-31, see Ant. XVIII. 1. 3 § 13 and Ab. 3. 15

[5]) Mk. 6. 56, Matt. 14. 36, see LXX on Num. 15. 38.

[6]) Matt. 14. 19, Mk. 6. 41, Luk. 9. 16 see T. Ber. 4. 1 (8. 20) on blessings before the meal, b. ib. 47a on breaking the bread and its distribution—a custom also prevailing among the Essenes, see I Q.S. 6. 5 and I Q. Sa II 18-21.

[7]) Mk. 6. 39, Luk. 9. 14, compare T. Ber. 5. 5 (12. 1) and I Q. Sa II. 11-15.

[8]) Luk. 4. 16, 17 and see J. Meg. 75a.

[9]) Mk. 1. 21 (He enters Capernaum so he can be there on the Sabbath).

[10]) See C.D. 11. 5 and M. Erub. 4. 3, 4, 11 (the explanation is in b. ib. 51a).

[11]) Luk. 4. 40 (only after sunset he heals the afflicted).

[12]) Jesus leaves for Jerusalem before Passover (so the Synoptics). John relates that Jesus left for Jerusalem before Passover (2. 13), before a festival (Tabernacles, 5. 1 and see 7. 2) compare Deut. 16. 16.

[13]) Matt. 26. 17-19, Mk. 14. 12-16, Luk. 22. 7-13; see Ex. 12. 3, 4 and the rules enumerated in M. Pes. 8. Refer to S. Zeitlin, Passover and the Last Supper in "the Passover Anthology" ed. P. Goodman (Philadelphia, 1961) and D. Chwolson, Das letzte Passamahl Christi und der Tag seines Todes, 2 ed. Leipzig, 1908.

[14]) Luk. 22. 17, compare M. Pes. 10. 2.

[15]) Matt. 26. 23, Mk. 14. 20, compare M. Pes. 10. 3.

the blessing over the wine after the meal [1]) and concluded with
the recital of Hallel [2]) (the Psalms of praise). He also adhered to the
priestly regulations. On one occasion he ordered the leper whom he
had just cleansed to present himself to a priest—so the priest could
affirm his state of cleanliness [3])—and to bring the prescribed offering.
On another occasion [4]) he asked his disciple, Peter, to deliver the
annual payment due the Temple treasury.

It also appears that Jesus during the period of his ministry adhered to the Pharisaic code of purity. A woman with a flow is considered a source of defilement causing impurity upon physical contact with the garments of the wearer. On such a circumstance Jesus
declared [Luk. 8. 46]: "someone (a woman with a flow) has touched
me, for I perceived that the power had gone forth from me"—since a
person in an environment of impurity is denied the power of healing
(see Ex. 8. 25, 26 [5]). A heathen woman was declared by the Pharisaic
academies a woman with a flow who can cause defilement. Thus,
Jesus, aware of the presence of a Syro-Phoenician woman [6]), re-
fused to associate with her. As an observant of a code of purity, he
frequented [7]) the homes of the Pharisees, where the meal was prepared
in a state of cleanliness. Thus, the Pharisaic masters recognized Jesus,
at first, as a colleague and the people address him with the title
"Rabbi" [8]). They did not reprimand his actions in the beginning, but
rather directed his attention to the disciples' [9]) negligence in obser-
ving the laws of purity and the Sabbath.

The Qumran scrolls, the testimonies of Josephus and Philo [10])

---

[1]) Matt. 26. 27, Mk. 14. 24, Luk. 22. 20, compare M. Pes. 10. 7.

[2]) Matt. 26. 30, Mk. 14. 26, compare M. Pes. 10. 6, 7. On the question which
passages were said on the night of Passover, see T. Pes. 10. 9 (173. 2, 3).

[3]) Matt. 8. 4, Mk. 1. 44, Luk. 5. 4 and see pp. 69, 125.

[4]) Matt. 17. 24-27. Since on Adar, a month before Passover, the half a shekel
was collected, see M. Shek. 1. 1, 3.

[5]) See Mid. Hag. Ex. 8. 25 (p. 138) and Mech. on 12. 1 (1, 2).

[6]) Matt. 15. 23. After a show of faith on behalf of the woman, Jesus fulfils her
wish and does not heal by contact as in Matt. 8. 3.

[7]) Luk. 7. 36; 11. 37; 14. 1.

[8]) Luk. 12. 13 (διδάσκαλος) or Mk. 10. 51 (ραββουνί) compare Sifre Num. § 96
(26b)—in Aramaic רַבּוּנִי. On different titles see T. Ed. 3. 4 (460. 4, 5) and refer to
Klausner, Jesus, p. 256, and Schürer, G.J.V. II, p. 375 ff. b. A.Z. 17a (Spanish
codex) reads ישׁוּ רבו.

[9]) Matt. 15. 2: "why do thy disciples transgress?", Mk. 7. 2 "when they saw
some of his disciples eat bread with defiled hands". Mk. 2. 25 and Luk. 6. 2,
see Klausner, Jesus, p. 364.

[10]) For the sources see Ch. Ginsburg, The Essenes (London, 1956) and Y. Yadin,
Hamegilloth Hagenuzoth pp. 205-223.

describe the Essene teachings which can indicate that Jesus adopted and preached Essenic doctrines. He [1]) spent a period of selfexamination in the desert prior to his ministry, as was practiced by the Teachers of Righteousness. He assumed the mission of preaching at the age of thirty [2]), a prescribed age limit for a teacher among the Essenes. He adopted a routine of prayer and meditation [3])—a routine observed by the members of the Essene communities. Thus, he prayed [4]): "I thank Thee O Father, Lord of heaven and earth, that Thou hast hidden these things from the wise and prudent and hast revealed them unto babes even so, Father: for so it seemed good in Thy sight". There is a recorded prayer of thanks by the Teacher of Righteousness declaring: "Blessed art Thou, my God who unveiled to the heart of Thy servant knowledge . . . and fulfil to the child of Your maid, as You have willed, that the chosen among men attend You for ever . . . for without Thy will no one can perform". He [5]) possessed the knowledge of healing and medication attributed to the Essenes [6]). He selected twelve men to carry his message comparable to the twelve men appointed to the council of the Essenes [7]). He prescribed a code of conduct for his disciples similar to the Essenic code on habit of dress [8]), talk [9]) and travel [10]). He pronounced a list of blessings and curses like it was pronounced by the priests and the Levites among the Essenes [11]).

Although the sources suggest that Jesus, who was raised in a Pharisaic and Essenic atmosphere, could not escape the teachings and the mode of life of these masters, yet during the course of his ministry he did deviate from the path of his contemporaries. The reason for

---

[1]) Matt. 4. 1-12, Mk. 1. 13-15, Luk. 4. 1-15, compare the activities of Bannus-Vit. 1. 2 § 11, 12. A two year requirement was necessary see I Q.S. 6. 17, 21; 8. 26.

[2]) Luk. 3. 23, compare I Q.Sa I 13, 14.

[3]) Luk. 6, 12, compare Bell. II. 8. 5 § 128 (prayers at sunrise) and I Q. S. 10. 2.

[4]) Matt. 11. 25, 26, Luk. 10. 21 compare I Q.S. 11. 15-18.

[5]) See K. F. Bahrdt, Ausführung des Plans und Zwecks Jesu (1784-1792), so H. Grätz, G.d.J., III, p. 216 ff. On Essene knowledge of healing see Bell. II. 8. 6 § 136.

[6]) Compare the manner of healing in Gen. Apoc., col. XX., 29 (p. 44) referred to me by Dr. O. Betz.

[7]) Matt. 10. 1, Mk. 3. 14, Luk. 9. 1; compare I Q.S. 8. 1—"the twelve of the council". Luk. 10. 1 refers, also, to seventy, the prescribed number for the Sanhedrin.

[8]) Matt. 10. 9, 10, compare Bell. II. 8. 4 § 126, 127.

[9]) Matt. 5. 37, compare Bell. II. 8. 6 § 135.

[10]) Matt. 10. 11, compare Bell. II. 8. 4 § 124, 125.

[11]) Luk. 6. 20-26, compare I Q.S. 2. 1-10.

Jesus' deviation from the path was the purpose of his mission, which he in his own words states [1]): "I am not sent but to the lost sheep of the house of Israel". These words echo the programme of ministry outlined by Isaiah and pursued by Jesus [2]): "The spirit of the Lord, Yahweh, is upon me for He has anointed me to bring good news; to the poor He has sent me, to proclaim to the captives release and sight to the blind, to set at liberty the oppressed, to proclaim the acceptable year of Yahweh and the day of recompense". Whereas John the Baptist preached in the desert, as was common with the other Essene teachers [3]), Jesus intended that his call to ministry will be in the towns and villages among his own people. In said manner his call was not to be accomplished as a Pharisaic teacher among the strict observers of a code of separation and purity. His intended mission required close contact with the sick, the poor, the unclean and the untouchable. Thus, in a reply to the Pharisaic masters he says [4]): "The healthy men do not need a physician but they who are sick", and in a reply to the disciples of John, he says [5]): "Neither do men put new wine (a new path paved by Jesus) into old skin-bottles (the old practices): else the bottles break and the wine runneth out, and the skin-bottles perish: but they put new wine into new skin-bottles [and both are preserved]". This can be concluded: although Jesus showed tendencies both as a Pharisaic and Essene teacher, a deviation from their ways emerged to clear the obstacles on the road of his proposed mission.

The Opposition to the Pharisees

The polemics with the Pharisees, the harsh "woes" addressed to their teachers were, in fact, directed at the zealous Pharisees, the disciples of Shammai's academy. On the other hand, the Pharisaic approach adopted by the disciples of Hillel's school—their humbleness, restraint, clear argumentative reasoning and liberal stand—was close in spirit to that of the teacher of Nazareth. Jesus' claim to hum-

---

[1]) Matt. 15. 24 (addressing the disciples, ib.10. 6), compare ib. 9. 36 and Mk. 6. 34.

[2]) Luk. 4. 17-22 and see further p. 155 ff.

[3]) Compare the activities of Bannus, Vit. 1. 2 see Klausner, Jesus, pp. 243, 244. See M. Friedländer, Die religiösen Bewegungen innerhalb des Judentums im Zeitalter Jesu, Berlin 1905 on the Baptist's movements.

[4]) Matt. 9. 12, Mk. 2. 17 and Luk. 5. 31 (teaching denotes healing see Mech. on 15. 26 and Sifre Deut. § 45).

[5]) Matt. 9. 17, Mk. 2. 22 and Luk. 5. 38. Note: the reply to the Pharisees is included with the reply to the disciples of John. Wine represents teachings see Cant. R. on 1. 2b (p. 33).

bleness, a reason for the acceptance of his teachings [1]), was a claim of Hillel's students who demonstrated humbleness and leniency in their teachings, a reason for their unanimous acceptance at Jamnia academy [2]). Jesus' praise [3]) of the seekers of peace whom he deservedly calls the sons of God—he also demonstrated [4]) with a coin in the presence of the Herodians—is praise of the advocates of Hillel's teaching [5]): "Be as the followers of Aaron loving peace, seeking peace, making peace between man and his wife and to love all creatures"—as noted in the actions of Gamliel I [6]) and R. Jochanan ben Zakkai [7]), the disciples of Hillel. Jesus practicing and preaching kindness to one's fellowman, especially to the needy, is so characteristic of Hillel and his household [8]). Jesus instructed his disciples [9]): "With what measure ye mete it shall be measured to you again", and restated this instruction at the time of his arrest [10]): "For all they who take the sword shall be punished by the sword". The identical theme was preached by Hillel upon seeing a skull floating on the waters [11]): "Because thou drownedst they drowned thee, and at the end they who drowned thee shall be drowned". Gamliel II, a descendant of Hillel's family, and his colleagues teach the same rule [12]): "With what measure one metes, it shall be meted to him". Jesus [13]) stressed and professed an absolute trust in the Almighty. Such a show of complete faith in the will of the benevolent God, on part of the master Hillel, was spoken of among his disciples [14]) and in all probability was adopted as a guide in their daily actions. A rule prescribed by the teacher of Nazareth was [15]): "Do not judge, that you may not be

---

[1]) Matt. 11. 29.

[2]) b. Erub. 13b. Compare Hillel's teaching, Lev. R. on 1. 1 (9) with Matt. 23. 12.

[3]) Matt. 5. 9.

[4]) Matt. 22. 16-21, Mk. 12. 14-16 and Luk. 20. 21-25.

[5]) Ab. 1. 12 and I A.D.N. 12 (p. 24b). Since "peace" is a by-name of God, so D.E.Z., the chapter on peace, in the name of R. Jehushua (c. 100 A.D.), therefore "the seekers of peace" are called the sons of God. (Matt. 5. 9).

[6]) See Acts 5. 34-39.

[7]) See b. Git. 56a, b.

[8]) T. Pea. 4. 10 (23. 27-29)—Hillel provides for the needy, D.E.R. 6—the wife of Hillel provides for the poor.

[9]) Matt. 7. 2, compare the statement in M. Sot. 1. 7 (μέτρον = מדה).

[10]) Matt. 26. 52.

[11]) Ab. 2. 6, I A.D.N. 27 (28a).

[12]) b. Sot. 15a, b based on M. Sot. 1. 7 see also Mech. on 13. 21 (30a) and b. Meg. 12b.

[13]) Matt. 17. 20; 6. 31; 21. 21.

[14]) b. Ber. 60a.

[15]) Matt. 7. 1, Luk. 6. 37.

judged", and as related by John (8. 11) when Jesus addressed the adulteress saying: "Neither do I condemn thee". The same rule was declared by Hillel [1]): "Do not judge your fellowman unless you find yourself in the same situation" and in an incident concerning his wife he says [2]): "I have not judged you with a leaning of guilt but that of merit". A show of unbiasness on part of Jesus in the propagation of his teachings was also the accepted rule in Hillel's academy [3]).

The controversial halachoth which are found in the list of "woes" [Matt. 23. 2-35] [Luk. 11. 39-48] apply only to the Pharisaic Shammaites. "Woe unto you, scribes [and Pharisees, hypocrites]! for ye shut up the Kingdom of Heaven against men" [4]). The Pharisees who denied the sinner a share in "the world to come" were the Shammaites. The school of Shammai classified the candidates for the "world to come" into three groups: to the pious ones was allotted eternal life, to the sinner, reproaches and everlasting abhorrence; to the average individual, a period of judgement in Gehenna. The Hillelites contested this artificial classification that not only denied the sinner a share in the "world to come" but also excludes the rest of humanity, the non-Jews. They based their argument on the attribute of the Creator which is kindness as attested to in Psalm 117 [5]).

"Woe unto you, scribes and Pharisees, hypocrites! for ye compass both sea and land to make one proselyte and when he is made, ye make him two fold more the child of hell than yourself". The Pharisees [6]) did advocate, prior to the spread of Christianity, a positive stand on proselytization, and even transversed both sea and land to convert the non-believer. They treated the proselyte as they would treat their own members of the academy, and outstanding proselytes were members of the academy, such as Aquila [7]), R. Meir [8]), and Jehuda, the Ammonite proselyte [9]). The harsh words addressed to the Pharisees concern, in the main, with the way the Pharisees accepted the

---

[1]) Ab. 2. 4.

[2]) D.E.R. 6.

[3]) Ab. 1. 12 and I A.D.N. 3 (p. 7b, 8a).

[4]) The Lost Gospel reads (see I.C.C. Matt. p. 245) "the key of the Kingdom they hid" (ṭamarun denotes they hid or they withhold, Luk. 11. 52). Kingdom denotes "the world to come" in rabbinic literature, so J. Lichtenstein, Kommentar zum Matthäus (Leipzig 1913) on Matt. 16. 19.

[5]) See T. Sanh. 13. 3, 4 (434. 11-20), compare b. R.H. 16b, 17a.

[6]) See A. Jellenik, Beth Hamidrash V (Vienna, 1873), pp. XLVI, L-LII.

[7]) See J. Dem. 25d and the article Aquila (J. Enc.) by L. Ginzberg.

[8]) b. Git. 56a; rather a descendant of proselytes, as was R. Aqiba.

[9]) M. Yad. 4. 4.

proselytes. In the acceptance of the converts, the Shammaites were very strict, whereas the Hillelites lenient. A major requirement was circumcision, a bone of contention even among the early Christians[1]). The Shammaites held that even an individual, who prior to his conversion had undergone such an operation (e.g. an Arab), must submit to the formal act of drawing blood, whereas the Hillelites maintained that this was unnecessary [2]).

"Woe unto you ye blind guides which say whosoever shall swear by the Temple it is nothing ... and whosoever shall swear by the altar it is nothing, but whosoever sweareth by δῶρόν (= corban) that is upon it, he is bound, ye fools and blind whoso therefore shall swear by the altar sweareth by it ... whoso shall swear by the Temple sweareth by it." This bitter statement cannot be explained as a cry of contempt to the Pharisaic teachings, since both academies held [3]) that a vow declared in terms of holy objects is as valid as a person who declares corban (an expression designating the object as a sacrificial offer). The reason for the above resentment can be illuminated through the polemic reply to the Pharisees; a reply which includes also the question of impurity and is parallel to this cry of contempt. It states [4]): "For Moses said: 'honour thy father and mother' (Ex. 20. 12), and: 'whoso curseth a father or mother shall be put to death' (ib. 21. 17). But ye say if a man say to his father or mother κορβᾶν as to whatsoever thou mightest be profited or enjoyed by me, than you require him no more to do ought for his father or mother." Jesus was in opposition to the Pharisaic circumvention of the Mosaic law. If the Mosaic ethical teaching requires the individual to show respect by providing for his parents—as the Pharisees maintained [5])— how can the same teachers state that through a vow, declared by the term "corban", one can be absolved from supporting them.

The regulation concerning the declaration of vows prescribes that a man can prevent his properties from being enjoyed or profited by his fellowman or even from himself by a declaraction of 'corban'. This implies that a father can preclude his son from inheriting his

---

[1]) Acts ch. 15.
[2]) b. Shab. 135a; eventhough an Israelite, who was born without a foreskin, is required to submit to the formal act (T. Shab. 15. 9 (133.13)). On the other hand, the Hillelites required the proselyte to be sprinkled, as one who is defiled by contact with a corpse, thereby he was excused from the rites of Passover (M. Pes. 8. 8).
[3]) M. Ned. 1. 3. (ναὸς = היכל; θυσιαστήριον = מזבח).
[4]) Mk. 7. 10, 11.
[5]) b. Kid. 31a.

properties by a vow or vice versa [1]). On the regulations governing
the declaration of vows the Shammaites adopted a strict stand
whereas the Hillelites were inclined to leniency [2]). The following
case [3]) demonstrates this point: "If one saw some people eating
figs and said: 'May they be corban to you', and they were found
to be his father and brothers and others with them, the school of
Shammai says: They (the father and brothers) are absolved but those
who are with them are bound. But the school of Hillel says: Both the
former and the latter are absolved". The Talmud (b. Ned. 25b in the
name of R. Aqiba) explains that the argument concerns the question:
"Is a vow invalid if one part is not valid?", since he did not in-
tend to prohibit the figs to his relatives but only to strangers. On
the other hand, the above argument does also pertain to the following
question: "Can a man make use of vows haphazardly with no regards
to his fellowman, and if he does so, are the vows binding or not?"
The Shammaites are of the affirmative opinion and the Hillelites
are of the negative. The opinion expressed by the Hillelites did, in
fact, in later generation introduce the law: "The court can compel
the son to support his father" [4]).

   Two statements of refute and contempt are especially directed
at the Pharisaic circles who adopted an ever increasing complex
code of purity and separation. The first states "Woe to you, [scribes
and] Pharisees, [hypocrites] ! for ye tithe mint (ἡδύοσμον = מִנְתָא),
dill (ἄνηθον = שִׁיבְתָא), cummin (κύμινον = כַּמּוֹנָא)—Luk. 11. 42 renders
"and every herb" (כָּלְמִינָא for כַּמּוֹנָא)—and have neglected the weightier
matter of the law". The second states: "Woe to you [scribes and]
Pharisees [hypocrites] ! for ye declare a state of purity (καθαρίζετε,
compare Matt. 8. 3 saying to a leper: καθαρίσθητι) for the outside
of a cup and the platter, but within they are full of rapacity and
wantoness". Special importance was attached to the rules governing
purity and the law of seeds among the Pharisees; one of the necessary requirements for initiation into the Pharisaic fold was the

---

[1]) J. Ned. 39b: a son is prohibited from his father's possessions, and M. Ned.
5. 6: a father is prohibited from his son's possessions. Refer to Büchler, Studies,
part II, p. 15 ff.
[2]) For example T. Nez. 1. 1 (283. 27) Hillelites maintained that declaring a vow
with a by-name of a holy object is not binding, whereas the Shammaites declared
it binding.
[3]) M. Ned. 3. 2.
[4]) J. Pea. 15d (R. Jonathan, 2nd Cent. A.D.) see also S.E.R. pp. 24, 26.

observance of these laws. Although differences existed between the
two academies on the question of initiation, even greater contrasting
opinions on the scope of the Pharisaic code prevailed among the
Shammaites and Hillelites. From the 310 [1]) halachic disputes recorded
in the Mishnah, Tosefta and both Talmuds, over three quarters of
them deal with the code of purity, festivals and seeds. The academies
served as organs for the teachers of the Pharisaic order and little or no
interest was placed on the study of judicature. Judgement of civil and
capital cases was not in the hands of the Pharisaic teachers but rather
in the hands of local administrators under Roman supervision—a
marked change from the period of Duumvirates. The men responsible
for civil affairs were the Judges of Gezeroth [2]) (civil regulations) or
Gezeloth [3]) (cases of theft), while capital offences fell under Roman
law. They delegated the religious questions to the Sanhedrin in the
presence of the recognized Roman authority, the High Priest, and
the Herodian representatives. Therefore, the area of study in the
academies of Hillel and Shammai was, in the main, concerned with
the structure of the Pharisaic code of observance. Pertaining to this
field of study, the Hillelites displayed leniency in their decisions,
whereas the Shammaites displayed strictness [4]), of whom it can be
said [5] "they bind heavy burdens and grievous to be borne".
Thus, R. Jehoshuah of Jamnia speaking of the behaviour of the
Shammaites in issuing Eighteen Measures on separation from the
heathens [6]), said that they "obliterated the pot of measure" and that
day was likened to the infamous day of the "Golden Calf".
Jesus cited only two essential questions concerning the Pharisaic
code, and they should suffice as a demonstration of the above distinction between the two academies. On the question of tithes, the
Mosaic law [Deut. 14. 22, 23] requires the delivery of a tenth of the
yield of the seed specifying corn, wine, oil and fruits of the land, i.e.,

---

[1]) Enumerated by I. H. Weiss, D.D. Wed. I, pp. 169, 170, in the notes. See
further A. Schwarz, Die Controversien der Schammaiten und Hilleliten, Karlsruhe, 1893, p. 2 n. 1, and J. Enc. III, p. 115.

[2]) M. Ket. 13. 1.

[3]) b. Ket. 105a.

[4]) M. Ed. 4; 5. 1-5 only knows of several exceptional cases where the Hillelites
are stricter then the Shammaites. Out of the 310 halachoth only 55 (or about
one-sixth) present the Shammaites on the side of leniency. Moreover, some of
the restrictive views of the Hillelites were rejected, adopting the moderate views
of the Shammaites.

[5]) Matt. 23. 4.

[6]) T. Shab. 1. 16, 17 (111. 2-5).

figs and pomegranates [see Lev. 27. 30 cf. Deut. 8. 8 where the fruits of the land are enumerated]—and as such was restated in the covenant of the Great Assembly [Neh. 10. 38]. In the pre-Pharisaic period the same rule of observance was in effect. Tobi states [Sin. Tob. 1. 7] "and the tithes of corn, wine, oil, pomegranates, figs and other fruits of the tree I have given to the Levites". During the Pharisaic period [1]), the teachers have included also the issuance of the tenth of the products of vegetation. The code states [2]) "Everything which is edible and is preserved and derives its nourishment from the soil is liable to be tithed". Rabbi Eliezer (c. 100 A.D.), upholding the views of Shammai's academy and thus nicknamed Rabbi Eliezer the Shammaite [3]), states [4]): "Of dill must one tithe the seed and the leaves and the stalks". The Shammaites also declared [M. Ukz. 3. 6]: "Hardened olives and grapes are susceptible to uncleanness and also are liable to tithe", whereas the Hillelites were of the negative opinion. Yet, when the Hillelites declared black cummin liable to tithe [passim], R. Ismael [5]) referred to it as an exception. In the same manner the Hillelites excluded balsam oil from the law of Demai [6]) and did not require—as the Shammaites did—a second apportionment of grapes made into raisins [7]).

On the question of purity concerning the hands: in pre-Pharisaic times [8]) the washing of the hands was a prerequisite to handling or associating with the holy objects of the Temple. The letter of Aristeas relates (305, 306) that the seventy elders sent by Eleazar the High Priest to translate the Pentateuch into the Greek tongue washed their hands prior to a day of prayer and writing the Holy Scriptures. The reason expounded by the elders was: "for every action is caused by the hands" and similarly quoted in the Talmud [b. Shab. 14a], "since the hands are always active". During the Pharisaic period

---

[1]) See also Jth. 11. 13 and Büchler, Studies, part II pp. 60-62.

[2]) M. Maas. 1. 1 see J. ib. 48c—the enactment of Ma'aser on vegetation stems from the academies.

[3]) J. Sheb. 39a; refer to Weiss, D.D.Wed. II, p. 76 and J. Bassfreund, Der Bann gegen R. Elieser und die veränderte Haltung gegenüber den Schammaiten, M.G.W.J., 42 (1898).

[4]) M. Maas. 4. 5 (See also the restriction declared by R. Eliezer, ib. 4. 6).

[5]) M. Ed. 5. 3, Thus the quote of Billerbeck, Kommentar I, p. 933, should be differently understood.

[6]) M. Dem. 1. 3.

[7]) T. Ter. 3. 16 (30. 3-8).

[8]) As explained in b. Shab. 14b—Since ancient times (referring to Solomon) the restriction was on holy objects.

Hillel and Shammai enacted a rule denying the handling of priestly food [1]—or more precisely even among the non-priests who observed a strict preparation of meals—to those of defiled hands. Thus, Judith explains to Holofernes [Jth. 11. 13] "And they are resolved to spend the first fruits of the corn and the tenth of the wine and oil which they had sanctified and reserved for the priests ... the which thing it is not fitting for any people so much as to touch with their hands."

The Hillelites were more liberal in the observance of the rule, whereas the Shammaites were very strict. The Mishnah [Ber. 8. 1] records the differences that existed between the two academies concerning the meal. The school of Shammai maintained: "First one washes the hands and then fills the cup" while the school of Hillel declared: "One may fill the cup at first and then wash his hands". The debate hinges upon a halachic question: "Can the drops of water on the outside of a plate or glass contaminate the utensil through handling with defiled hands?" [2]. Thus, Jesus in a reply to the Pharisaic teachers says [3]: "Ye Pharisees declare a state of purity for the outside of the cup or platter". This was the reasoning of the Shammaites: The outside of the cup in the state of purity can be contaminated through defiled hands. Therefore one had to first wash his hands and with undefiled hands fill the cup. The Hillelites maintained however that the outside of the cup can be in a state of impurity and the contents are still considered clean. Thus, one can fill the cup then wash his hands, and drink the clean contents.

Another saying of grievance directed to the Pharisees states: "But all their works they do to be seen of men ... enlarging the borders of their garments [4] or (as Matt. 23. 5 reads) the fringes (κράσπεδα)". This undoubtedly refers to the acts of the Shammaites. They maintained that in order to fulfil the Mosaic requirement (Deut. 22. 11): "Thou shalt make thee twisted cords upon the four corners of thy covering" one should extend the fringes of the garment to a length of four fingers with four twisted cords at each corner. The Hillelites, on the other hand, maintained that a measure of three is sufficient for the fringes of the garment with three twisted cords at each corner. Furthermore, at Jochanan ben Bathyrus' chamber the elders of both

---

[1] As explained in b. Shab. 15a.
[2] See T. Ber. 6 (5). 2 (13. 10-13).
[3] Luk. 11. 39, Matt. 23. 25.
[4] Luk. 20. 46 reads: στολὶς (אצטלא).

academies decided—probably following Hillelites' opinion—that
the fringes have no prescribed length [1]).

The last recorded statement of contempt states: "Woe unto ye,
[scribes and Pharisees, hypocrites !] ... ye are the children of them
who killed [2]) the prophets ... wherefore behold I send unto you
prophets and ḥakhamim[and scribes] and some of them ye shall kill [and
crucify] and some of them shall ye scourge [3]) in your synagogues
and persecute them city to city". Jesus must have seen or heard how
the Pharisees dealt with the hakhamim (teachers) who opposed their
decisions. The Pharisees who acted in this manner at the time of
Jesus are said in rabbinic sources to have been the Shammaites.
Two incidents are recorded of Hillel, an older contemporary of
Jesus. Hillel [4]) contested the decision of Shammai who maintained
that "Peace-offerings may be brought on the festival day but hands
are not to be laid on them"—these offerings were shared with the
owner. Thus, a sacrificial rite could be administered on the holiday (a
day which requires abstention from any laborious activity) since food
is permitted to be prepared on the holiday. Yet the act of laying the
hands was considered a laborious act. Shammai further maintained "but
not burnt-offerings"—burnt-offerings could not be brought alto-
gether on a holiday since they were not shared with the owner. Hillel,
in order ro demonstrate that burnt-offering could be brought on the
holiday, presented a burnt-offering in the Temple. The disciples of
Shammai, who witnessed the demonstration, have gathered in protest
to the master's act and only through clever persuasion was Hillel able
to hold back the raging Shammaites. On another occasion [5]), when
Hillel disputed Shammai's decision that "Grapes which are pressed
into a vat, their juice can make the food products susceptible to ritual
impurity", the disciples of Shammai planted a sword in the academy's
hall as a sign of warning thereby forcing Hillel to accept Shammai's
decision. That day was likened by the followers of Hillel to the infamous day of the "Golden Calf". Thus, the Shammaites, who demonstrated a zealous and violent attitude in enforcing their master's
decisions, had in the last years prior to the destruction of the Temple

---

[1]) See b. Men. 41b.
[2]) Matt. 23. 31 reads: בְּנִין אַתּוּן לְקִבְרֵיהוֹן; Luk. 11. 48 reads: בְּנִין אַתּוּן לְקִבְרֵיהוֹן.
[3]) Compare Ex. R. on 22. 24 (p. 398) [μαστιγώσετε = בזו, תלקו].
[4]) T. Hag. 2. 10, 11 (235. 21-236. 5), compare M. Hag. 2. 3 and b. Bez. 20a.
[5]) b. Shab. 17a.

massacred the Hillelites [1]) who opposed the enactment of the Eighteen Measures against the heathens. On the other hand [2]), Hillel preached and demonstrated peaceful coexistence. Gamliel I, his grandson, demonstrated tolerance of the early Christians and Rabban Jochanan ben Zakkai, his disciple, negotiated peace-terms with Vespasian at the time of the Jewish war.

Matthew includes in the above statement of contempt another demonstration of violence on the part of the zealous Pharisees. He states: "That upon you may come all the righteous blood shed upon the earth from the blood of Abel [Gen. 4. 8] unto the blood of Zacharias son of Barachias (Βαραχίας) whom ye slew between the temple-hall and the altar". The old tale [3]) [II Chr. 24. 20, 21] of the murder of Zechariah the son of Jehoida (so does Ev. Sec. Hebraeos read in Matt. 23. 35) was linked with the murder of Zacharias the son of Baruch (Βαρούχ), a pacifist Pharisee who, like R. Jochanan mentioned above, negotiated with Vespasian. Josephus [Bell. IV. 5. 4] relates that the Zealots summoned seventy of the leading citizens—the prescribed number of a Jewish Sanhedrin—to judge Zacharias. When the Sanhedrin acquitted the accused, two of the Zealots set upon Zacharias and slew him in the midst of the Temple". A violent act, which as we have seen was the way of the Shammaites, is recorded in Matthew and rabbinic sources [4]). Both designate the place where Zacharias met his death.

The Jewish Practices at the Time of Jesus

On the synagogue and reading of the Law [5]).

The synagogue, a place of assembly, which in all probability finds its primal origin in Babylonian exile and was later introduced in Judea by Ezra, emerges at the beginning of Christian era as really full grown and firmly established institution. The home of a learned

---

[1]) J. Shab. 3b.
[2]) See above p. 136.
[3]) See Klausner, Historia V, p. 215.
[4]) See Lam. R. on 2. 2 (p. 163 ff), Ecc. R. on 3. 16 (p. 101), b. Git. 57b and J. Taan. 69a, b.
[5]) See L. Rabinowitz, The Synagogue and its Worship, in Manson's Companion to the Bible (Edinburgh, 1945), G. F. Moore, Judaism III, p. 88, S. Krauß, Talmudische Archäologie III, p. 204 ff (Leipzig, 1912) and idem, Synagogale Altertümer (Berlin-Vienna, 1922).

scribe ¹), the city square ²) or a designated building ³) in a town
served as a synagogue. The function of the synagogue is noted by
Travers H. Herford ⁴): "The synagogue was a local assembly for
the promotion of the religion through the two main functions of
worship and instruction". This place of assembly, indeed, has served
as a channel for the propagation of the Jewish religion by familiarizing
the people with the Holy Scriptures. It is recorded (Neh. 8. 1-3) that
in the days of Ezra: "All the people gathered themselves together as
one man into the square that was before the Water Gate and they spoke
unto Ezra, the scribe, to bring the book of the Law of Moses ... and
Ezra, the priest, brought the Law before the congregation both men
and women ... and he read therein ... from early morning until
midday ... and the ears of all the people were attentive unto the book
of the Law". The above narrative portrays a model of a synagogue
centered about the reading of the Books of Moses. Thus, the Jewish
tradition ⁵) ascribes to Ezra's generation the introduction of lectionary
readings on the Sabbath, Monday and Thursday—a modification of a
custom, also assumed, originating in antiquity ⁶). Three centuries later
in the days of the Hasmonaean revolt, it is related (I. Macc. 3. 46-48]:
"And they gathered themselves together and came to Mizpeh (since
Jerusalem was uninhabited and the sanctuary was trodden down) over
against Jerusalem, for in Mizpeh there had been aforetime a place of
prayer (τόπος προσευχῆς) ⁷) for Israel and they fasted that day ... and
they spread out the roll of the Law". Again we have a narrative describing a model of a synagogue which reveals that the reading of the
Law was a main feature in the place of worship. It is also recorded [II
Macc. 2. 14] that in the days of Judah the Maccabean an effort was
made to collect and preserve the existing prophetic and other writings.
Thus, it can be assumed that an equal effort was made to include the
Prophets in the public reading at the synagogue. Abudrahim ⁸),
a learned rabbi of the 14th century, transmits a tradition that the origin

---

¹) As described in Ez. 8. 1.
²) See Ezr. 10. 9, Neh. 8. 1, 13, M. Meg. 3, 1, M. Taan. 4. 2, 3 and J. Meg. 73d.
³) Synagogues are mentioned in Philo, De Som. II § 127 compare T. Suk. 4. 6
(198. 20), in Alexandria; Matt. 13. 54, in Galilee; Mk. 1. 21, at Capernaum and
Luk. 4. 16, at Nazareth; Bell. 2. 14. 4, in Caesarea; ib. 7. 3. 3, at Antioch; Ant.
19. 6. 3, at Dora and J. Meg. 73d, in Jerusalem.
⁴) The Pharisees, p. 92.
⁵) See b. B.K. 82a compare J. Meg. 75a and Mech. on 15. 22 (52b).
⁶) Compare above with Cont. Ap. II. § 175, De Op. Mund. § 128 and Acts 15. 21.
⁷) Cf. LXX on Is. 56. 7 and I Macc. 7. 37 (οἶκος προσευχῆς).
⁸) L. Zunz, G.V.d.J., p. 6.

of concluding the weekly reading with a selection from the Prophets (known as Haftarah) is traceable to the troublous period of the Hasmonaean revolt. At that time, the reading of the Scriptures had been interdicted and the Jews substituted for it the reading of similar passages from the prophetic books [1]). The New Testament sources affirm the existence of a common Jewish practice in the first Christian century, that of lectionary readings from the Pentateuch with a concluding section from the Prophets on successive Sabbaths. Further evidence affirming the practice of lectionary readings is found in the works of Philo, Josephus [2]) and the Tannaim [3]).

A later development, following the canonization of the Holy Scriptures at Jamnia, can be traced to the early part of the third century A.D. at Nehardeah in Babylon. There [4]), a selection from the Hagiographa was read in addition to the lection and prophetical portion, at Saturday afternoon services, thereby acquainting the people with the whole of the canonical Scriptures and emphasizing the fact that they represent a unity. It is for this reason that the Homiletic Midrash to Pentateuch, almost without fail opens its exposition with a verse from the Hagiographa. In the same manner, the books of Ecclesiastes, Canticles, Esther, Ruth and Lamentation were grouped together, regardless of the date of their authorship, since they were designated on special occasions for public reading. Thus, it has been suggested by E. G. King [5]), J. Thackeray and A. Guilding that the Psalms were recited over a three year period—a number of Psalms corresponding to the number of Sabbaths in three lunar years—an arrangement which betrays a liturgical consideration.

Since the origin of the lectionary system remains in obscurity owing to its very antiquity different opinions have been expressed as for its motivation. A. Büchler [6]) claims a polemical and apologetic motives arising from the situations in different eras—the struggle with the

---

[1]) J. Thackeray, The Septuagint and the Jewish Worship (London, 1921) pp. 10, 14 ff, suggests that the lectionary needs of the Jewish community in Alexandria provided a stimulus for a translation of the Prophets and other Writings, which was achieved in the course of two centuries after the rendering of the Pentateuch in Greek.

[2]) See A. Guilding, The Fourth Gospel, part I, ch. 2, and R. G. Finch, The Synagogue Lectionary and the New Testament (London, 1939) p. 6.

[3]) See p. 144, n. 6, Bacher's Terminologie, סדר, and H. Grätz, Über Entwicklung der Pentateuch-Perikopen-Verlesung, M.G.W.J., 18 (1869).

[4]) b. Shab. 116b. See Oṣar Hageonim, ad loc.

[5]) Journal of Theological Studies, oct. 1903.

[6]) The Triennial Cycle, J.Q.R.O.S.:V (1893), p. 420-68 and VI (1894), p. 1-73

Samaritans, the spread of Hellenism and the appearance of Christianity—point to its development. J. Mann [1]), on the other hand, suggests a positive aim of familiarizing the ordinary Jew with a knowledge of his religion on the leisure days of the Jewish calendar. If we accept the opinion of A. Büchler on the development of the lectionary reading from readings of the Pentateuch to the selections from the Prophets and Hagiographa, and the opinion of J. Mann on the reason for adopting a lectionary reading, the problem still remains. If it is solved light would be shed on the practice in the days of Jesus. How was the Pentateuch subjected to a division of pericopes in the years prior to the destruction of the Temple? and what was the period of time required to complete the reading of the whole Pentateuch?

The universal practice among the Jews today is to read the Pentateuch subdivided into 54 weekly portions [2]) during a span of one year. A practice based on a Babylonian tradition which replaced all other practices due to the hegemony of the Babylonian Gaonate over the Jewries of dispersion. Yet, evidence from the Masoretic division of pericopes [3]), the Geniza lists [4]) the structure of Midrashic literature based on Palestinian tradition [5]), and the statement in b. Meg. 29b point to a different practice. A practice, which was traced to Palestinian origin by the scholarly efforts of J. Theodor, A. Büchler and J. Mann, was based on a triennial cycle, i.e., the reading of the Pentateuch over a period of three years presented in 154 successive lections. The above results have prompted the erudite A. Guilding to study the Gospel acc. to John in connection with the triennial cycle [6])—a study which was anticipated two decades prior to the publication of her book in the Work "The Synagogue Lectionary and the New Testament" by R. G. Finch (London, 1939). As her predecessor, A. Guilding with much effort reconstructs a lectionary calendar [7]) prevalent in the days of Jesus and, above all, arrives to the conclusion that [8]) "early in the

---

[1]) "The Bible as Read and Preached in the Old Synagogue (Cincinnati, 1940) in the prolegomena.

[2]) See R. G. Finch, The Synagogue Lectionary, p. 34-37.

[3]) Indicated in Kittel's Biblia Hebraica by ס for Seder.

[4]) Discussed in Ginsburg, Introduction, ch. IV.

[5]) See J. Theodor, Die Midraschim zum Pentateuch und der dreijährige palästinische Cyclus, M.G.W.J. 34-36 (1885-1887).

[6]) Already noted by Büchler, J.Q.R.O.S., V p. 436 n. 2.

[7]) The Fourth Gospel, p. 10 ff and the appendix, and R. G. Finch, The Synagogue Lectionary, p. 22-34.

[8]) The Fourth Gospel, 229 ff, cf. p. 24 ff

4th century B.C., or perhaps a little later, the constituent documents of the Pentateuch were finally adapted to suit a triennial cycle of synagogue lectionary readings."

A closer examination can suppose a prevalent Palestinian custom quite different from a triennial cycle. A gloss [Sof. 16. 10] on a pre-third century A.D. passage speaking about the 175 portions (פָּרְשִׁיּוֹת) found in the Pentateuch states: "Therefore (the Rabbis) instituted 175 pericopes (Sedarim) for the Sabbaths to be binding as the Tamid—sacrifice", i.e., an uninterrupted practice of lectionary readings on successive Sabbaths. The 175 pericopes of the Pentateuch correspond, therefore, to the Sabbath lessons of a 3 1/2 year cycle, allowing for 50 lections a year in addition to the four readings allocated to the four special Sabbaths—as prescribed in M. Meg. III. 4 which continues "on the fifth (Sabbath) we return to the ordinary cycle"—thus designating 54 lections per year. A supplement to Rabbi Luria's "Yam shel-Shlomo" on tractate B.K. [1]), which enumerates the contrasting customs that prevailed among the Palestinian and Babylonian Jewries, states: "We in dispersion conclude the readings of the Pentateuch in an annual cycle, whereas the Palestinians conclude the Pentateuch twice in seven years, that is to say the Pentateuch is read over a period of 3 1/2 years."

Further evidence does point to a septennial cycle [2]) (i.e., twice in seven years: one commencing in Tishri of the first year and concluding in Nisan of the fourth year and the second concluding in Tishri of the eighth year) in the pre-Destruction of the Temple period. a) On two occasions in a seven years period a greater turnout of the population was witnessed at the Temple. Once [3]) on the Passover of the fourth year, when the Mosaic Law requires the appearance of all farmers to declare the back payments of tithes (known as Biʿur) in the presence of the priests at the Temple court and the presentation of first-fruits. At that time the farmer read the passages in Deut. 26. 13-15 as prescribed in the Mosaic law. The other occasion [4]) was the Festival of Assembly, attributed to Moses (Deut. 31. 10-12),

---

[1]) Mentioned by L. Zunz, G.V.d.J., p. 3 n. f, Bacher, Terminologie, p. 134 see also Naḥlat Jaʿacob on Sof. 16. 10; and compare I. Elbogen, Der jüdische Gottesdienst 2 ed., p. 161, 162.

[2]) Ant. IV. 8. 12 § 209.

[3]) M. M. Sh. 5. 6, 10, 11, 12, 13.

[4]) M. Sot. 7. 8.

which occurred on the Feast of Tabernacles at the outset of the eighth year. At the gathering of the multitudes of men, women and children on the Temple mount, the head of state received the Torah from the High Priest who in turn had received it from his adjutant who had received it from the archesynagoge, who in turn had received it from the Reader of the synagogue. Then the head of state proceeded with the reading from Deuteronomy 1. 1-6. 10 and 11. 13-22 (corresponding to the "Ten Commandments" and the "Shema", as it was the daily priestly reading [1]) during the morning Temple services); 14. 22-16. 17 (corresponds to the post-Second Temple era allocated lectionary reading for the Festival of Weeks [2])); 26. 12-15 (the lesson on clearance of back payments as a reminder to the farmer); 17. 14-20 (lesson on monarchy of which verse 15 is said to have caused Agrippa [3]) to shed tears); and 27. 1-26 (the list of curses which does indicate a pericope [4])). This ceremony manifests an occasion on which the whole structure of lectionary readings rotated, a septennial cycle corresponding to that of the days of Moses and Ezra. On the feast of the eighth year the head of state initiated the cycle by reading selections from the last Book of Moses.

b) There is a question on which month the triennial cycle began: in Tishri (which begins with the New Year festival, see M. R. H. 1. 2) or in Nisan (see Ex. 12. 2). Jewish scholars seem to disagree. A. Büchler reconstructed a triennial cycle based on calendaral considerations in rabbinic literature, resulting in the conclusion that the reading of the Pentateuch began in Nisan. I. Elbogen [5]) and J. Mann [6]) raised serious objections to Büchler's theory and saw it more fit to commence in Tishri. A. Guilding [7]) weighing both arguments champions Büchler's theory. In accepting a septennial cycle both opinions are validated since the months Nisan and Tishri served as starting points for the lectionary readings [8]).

---

[1]) M. Tam. 5. 1. R. Jehudah's omission of the Decalogue (T. Sot. 7. 17 (308. 11)) is based on the explanation given in b. Ber. 12a.

[2]) As found in Pesiqta, pis. 11 (p. 95a) and M. Meg. 31a.

[3]) M. Sot. 7. 8.

[4]) As indicated in Kittel's Biblia Hebraica, p. 304.

[5]) Der jüdische Gottesdienst in seiner geschichtlichen Entwicklung, p. 162 (2 ed., Frankfort, 1924).

[6]) The Bible as Read and Preached in the Old Synagogue, p. 6 ff.

[7]) The Fourth Gospel, pp. 10 ff, 27 ff.

[8]) Thus the enactment attributed to Ezra (b. Meg. 31b) that the admonitions in Lev. 26. 3-46 should be read before Pentecost and those recorded in Deut. 28 before New Year, can fall within septennial cycle.

c) Ch. D. Ginsburg in his important work "Introduction", ch. IV, p. 33, discussing the Masoretic division of pericopes, states: "But though the Massoretic treatise referred to above distinctly tells us that the Pentateuch is divided into 154 sedarim, yet the analysis of each book as well as in the separate enumeration of each seder distinctly specifies 167 such sedarim." Further evidence from Yemenite and Persian manuscripts and the divisions according to the Tanhuma fluctuate between 154 and 175 pericopes. Thus, several pericopes designated in the Tanhuma, for example, Gen. 42. 1, Ex. 12, 1, and Lev. 16. 1 coincide with the Persian recension and not with the common Masoretic lists. The Tannaitic prescription of a minimum of 21 verses per lection does point to shifting the beginning of particular seder in some localities but this represents the view of later scribes of post — Temple era and does not reflect the exact division of the earlier period as A. Guilding supposes.

We may now conclude that there is no definite solution to the exact lectionary system during the Temple period and consequently to the time of Jesus and Paul. However, there did exist a definite pericope text on which the weekly lectionary reading of Palestinian Jewry was based. At Jamnia academy the lectionary system of the past, in all probability, was subjected to a change as a result of the destruction of the Temple; the Bi'ur-ceremony and the Festival of Assembly were eliminated. Similar change to one year cycle took place during the Gaonate period. Our task is to examine pericopes' text used in pre-Destruction period and to determine their relation to the rabbinic form of a homily, which in turn will shed light on the type of homily presented by Jesus.

THE PERICOPES' TEXT AND THE HOMILY

Two accepted practices arising from public need and a desire to acquaint the people with the Jewish religion accompanied the lectionary reading in the synagogue on the Sabbath morning. One was a verse by verse rendition in the spoken language (in Palestine, Aramaic, in the Diaspora, Greek) by an appointed Meturgeman (translator). This custom, which is alluded to in Neh. 8. 8, later resulted in Aramaic and Greek translations of the Pentateuch at Jamnia seminary. The other convention was the delivery of a homily by a competent scholar following the prophetical reading which concluded the allotted day's scriptural reading. Two incidents in the New Testament and one in rabbinic literature point to a pre-Destruction presentation of a homily in the synagogues. The examination of these accounts will produce certain conclusions as to the methods adopted in presenting a homily in the days prior to the destruction of the Temple; and which, in turn, will shed light on certain teachings of Jesus recorded in the four Gospels.

The account in rabbinic literature, based on several recensions [1]), relates that Eliezer ben Hyrcanus, a prominent scholar at Jamnia, entered the school of Rabban Jochanan ben Zakkai which at that time was located in Jerusalem prior to the destruction of the Temple. The account states:—I designate the variants with brackets—"After some time his father came up [to Jerusalem on the Sabbath eve] to disinherit him (Eliezer, because he had deserted his father in time of need and the father yielded to the pressure of his sons to disinherit Eliezer), [on the Sabbath day, he arrived in the house of learning as the custom prevailed, in order to hear the customary homily]. There he found Eliezer preaching a sermon (who had been persuaded by his teacher to do so), [the Reader was standing near by] and the most prominent men of the land, Ben Ṣiṣṣith Hakeseth, Niqodimon ben Gurion and Ben Kalba Sabua (the richest men in Jerusalem at that time) sitting before him. He [opened the homily (פָּתַח וְדָרַשׁ)] with the

following saying: ["This is what the scripture says (זֶה שֶׁאָמַר הַכָּתוּב)"]

Ps. 37. 14, 15 (linking the proem with the opening passage of the day's pericope (Gen. 14. 1): 'The wicked have drawn out the sword and have bent the bow" this alludes to Amraphel and his companions (Gen. 14. 1); 'To cast down the poor and the needy'—to Lot (Gen. 14. 12); 'To slay such as are upright in the way'—to Abraham (Gen. 14. 13, 14); 'Their sword shall enter into their own heart' as it is written (Gen. 14. 15) 'And he fought against them by night, he and his servants and smote them' " [2]).

The main feature of the above homily, which is also noted in the homilies presented by the Rabbis in the following years, is the opening of a homily (Pithḥa) [3]) based on a proem text—a quo-

---

[1]) Gen. R. 41 (p. 397), Pirqe I, II, I A.D.N. 4 (15b), II A.D.N. 13 (15b); Tanh. on Gen. 14. 1 (p. 34). Yalqut Shim'oni § 72. Tanhuma states "and all of Israel entered as the custom prevailed to hear the homily".

[2]) J. Mann, op. cit., p. 105, relates it to the Haftarah (Is. 41. 2), demonstrating a unity. Compare the Pesher in Haberman's Megilloth, p. 155.

[3]) See J. Mann, op. cit., Zunz, G.V.d.J., chs. 10-22 and S. K. Mirsky, Haderashah Bitqufat Hamishnah Ve-hatalmud, Horeb, 1943, pp. 75-90.

tation from the Prophets, in some cases that of the Haftarah, or more commonly from the Hagiographa. The proem text was then linked to the opening phrase or another passage (in some cases) of the pericope text. The preacher, who adopted this form of homily, began in most cases with the introductory Hebraic of Aramaic expression: "This is what the Scripture says". A collection of this type is found in the Homiletic Midrashim (Tanḥumas and Pesiqtas) and in the Rabboth. The text was interpreted by projecting the words of the Prophets or of the Writings to contemporary situations, customs and persons or by bringing into relation the proem text and the Pentateuchal pericope text. Thus, a presentation of the Scriptures as a unity was common practice of the early Rabbis, a practice known as pearl-stringing (חָרוּזִים) [1]). It is related [2]) that in the last days of the

Temple era at the circumcision-feast of Elisha ben Abuyah, Rabbi Eliezer and Rabbi Jehoshua, the disciples of Jochanan ben Zakkai, were sitting and stringing the words of the Pentateuch with those of the Prophets and the Hagiographa. The method of projection is noted above in Eliezer's homily which related the Pentateuchal personalities with the words of the Psalter and at the same time alluded to the present situation—the oppressions of the Jews by Romans. The Biblical Amraphel and his companions represent the Romans; the common people Lot and the learned individuals Abraham, through whose guidance the Roman yoke will be finally overthrown. This mode of interpretation is indicated by the Hebraic expression Patar [3]) or Pashar (to unveil the hidden meaning of the text, as it is denoted in Gen. 40. 8, 16, Dan. 7. 16, Ecc. 8. 1 to unveil the hidden meaning of a dream). Thus, the formula "Rabbi × patar qera (qaraya)..." refers to an interpretation through a projection of the words of the Scriptures to a given case. This formula introduces the interpretation of the pericope's text Gen. XLIX. 27 [4]) in connection with the proem text Ps. LXVIII. 17 by Rabbi Jose the Galilean and Rabbi Aqiba in the beginning of the second century of Christian era. "R. Jose the Galilean 'patar qera' in reference to the mountains.

---

[1]) See W. Bacher, Die Proömien der alten jüdischen Homilie (Leipzig, 1913), p. 9 ff.

[2]) J. Hag. 77b.

[3]) See Bacher, Terminologie פתר.

[4]) Gen. R. on 49. 27 (p. 1271), whereas Mid. Hag. on Gen. 49. 27 introduces the formula, זֶה שֶׁאָמַר הַכָּתוּב; compare Targum on Jud. 5.5. The reference to the mountains and Benjamin is found in the Haftarah (Zech. 14. 1-11).

When the Holy One blessed be He came to reveal the Torah on Sinai, the mountains presented the following arguments (a play on the words Teraṣdun and Teraṣu din), each claiming, 'The Torah shall be revealed on me', Tabor came from Beth Elim and Carmel from Apamor... Said God to them 'Why look ye askance (Ps. 68. 17)'—ye are all indeed high mountains but 'ye are rather gabnunim (which denotes in Lev. XXI. 20 'crook-backed' or 'dwarf'); idolatrous worship has been performed on the tops of all of you. But Sinai upon which no idolatrous worship has taken place is the mountain which God hath desired for His abode'. Therefore, 'The Lord came down upon Sinai' (Ex. 19. 20), nevertheless, yea, the Lord will dwell in it for ever in the eternal house (the Temple). R. Aqiba 'patar qera' in reference to the tribes. When Solomon came to build the Temple, the tribes delivered the following argument, 'Let it be built in my territory'... Said the Holy One blessed be He to them: 'ye tribes (described in the verse as mountains) why look ye askance?' Ye are all righteous, yet ye are 'gabnunim'. What does 'gabnunnim' mean? Gannabim (thieves —a transposition of letters). Ye were all associated in the selling of Joseph, his is 'the mountain which God hath desired for His abode (territory of Benjamin)' ".

The secret knowledge in unveiling the hidden meaning of the text as demonstrated by R. Jose the Galilean was later referred to as "Bath-Qol" in the homily of Bar Qapara. Bar Qapara (c. 250 A.D.) [1] delivered the following homily (דָּרַשׁ): "What is the meaning of the verse [Ps. 68. 17] 'Why look ye askance mountains of peaks (Gabnunim)'. A 'Bath-Qol' went forth and said to them (the mountains) 'Why do ye desire litigation (a play on the words Teraṣdun and Teraṣu din) with Sinai?' ye are all deformed as compared to Sinai, as it is written in the above verse 'gabnunnim' and it is written in Lev. 21. 20 'gibben' (deformed)".

In a similar manner the Teacher of Righteousness and the apostles unveiled the hidden meaning of the Scriptures to describe current events and personalities. The Teacher of Righteousness believed to have possessed full knowledge in unveiling the hidden (הוֹדִיעוֹ אֵל אֶת כּוֹל רָזֵי ...הַנְּבִיאִים)[2] words of the prophets and to do so he applied "pesher" to disclose the hidden meaning. Two selections from the Pesharim material found at Qumran will suffice to demonstrate the

---

[1] b. Meg. 29a.
[2] I Q p. Hab. 7. 4, 5.

method of interpretation which was akin to the "patar qera" of the early Rabbis. On Hab. 1. 4b-6a [1]), it explains: " 'For the wicked hath beset the righteous'—[the wicked is the wicked priest and the righteous] is the Teacher of Righteousness [whom God has placed among His people. And that which the Scripture says]: 'Therefore right goeth forth perverted... For behold, a work shall be wrought in your days, which ye will not believe though it be told you'— [its "pesher" refers to] the disobedient people who with the man of falsity [did not believe what] the Teacher of Righteousness [unveiled] from the mouth of God ... and have desecrated His (the Lord's) holy Sabbath ... and that which the Scripture says, 'For lo, I raise up the Chaldeans that bitter and impetuous nation' its "pesher" refers to the Kittim (a sobriquet for the Romans) [who are] quick and mighty in war in order to destroy the wicked [and sinners]". Another "pesher" employed by the Teacher of Righteousness to interpret Nah. 1. 12b, 13 displays a projection to personalities who played an important role in his time. Nah. 2. 12b reads [2]) " 'Where a lion and a lioness walked and the lion's whelp and none made them afraid" [its "pesher" refers to] Demetrius (III Eukarios in 88 B.C.) the Greek king (of the Seleucid line) who sought to enter Jerusalem on the advice of "those who seek smooth things" (see Ant. XIII. 13. 5 § 376 = Bell. I. 4. 4 § 92) and he sought to deprive the Greek kings (the other claimants to the throne see Ant. 13. 13. 4; 14. 3) of Antioch until the rise of the Kittim rulers (the Romans under Pompey, 64 B.C.) ... 'The lion did tear in pieces enough for his whelp and strangeled for his lioness' its "pesher" refers to the "lion of wrath" (Alexander I Jannaeus) who smote his (Jewish) great men and the men of his council (see Ant. XIII. 14. 2 §§ 380-383)".

The apostles, too, used the above tool of interpretation when seeking a fulfilment of the Scriptures for the coming of Jesus. Peter, in the presence of the High Priest, the elders, and the scribes, replied [3]): "Be it known unto you all and to all the people of Israel that by the name of Jesus Christ of Nazareth, whom ye crucified, whom God raised from the dead, even by him doth this man stand here before you whole. This is 'The stone which was set at naught of you builders which is become the head of the corner'. Neither is there salvation in any other". The words of the Psalter (Ps. 118. 22 in conjunction with

---

[1]) I Q p. Hab. 1. 11-2. 13.
[2]) See Haberman, Megilloth, p. 153.
[3]) Acts 4. 10-12.

v. 21) was interpreted by a pesher formula, "this is": the stone (a play on
the words 'eben' and 'ben') [1]) is Jesus, the builders who had rejected
it are the Pharisees, and "the stone has become the chief corner-stone"
(Ps. 118. 22), therefore those who confessed unto him found salvation
(v. 21). The identical phrase from the Psalms is recorded to have been
used by Jesus in the same manner of interpretation in the presence
of the high priests and the Pharisees [Matt. 21. 33 ff].

Another account found in Acts 13. 14-41 describes a homily
presented by Paul on the Sabbath morning after the reading of the
Scriptures at Antioch. It relates: "Then Paul stood up and beckoning
with his hand said: Men of Israel and ye that fear God give audience
'The God of His people of Israel chose our fathers and exalted the
people . . . and with a high arm brought He them out of it (Egypt) . . .
and when He had destroyed seven nations in the land of Canaan, He
divided their land to them' (a parallel to the pericope text Deut. 4. 37,
38) [2]) . . . He raised up unto them David to be their king, to whom
also He gave testimony [3]): 'I have found [David the son of Jesse] a
man after Mine own heart' (a parallel to the proem text from the
work of the Prophets, I Sam. 13. 14) of this man's seed hath God
according to His promise raised unto Israel a saviour, Jesus: "When
John had preached before his coming the baptism of repentence to all
the People of Israel. And as John fulfilled his course, he said whom
think ye that I am? I am not he. But, behold, there cometh one after me,
whose shoes on his feet I am not worthy to loose" (a parallel to common source used by Luke 3. 16, Mk. 1. 7, Matt. 3. 11 and John 1. 27).

Paul employed a "Pithḥa"—a pericope text correlated to a proem
text, that of the Prophets—with the introductory formula "to whom
also He gave testimony", and then he followed with a probable existing
text from the early Christians. This, in fact, is the rabbinical method
of "pearl-stringing", but Paul substituted a Christian writing for the
Hagiographa. In this manner Paul expounded and testified to the
arrival of the Kingdom of God; persuading the Jewish public in

---

[1]) It is also alluded to in Matt. 3. 9; note the parable of the wicked husband-
man, Matt. 21. 33-41, which precedes the interpretation of Ps. 118. 22.

[2]) A pericope beginning with Deut. 4. 25 is found in the Masoretic text and
Tanhuma. A. Guilding The Fourth Gospel, p. 7, however, ascribes the parallel
to Deut. 1. 31 on the account of LXX reading, yet the whole phrase is out of
place.

[3]) A parallel to the formula: זֶהוּ שֶׁאָמַר הַכָּתוּב or וְכֵן הַכָּתוּב מְשַׁבְּחוֹ בְּקַבָּלָה
(Sifra on 1. 1 (p. 4a)) which ushers the proem text I Sam. 13. 14, not as Guilding
believes Jer. 30. 4.

the synagogues on the Sabbath to accept Jesus as a saviour from the Scriptures.

Paul follows the above "Pithḥa" with the common message outlined by the preachers of the early Christian circle. Thus, he again introduces the message with an introductory note: "Men and brethren, children of the stock of Abraham and whosoever among you feareth God,[1]) to you is the word of salvation sent". Then he proceeds to explain the outline of the message a) the glorious fact that the crucified Messiah has arisen by God's will from death, b) therefore, he is the true Messiah; indeed even more so than David who saw death, c) therefore, all who hear the message believe in him, repent and be baptised.

THE PROEM HOMILIES ATTRIBUTED TO JESUS

Before examining the proem homilies attributed to Jesus let us review their main features: a) The pericope text was linked with a proem text and usually was introduced with the formula "This is what the Scripture says". b) The preacher followed with either a "pesher" or a message derived from the text. c) A general practice found in most rabbinic proem homilies was concluding the sermon with the introductory Scripture or with words of comfort.

The Proem Homily in Luke 4. 17-22

In Luke 4. 16 we read that Jesus preached on the Sabbath day in the synagogue at Nazareth after the "Reader" has presented him the Isaiah roll. He opened it reading: "The spirit of the Lord is upon me: Because He hath anointed me, to bring good tidings unto the poor. He hath sent me to bind up the broken-hearted. To proclaim liberty to the captives and the opening of the eyes to them that are bound... To proclaim the year of the Lord's good pleasure" [Is. 61. 1-2]. The contents of the sermon is left unrecorded, yet, the following is stated "And he began to say to them: 'This day is this Scripture fulfilled in your ears". Whereupon, the congregation reacted with a desire to witness the same marvel doings as he had performed in Capernaum. The concluding remark points to the type of homily used by Jesus, a proem text of the Haftarah [2]) (the concluding prophetical lection)

---

[1]) They were considered semi-proselytes, see J. Klausner, From Jesus to Paul, I § 3. Pauls' message was, in this sermon, similar to the apostolic kerygma.

[2]) A possible Haftarah to Gen. 35. 9, see Mann, op. cit., p. 283 ff. Blessing (mentioned in v. 9) is the theme. On Blessing of those who mourn see J. Targum on v. 9 and compare Is. 61. 3.

with an interpretation in the form of a pesher, projecting the words of the prophet to represent his actions and the purpose of his mission. The contents of the homily can be reconstructed from other sources in the Synoptics.

The list of beatitudes found in the Sermon on the Mount are composed of nine statements beginning with the formula "Happy are" and two beginning with "Ye are". For "Ye are" statements we find parallel passages in the other two Synoptics but in a different arrangement and with another connotation. The statement "Ye are the salt of the earth" [Matt. 5. 13] refers to a special Sodomite salt [1]) used on the sacrifices; to which the Sifre Num. § 118 (p. 39a) on 18. 19 states: "The Scripture declares a covenant with Aaron with a non-decaying substance, which also conserves other (substances)". Thus, the illustration of salt implies two related ideas: a) Ye are the salt with which to preserve humanity; b) Ye should apply the salt unto yourself in order not to be decayed. Matthew adopts the former explanation [5. 13] and Luk. 14. 34 f and Mk. 9. 49, 50 the latter. As for the statement, "Ye are the light of the world", Matthew 5. 15 records the illustration of the candle and states [v. 16]: "Let your light so shine before men, that they may see your good works and they will praise your Father which is in heaven" [2]). While the other two Gospels [Mk. 4. 22, Luk. 8. 17] in presenting the illustration of the candle state, "For there is nothing hidden, which shall not be manifested, neither was anything kept secret but that it should come to light". Therefore two different explanations are given for the illustration of the candle which was portrayed by Jesus. Matthew explains that the disciples should set a shining example on this earth whereas the other two Gospels [3]) refer to the day of judgement where the doings of men will be revealed in the open. The above evidence already implies that Matthew made use of excerpts from an existing collection of Jesus' sayings (Logia) [4]) to construct the beatitudes.

As for the nine statements beginning with the formula "Happy are" we do find a parallel in Luk. 6. 20-26. Luke lists only four of the Blessings with slight variations, and he then follows with four parallel "Woes", recalling the pronouncement of the Blessings and

---

[1]) See Billerbeck, Kommentar I, p. 232.
[2]) On praising "The Father which is in heaven" in reference to a wise pupil, see II A.D.N. 13 (10b). Light denotes teachings see b. Taan. 7b.
[3]) Mk. 4. 22, Luk. 8. 17, compare Luk. 12. 2, 3 with Matt. 10. 26.
[4]) As stated by Papias preserved in Eusebius, Hist. Eccl. III. 39. 16.

NOS.	IS. 61. 1-7	Matt. 5.3-12	Luk. 6. 20-23	Rabbinic parallels to the Beatitudes acc. to Matt.
1.	The spirit of the Lord is upon me, Because the Lord hath anointed me: To bring good tidings to *the poor*. ('aniyim for 'anavim)	Happy are *the poor* in spirit for theirs is the Kingdom of Heaven	Happy are *the poor*, for yours is the Kingdom of God	
2.	He hath sent me to bind up the broken hearted, to proclaim liberty to the captives and the opening of the eyes to them that are bound . . . (Materialistic hunger for help)	Happy are they which do hunger and thirst after righteousness for they shall be filled. (The spiritual hunger is followed by three blessings on the 1) merciful, 2) pure in heart (bare leb for nishbere leb) 3) peacemakers)	Happy are ye who hunger now, for ye shall be filled (The materialistic hunger)	Merciful: see Sifre Deut. § 96, b. Shab. 151b, see Ps. 18. 26. Pure in heart: see Ps. 24. 4, 6 and D.E.R. II. Peacemakers: see loc. cit. and Ps. 34, 12, 15.
3.	To *comfort all that mourn.* To appoint unto them that mourn in Zion. To give unto them a garland for ashes, the *oil of joy* for mourning . . . and they *shall be called terebinths* (or rams) of *righteousness, and they shall renew the waste cities*	Happy are they that *mourn for they shall be comforted* (adding the blessing on the meek *for they shall inherit the earth*-the land of Israel (see Ps. 37. 11 LXX rendition)	Happy are ye that weep now, for ye shall laugh —(*that is of joy*)	
4.	But ye shall be named the *priests of the Lord* . . . ye eat the wealth of the nations . . . for *your shame* which was double. And for that *they rejoiced* . . . Therefore in their land they shall possess double *everlasting joy shall be unto you*	Happy are they which are *persecuted* . . . for theirs is the *Kingdom of Heaven* (the heavenly land). Happy are ye, when men shall *revile you* . . . *rejoice and be exceeding glad*	Happy are ye, when men shall *hate you* and when they shall separate you . . . *rejoice ye* in that *day and leap for joy.*	See b. Shab. 88b = b. Jom. 23a = b. Git. 36b = D.E.R. II

the Curses by the priests on Mount Gerizim [Deut. 27. 15-26 and Josh. 8. 33-35] and as practiced among the Essenes [IQS. I. 18-II. 19]. The list of Blessings, on the other hand, can be correlated with the words of Is. 61. 1-7, the program of Jesus' ministry, and the theme 'blessing' is drawn from the day's Pentateuchal pericope, Gen. 35. 9 (see p. 155 n. 2). It can be constructed under 4 headings of blessings as found in Luke and presented on p. 157 [The italics indicate the comparison. Note that the additional blessings found in Matt. are based on Psalms. Thus Matt. included additional Blessings to those demonstrated by Jesus. The correlation of words of the Psalms beginning with אשרי= μακάριοιwith the pericopial text Gen. 34. 9 is found also in Mid. Hag. Gen. 18. 1 (pp. 283, 284).]

Apparently both Matthew and Luke drew from a common source where the statements of blessings followed the proem text of Jesus' homily at Nazareth on the Sabbath day as recorded in Luk. 4. 16-20. In presenting the blessings, Luke records the materialistic interpretation of the text and Matthew the abstract and spiritual. A similar collection of statements of praise and condemnation correlated with different proem texts and compiled from the massive rabbinic literature is found in Derekh Ereṣ Rabba (a pre-Gaonic work), chapter II.

A Proem Homily as Found in John 6. 30-59 [1])

Another pesher-homily based on a pericope and a proem text is recorded in the Gospel according to John [6. 32-58] which was preached in the synagogue on the Sabbath day at Capernaum [2]). The congregation demanded of Jesus: "a sign shewest thou then we may see and believe thee" [3]) as it was told in the day's reading-pericope text, Ex. 16. 4, that Moses beckoned God to produce manna from heaven. Jesus proceeded with a "pesher" to explain the proem text [Ps. 78. 24]: "And he gave them bread from heaven". God and not Moses was responsible for the miraculous bread and that bread referred to in the Scripture denotes Jesus, the bread of life [4]). "And he

---

[1]) See also the analysis of Guilding, The Fourth Gospel, ch. 5.

[2]) See Mk. 6. 1-6: "He came to his country on the Sabbath day to teach in the synagogue". Then it relates: "and many hearing him were astonished", the sermon is lacking. To which they said: "Is not this the carpenter the son of Mary" compare Matt. 13. 54 and John 6. 42. The sermon appears to be preserved only in John.

[3]) A σημεῖον (= אות, סימן) is asked of a true prophet see Deut. 18. 15 ff, and b. Sanh. 89b.

[4]) Bread representing teaching is also implied in the parable: "the Kingdom

that cometh to me shall never hunger and he that believeth in me shall never thirst [1]) . . . for I came down from heaven not to do mine own will but the will of Him that sent me".

Hearing a "pesher" employed by Jesus to denote that he is the manna, the angry congregation said: "Is not this Jesus, the son of Joseph, whose father and mother we know?" Then Jesus continued with a parallel exposition, quoting probably from the day's Haftarah [2]) Is. 54. 13: "Every man (the text: son) therefore that have learned of the Father" (in the text: Yahweh, since the name of God was not pronounced)—that not every one can come to me, only the ones who were chosen by God and to whom He has sent me. Thus in a reply he rejected the congregation that it will not nourish from the bread of life. He further proceeded with the same idea expounded earlier in a "pesher": "I am the bread of life (whereas) your fathers did eat manna in the wilderness and are dead, (yet) this is the bread which cometh down from heaven that a man may eat thereof and not die". The consequent teaching is "whoso eat of this bread shall live for ever and the bread that I will give for the life of the world". Again he was interrupted. Yet he was still able to conclude the pesher-homily with the opening statement: "This is that bread which came down from heaven. Not as your fathers did eat manna and are dead. He that eateth of this bread shall live for ever".[3])

Thus, a proem-homily based on a "pesher" of the word "bread" —which also in rabbinic literature denotes "teaching" [4])—is preserved within the framework of a lively synagogical debate.

The Pericope Homily in the Sermons on the Mount and the Plain

Comparing the Sermon on the Mount (Matt. 5. 3-7. 27) with the Sermon on the Plain (Luk. 6. 20-49) a pericope and a proem homily (the latter was described above pp. 155-158) are to be found. The Sermon on the Mount consists of the following parts: a) the beatitudes (Matt.

---

of Heaven is like unto leaven" Matt. 13. 33, Luk. 13. 21. Leaven (שְׂאוֹר) means good actions or teaching, see D.E.Z., the chapter on peace, and also bad teaching, Matt. 16. 12, Luk. 12. 1 (hypocrisy) and see J. Ber. 7d and Mech. on 14. 11 (33b).

[1]) The theme: "Confidence in God's provision" is derived from the story of manna see Philo Leg. Alleg. III. 56 and Mech. on 16. 4 (p. 55b).

[2]) The Haftarah including Is. 55. 1, 2 tallies with the general contents of Ex. 16. 4 ff.

[3]) Probably Jesus employed a play on the words, lehem (Ps. 78. 24) and lehayyim, a common rabbinic practice. Note also the same method described p. 154.

[4]) Gen. R. on 14. 18 (421) and b. Hag. 14a in reference to Pr. 9. 5.

5. 3-16) with the formulas "μακάριοι" and "Ὑμεῖς ἐστε"; b) an introductory note to the effect that the subsequent teachings "did not come to decrease from the Law or Prophets but to add (Matt. 5. 17-20 compare v. 17 with the Aramaic rendition in b. Shab. 116b); c) the teachings on the manner of addition: a prescription of added precautionary measures in regard to the three commandments of the Decalogue and the rule of lex talionis as found in connection with Dt. 19. 21. Each teaching in reference to the Pentateuchal commandment begins with the formula "ye have heard that it was said (by them of old)" and is correlated to an explanation of yet another verse from the Scriptures with the formula "It hath been said". In three cases the formula is omitted [Matt. 5. 21 in reference to Ex. 20. 13 with vs. 25, 26 to Pr. 6. 3 and 25. 8; Matt. 5. 27-30 in reference to Ex. 20. 14 with v. 32 to Deut. 24. 1; Matt. 5. 34-37 (to Ex. 20. 7) with Lev. 19. 12 and Deut. 23. 23, and Matt. 5. 39-42 on Dt. 19.19 and Pr. 20. 22]. d) The pericope homily on Lev. 19. 18 (parallel to Luk. 6. 27-45): a teaching on the manner of fulfilment by adopting the ways of God those of love and perfectness [1]) demonstrated by three acts (Matt. 6. 1-4, charity; ib. 6. 5-15, prayer; ib. 6. 16-18, fasting), by the three parts of the body (Matt. 6. 19-20, the heart; ib. 6. 21-23, the eye; and the body, ib. 6. 24) [2]) with three teachings beginning with "Do not" (Do not worry, Matt. 6. 25-34; Do not judge, Matt. 7. 1-5; Do not give the holy to the dogs, Matt. 7. 6) which concludes with the explanation of the opening verse Lev. 19. 18; e) The concluding note on teachings and disciples illustrated by three parables: 1) parable of the two paths demonstrating how one discerns the way of life (Matt. 7. 13, 14), 2) parable of the tree and its fruit demonstrating how one should recognize the true teacher (ib. 7. 15-24), 3) parable of the builders describing the good disciple (ib. 7. 14-27).

The Sermon on the Plain, on the other hand, is arranged differently than the Sermon on the Mount and consists of the following parts: a) the beatitudes with a list of blessings and woes [Luk. 6. 20-26]; b) the pericope homily on Lev. 19. 18 on the three related subjects; a show of love to one's fellowman (demonstrated by the Golden Rule, an interpretation of Lev. 19. 18 (Luk. 6. 27-31); by a sensible deduction (ib. 6. 32-34) and the resulting reward (ib. 6. 35)); a show of

---

[1]) On grouping in three, see L. Ginzberg, Genizah Studies I, p. 24.

[2]) The three acts are grouped together (J. Taan. 65b) and so the parts of the body (Ab. II. 9).

mercy (demonstrated by the way of God (ib. 6. 36); the teaching of "Do not judge" (ib. 6. 37) and generosity (ib. 6. 38)) and a show of perfectness demonstrated with a parable of the blind leader (ib. 6. 39, 40), a parable of the beam and the mote (ib. 6. 41, 42) and a parable of the tree and its fruit (ib. 6. 43-45). c) A concluding note on teachings and disciples demonstrated with a parable of the builders (ib. 6. 46-49)).

The list of beatitudes found in both sermons was demonstrated above as a proem-homily—the first sermon found in the Sermons on the Mount and the Plain.

The second part, found only in the Sermon on the Mount, is an introductory note to the following teaching on addition to the Law in part c. The introduction, which also includes the statements [1] "It is easier for heaven and earth to pass, than one jot or one crown (of the letter) of the law to be superfluous", is parallel to the teachings expounded during mealtime [Luk. 16. 17]. In both Gospels the note introduces a teaching of fulfilment of the Law, "which should exceed the fulfilment of the Law by the scribes and the Pharisees". The teaching as recorded in part c of the Sermon on the Mount states: "Whosoever shall put away his wife saving for the cause of fornication causeth her to commit adultery", which is verified in the Pauline letters [Rom. 7. 3 and I Cor. 7. 10 and compare Mk. 10. 11]. The teaching portrays a stricter approach than that of both Pharisaic academies, i.e., on no occasion a man should put away his wife and take another.

To demonstrate the strict teaching—Mk. 10. 11 but not Matt. 19. 9, the latter is similar to the Shammaite opinion—Jesus recalls the story of creation (Gen. 1. 27b) "(God) created them a male and female" followed by (Gen. 2. 24)—"Therefore shall a man leave his father and his mother and shall cleave unto his wife and they shall be one flesh"; therefore, what God hath joined together let not man put asunder. This resulted in the strict teaching—as the Essenes taught [C.D. 4. 20, 11]—a man can not keep two women in his life while both are alive even though one of them is divorced.

The above analysis indicates that Matthew collected several examples of interpretation of the Law committed by Jesus and rearranged them in the Sermon on the Mount following the introduction. The author's motive was to issue a new code of law based on interpreta-

---

[1] Matt. 5. 18, compare Cant. R. on 5. 11 (p. 242).

tions of the Mosaic law—as the rabbinic expositional Midrashim [1]) are related to the Pentateuchal scriptures. Therefore he proceeds with the most venerated set of laws, the Decalogue. The narrative in b. Shab. 116 describes an incident when a Christian was confronted by the Rabbis, about the time of the composition of the Synoptics. He quoted an Aramaic passage—identical with Matt. 5. 17—from the end of a similar collection. The Judaeo-Christian member also remarked to the Rabbis: "From the day you were exiled from your country (the time of the Destruction) the Mosaic Law was removed and instead was given a Gospel".

Part c of the Sermon on the Mount contains the following expositions with a formula [2]), "ye have heard that it was said [by the old]", introducing the Decalogue passages and "It hath been said" for another Pentateuchal passage (Deut. 24. 1).

α) Ex. 20. 13 declares: "Thou shalt not kill"—the transgressor of the law was brought to the Sanhedrin during the Hasmonaean and Herodian times [see Ant. 14. 9. 4 (the trial of Herod) compare b. Sanh. 19b, the trial of the Governor of Hyrcanus (Herod?) and the judge Shimeon (Σαμαίας?) ben Shetach].

The exposition follows: A transgression of "thou shalt not kill" does not imply only the act of slaying, but it also includes preliminary steps which lead to murder, such as hatred and causing shame. Thus, three consequent rules follow this commandment in the order of their severity: a) "Whosoever is angry with his brother without cause shall be liable to stand trial in court". Since anger, as R. Eliezer ben Hyrcanus explains [3]), is regarded as" he who spills blood", therefore the person is to be judged in the same light as the killer. b) "Whosoever shall say to his brother רֵיקָא [4]) (a vain fellow) shall be in guilt before the Sanhedrin". This abusive remark רֵיקָא which indicates the disability and untrustworthiness of the individual is as violent as the expression bastard, about which the Rabbis state [5]): "Whosoever calls his fellowman bastard is to receive forty stripes". Thus, Jesus says "he is guilty before the Sanhedrin" who can ad-

---

[1]) On expositional Midrash see D. Hoffman, Einleitung in die halachischen Midraschim (Berlin, 1888), Ch. Albeck, Introduction to Bereshith Rabbah (Berlin, 1920) and J. Theodor, Midrash Haggadah, J. Enc.

[2]) On the formulas see Billerbeck, Kommentar I, p. 253, and Daube, op. cit. II § 1.

[3]) D.E.R. 11, Sifre Deut. § 187 (108b) and b. B.M. 58b.

[4]) The expression is found in D.E.R. 4; 5.

[5]) b. Kid. 28a (Beraitha).

minister the punishment of stripes [1]). c) "Whosoever shall say μωρός (denotes ethical ugliness) shall be guilty of fire of Gehenna". The abusive remark μωρός or רָשָׁע (a wicked man) addressed to a fellowman is to be punished by God alone, or as the Rabbis explain [2]: "They bring witnesses, a notary, a pen and ink, then they record and attest (a document stating): that and that person (who abused his fellowman with the remark רָשָׁע) has denied the God of Israel".

From the above teaching, it follows that an individual must be careful in his daily dealings with his fellowmen, and when even slight differences arise, he must resort to reconcilation lest he be not favoured by God at the time of worship [3]). Thus follows the exposition on Pr. 6. 3 [4]) in conjunction with 25. 8, "Agree with thine adversary quickly while thou art on the way with him: lest at any time the adversary deliver thee to the judge and the judge deliver thee to the officer and thou be cast into prison . . . Thou shalt by no means come out thence, till thou hast paid the uttermost farthing"—i.e., seek a compromise lest you will be punished on earth in court.

β) Ex. 20. 14 states: "Thou shalt not commit adultery". The exposition is: the commandment does not only apply to the act itself but it also includes all preliminary actions which can lead to adultery, e.g. to lust after a woman by looking at her. The exposition, like the one above, displays a measure of precaution. Both examples follow the introductory note that the new code of Jesus teaches how to fulfil the Law—πληρῶσαι is rendered in the Aramaic recension לְאַסוּפֵי [5]) (to add), i.e., to preserve the literal meaning of the Law by including all preliminary acts. So did the Men of the Great Synagogue teach [6]): "And ye

---

[1]) M. Sanh. 1. 2. χρίσις = דינא; συνέδριον = סנהדרין .

[2]) b. B.M. 71a.

[3]) Compare Sifra on 16. 30 (83a).

[4]) The Hebrew text reads לֵךְ הִתְרַפֵּס וּרְהַב רֵעֶיךָ. The difficult text is explained by critics as לֵךְ הַתֵּר־פַּס וְהַב לְרֵעֶךָ (see Kittel's apparatus, p. 1161), LXX renders μὴ ἐκλυόμενος = וְאַל תִּתְרַפֵּה. The Rabbis explain b. Yom. 87a, הַתֵּר לוֹ פִּסַּת יָד. הַרְבֵּה עָלָיו רֵעִים. Thus in Matt. 5. 25 it is explained as לֵךְ הִתְפַּיֵּס רִיב רֵעֶךָ and in Luk. 12. 68 as הַתֵּר־פַּס, רִיב רֵעֶךָ.

[5]) b. Shab. 116b, quoted in the Kuzari, I. 83. E. Bischoff, Jesus und die Rabbiner (Leipzig, 1905), p. 26, only knows of the quotation in the Kuzari (a work of the 12th cent.) and not the quotation in the Talmud (of 1st cent.). Compare the saying of Hillel (Ab. I. 13); "He that adds not (מוֹסִיף) decreases it".

[6]) Ab. 1. 2.

shall make fences", i.e., produce measures of precaution to the Law. Thus, the early elders taught [1]: "Lev. 18. 19 states: 'And thou shalt not approach (copulate) unto a woman ... in the impure period of menstruation'. I would say one may hug her or kiss her and speak vain things, therefore it states 'thou shalt not approach'—any act which may lead to copulation' ".

The above exposition attributed to Jesus is correlated to a related interpretation of yet another law found in Deut. 24. 1, "When a man taketh a wife ... then it cometh to pass ... he hath found she had committed an unseemly act then he writeth her a bill of divorcement". The interpretation of the law can lead to two consequent rules: a) A bill of divorcement can be issued only in case of fornication [עֶרְוָה see Lev. 18. 6]; b) A bill of divorcement issued for other reasons is not valid and the divorced woman, still considered married, commits adultery upon marrying another. Matt. 5. 32 presents the former interpretation whereas Mk. 10. 11 and Luk. 16. 18 present the latter —indicated on p. 161. The author of the Gospel according to Matthew [5. 28] correlates the precaution against adultery, that is, "Whosoever looketh on a woman to lust after her hath committed adultery [2])" with the precaution against divorce [5. 32]. In the same manner the Palestinian Amoraim [J. Git. 50d] correlate the precaution against a menstruant (described above) with the precaution against divorce according to the Shammaite opinion (M. Git. 9. 10).

γ) Ex. 20. 7 states: "Thou shalt not take the name of Yahweh, thy God, in vain" which is rendered in Lev. 19. 12 "Ye shall not swear by My name falsely". This commandment bears upon the law in Deut. 23. 23, 24, "When thou shalt make a vow unto Yahweh, thy God ... do accordingly as thou hast vowed unto Yahweh, thy God".

The exposition on the commandment and its related law is: "Ye shall not swear by My name falsely" does not only imply profaning the names of God but it also prohibits swearing falsely by the holy objects [3]). Whereas the law, "Do accordingly as thou hast vowed unto Yahweh, thy God", indicates that even if a person declare an oath with the words "yea, yea and nay, nay" [4]) he must abide by his promise. Thus, the separate yet related interpretations of the law

---

[1]) I A.D.N. II (4b) compare Sifra on Lev. 19. 33 (79c) and M. Git. 9. 9.

[2]) Compare Mech. of R. Shimeon ben Yochai (ed. Hoffman), p. 111, on Ex. 20. 14.

[3]) Compare Sifra on 19. 12 (88c). For the types of vows which are binding see M. Ned. 1.

[4]) Compare Sifra on 19. 36 (91a) and b. B.M. 49a.

concerning oaths are based on two separate yet related laws of the Books of Moses.

δ) Dt. 19.21 states the rule of lex talionis: "eye for eye, tooth for tooth etc."

The exposition is in connection with Pr. 20. 22: "Say not thou: 'I will requite evil' [compare Matt. 5. 38 "But I say unto you that 'ye resist no evil' "] in reference to the law of torts, "Diverse weights are an abomination to Yahweh and a false balance is not good" [Pr. 20. 23 compare Lev. 19. 35, 36]. Thus, Jesus teaches one should not judge in accordance with the strict letter of the law (the rule of lex talionis) but instead one should resort to a solution beyond the reach of the law [לִפְנִים מְשׁוּרַת הַדִּין, see Mech. (67b) on Ex. 18. 20] in the following civil cases: a) bodily damages [Matt. 5. 39, cf. M.B.K. 8. 6], b) property damages [Matt. 5. 40 cf. Mech., Kaspa, (102b) on 22. 25], c) forced labours [Matt. 5. 41 cf. M.B.M. 7. 1 (workers); M. ib. 6. 5], and d) withholding loans [Matt. 5. 42, cf. Sifra, Kedoshim, on 19. 18 (89a)].

The above analysis of part c leads to the following conclusions: a) The author of the Gospel acc. to Matthew presents illustrations to the introductory note on the fulfilment of the law. b) These explanations introduce measures of precaution in reference to the Decalogue and 'lex talionis' in conjunction with related Scriptures. c) The type of interpretation is in the form of expository Midrash [1]).

Part d of the Sermon on the Mount exhibits a different feature which appears to be a type of a pericope-homily. The homily opens with the pericope Lev. 19. 18: "Thou shalt love thy neighbour" and is followed with the teaching: "Thou shalt love thy enemy" which is based on two reasons. a) This is the way of God who also shows His love to both just and unjust. b) To love only a friend is of no credit for it is the natural reaction of everyman. To the teaching: one should adopt the way of God [compare Sifre Deut. § 49 (p. 85a) on 11. 12], a related teaching is added: "to be perfect even as your Father which is in heaven is perfect". To illustrate the virtue of perfection three groups of three examples [2]) each are presented. It then concludes with a definition of the opening verse: "Therefore all things whatsoever ye would that men should do to you, do ye even so to

---

[1]) For exposition on harlot's hire (Deut. 23. 19) attributed to Jesus and not found in the Gospels, see b. A.Z. 17a, which follows the opinion of the Hillelites (b. B.K. 94a).

[2]) On the triads employed by the author see I.C.C. Matthew, Introduction.

them: for this is the Law and the Prophets". Thus, the structure
betrays a pericope homily; beginning with the Pentateuchal verse,
declaring a moral and ethical teaching, and concluding with an interpretation of the opening verse. Comparing the Sermon on the Mount
with the Sermon on the Plain we can reconstruct the original pericope-
homily. Both sermons begin with the beatitudes which was shown to
have been based on a proem-homily preached at Nazareth. Matthew
continues with an introductory note on the fulfilment of the law and
follows with an expository Midrash which is lacking in Luke. In the
latter only the exposition on Ex. 21. 24 is introduced to the homily on
Lev. 19. 18. Similarly in the homily of the Sermon on the Mount two
teachings are inserted: a) the form of prayer with the explanation of
forgiveness which is to be included in the prayer [Matt. 6. 9-15 but
Luk. 11. 1-4 and Mk. 11. 25, 26 in a different arrangement]. b) on
materialistic worries with illustrations [Matt. 6. 25-34 but Luk. 12.
21-31]. Yet, from the contents of the parallel sermons the following
homily is to be reconstructed:

Ye have heard that it hath been said[1]): Lev. 19. 18 "thou shalt love
thy neighbour"—from which may be derived [2]): "hate thine enemy".

But I say unto you[3]): "Love your enemies, bless them . . ., pray for
them . . .". Two reasons are given:

> a) "That ye may be the children of your Father which is in
> heaven: for He is kind unto the unthankful and to the evil [4]).
> b) "For if ye love them which love you, what reward have ye?
> do not even the publicans (do) the same?"
> a derivative of a): "Therefore be ye perfect (merciful) as
> your Father [5]) . . .".

The acts of perfection are outlined in negative and positive teachings
with formulas (italicized) for each. On alms:

The negative teaching: "When thou doest thine alms do not sound
the trumpet before thee . . .

---

[1]) A rabbinic formula, הֲרֵי הוּא אוֹמֵר, see e.g. M. Ned. 10. 7.

[2]) The method of exposition is known as מְעוּט (exclusion). Similarly Matt.
22. 32 according to J. W. Doeve, J. Hermeneutics, p. 106, compare b. Sanh. 90b.

[3]) A rabbinic formula אֲבָל אֲנִי אוֹמֵר לְךָ see II A.D.N. XIII (p. 16a); see further
Abrahams, Studies I, p. 16. This formula introduces an antithesis, whereas
שׁוֹמֵעַ אֲנִי introduces a thesis, as found in the Rabbinic halachic Midrashim.

[4]) Compare Mech. on 18. 12 (67a).

[5]) Compare Sifre Deut. § 49 (85a) on 11. 22 "to walk in His ways" is explained
"as He is merciful so ye should be etc.".

Verily I say unto you [1]): *they have their reward.*

The positive teaching: based on negative formulation	"But when thou doest alms, let not thy left hand know what thy right hand doeth. . . *and thy Father which seeth in secret shall reward thee openly*" [2]).
	On prayer:
the negative teaching:	"When thou prayest, thou shalt not be like the heathens . . . *Verily I say unto you: they have their reward.*"
the positive teaching:	"But when thou prayest, enter into thy closed chamber . . . *And thy Father which seeth in secret shall reward thee openly*".
	On fasting:
the negative teaching:	"When ye fast, be not like the hypocrites of a sad countenance . . . *Verily I say unto you: they have their reward*".
the positive teaching:	"But when thou fastest, anoint thine head and wash thy face . . . *And thy Father which seeth in secret shall reward thee openly*".

Take heed what ye hear: introduces a popular gnomic saying found in rabbinic sources [3]): "With what measure ye mete, it shall be measured to you". Therefore: "Give, and it shall be given unto you, good measure"—another explanation of perfectness in dealings with one's fellowmen. Three parables are given:

The first parable [4]):	"Can the blind lead the blind? shall they not both fall into a ditch? the disciple is not above his master: but everyone that is perfect shall be his master."
The second parable [5]):	"How canst thou say to thy brother:

---

[1]) אָמֵן וְאָמֵן or Amen denotes a form of a vow or assurance, see b. Sheb. 36a and Billerbeck, Kommentar I, p. 242. Similar terms for assurance in reference to teachings are used by the early Rabbis as "Heaven", T. Hul. 2. 24 (503. 25); "Abode" (the Temple), M. Ket. 2. 9; "The Covenant" (refers to the Torah, the covenant with Israel, T. Pea. 3. 2) see T. Hal. 1. 6 (97. 25) and "I attest by the Heaven" in a letter of Bar-Kosiba, see Discoveries in the Judean Desert II (Oxford, 1961), p. 160.

[2]) See Sifra on 19. 37 (91a).

[3]) Mech. on 13. 19 (30a) and Sifre Num. § 106 (28b) compare Mk. 4. 24, 25.

[4]) Introduced in Luk. 6. 39 with the statement "And he spoke a parable unto them" which is found in Matt. 15. 14 on the question regarding the washing of the hands—lacking in Mk. 7. 1 ff.

[5]) Compare b. Ara. 16b (R. Tarfon).

'brother let me pull out the mote that is in thine eye', when thou thyself beholdest not the beam that is in thine own eye? Thou hypocrite cast out first the beam out of thine own eye, and then shalt thou see clearly to pull the mote that is in thy brother's eye".

The third parable [1]:   "For a good tree bringeth not forth corrupt fruit, neither doth a corrupt tree bringeth forth good fruit . . . A good man out of the good treasures of his heart bringeth forth that which is good, and an evil man out of the evil treasure of his heart bringeth forth that which is evil [2])".

The closing statement is an interpretation of the opening verse [3]), "And as ye would that men should do to you, do ye also to them likewise".

Part e of the Sermon on the Mount compared with the Sermon on the Plain contains a parable on the two types of disciples [4]). The one who hears and does is likened to a house built on a rock, the other who hears and does not is likened to a house built on sand. A similar parable, that of the sower, [Matt. 13. 1-23, Mk. 4. 1-20, Luk. 8. 1-18] presented by Jesus demonstrates four types of a disciple. One who hears and does not understand is likened to seeds planted on the road; the second who hears, yet circumstances can uproot his teachings, is likened to seeds sowed between the rocks; the third who hears and is persuaded by the riches of the world is likened to seeds among the thorns, and the fourth who hears and understands is likened to seeds planted in good ground. The early Pharisees [5]) also used common objects from daily life to demonstrate four types of discipleship. Rabban Gamliel I, a contemporary of Paul, employs the parable of the fish [I A.D.N. 40 (p. 64 a)]. In this respect one phase of the Kingdom of Heaven is to be explained with the identical term

---

[1]) Compare J. Pea. 15b, 16a (Munbaz, the converted king).
[2]) Luk. 6. 43, 45, compare Matt. 7. 16, 17 and ib. 12. 33, 34, which adds "of the abundance of his heart" as found in Luk. 6. 45. See also Luk. 11. 24 ff and Mk. 3. 25 ff.
[3]) Compare b. Shab. 31a (Hillel). Sifra on Lev. 19. 18 (89b)—R. Aqiba.
[4]) Compare Ab. 3. 17.
[5]) Ab. 5. 12 and I A.D. N. 40 (64a).

מַלְכוּת שָׁמַיִם employed by the Rabbis [1]) which meant "the sovereignty of God", i.e., the acceptance of the Jewish precepts. In the same sense Jesus demonstrated the types of disciples who can receive the Kingdom of Heaven, i.e., the teachings of Jesus on Theocracy.

THE YELAMMEDENU-HOMILY AS PRESERVED IN THE SYNOPTIC GOSPELS

Along with the weekly readings of the Pentateuch and the customary pericope-homily there also existed a tradition whereby to acquaint the people with the Jewish religion the preacher would deliver expositions on the important festival months as to the regulations and laws concerning the holiday. In later times, this type of a homily was called Yelammedenu (teach us, O master) [2]) based on the opening remark made by the members of the synagogue to the teacher which was customary on any Sabbath day [3]). The rabbinic tradition [b. Meg. 32a, J. Meg. 75a and Sifra on Lev. 33. 44 (103a)] states: "Moses (thereby referring to a pre-Destruction practice) made the following innovation in Israel that they should ask and expound (שׁוֹאֲלִין וְדוֹרְשִׁין) on the topic of the day; the laws of Passover on Passover, the laws of Pentecost on Pentecost and the laws of Tabernacles on Tabernacles". We find a very fine example of a Yelammedenu homily dating from the early days of Hillel's ministry (c. 34 B.C.). It is related [T. Pes. 4. 12 (162, 21-163. 4), b. Pes. 66a and J. Pes. 33a] that Hillel was confronted by the leaders of Bathyra on the Sabbath day which also occurred on the day of Slaughtering the Paschal Lamb. They posed the following

---

[1]) As explained in Deut. R. on 3. 23 (p. 60). Yet the Rabbis also refer to the Kingdom of Heaven as an actual manifestation of God's presence on earth after the elimination of the heathen rule. See Cant. R. on 2. 13 (p. 125): הִגִּיעַ זְמַנָּה שֶׁל מַלְכוּת

כִּיתִים שֶׁתִּכְלֶה, הִגִּיעַ זְמַנָה שֶׁל מַלְכוּת שָׁמַיִם שֶׁתִּגָּלֶה, in reference to Zech. 14.9. The Targum renders: וְתִתְגְּלֵי מַלְכוּתָא דַיְיָ (Kingdom of God) as found in the prayer (S. Baer, Abodath Israel, p. 132): וִיקַבְּלוּ כֻלָּם אֶת־עוֹל מַלְכוּתֶךָ. These are also the expectations of the Teacher of Righteousness in the scroll of "the War" ed. Yadin, cols. 1. 6; 19. 6, 2; compare Midrash on Samuel ed. S. Buber, p. 42a, in the name of R. Simeon ben Yochai.

[2]) The same form is found in the Hindu literature such as the Upanishads "ahīhi bhogavo" (teach me, sir).

[3]) Examples of Yelammedenu homilies are found in Tanhumas, Pesiqtas and in Deut. R. The formula begins simply with "Halachah" quoting the Jewish law. See further J. Mann. op. cit., p. 13, who explains that the choice of Halachah was based on the days reading, thereby demonstrating the unity of oral and written Tradition.

question, "Can the Paschal lamb be slaughtered on the Sabbath (a day which requires a complete abstention from any laborious act)?" He then proceeded to show by use of three modes of hermeneutics that it is permissible to do the rites on the Sabbath. In the conclusion, he listed the opinion of his teachers, Shemayah and Abtalion, the authorized Halachah as proof, and as a result he was appointed head of the community. The account also includes, "Then he continued in his delivery of exposition (וְהָיָה דוֹרֵשׁ) concerning the Passover throughout the day".

From the above account it can be concluded that the yelammedenu homily was in use as early as the beginning of the Schools of Exposition. The yelammedenu homily contained the following features: 1) A question pertaining to the reading posed by the leaders of the congregation. 2) An answer delivered by the teacher which, in most cases, was based on proof derived from the application of hermeneutics (Midrash) and the authorized opinion of the Rabbis (Halachah).

The Gospels list five cases dealing with the violation of the Sabbath in which Jesus with a yelammedenu homily explains the justification of work on Sabbath based on the use of hermeneutics.

Case A [Matt. 12. 1-8, Mk. 2. 23-28, Luk. 6. 1-5]:

Plucking the ears of corn on the Sabbath.

Question posed by the Pharisees: "Behold, thy disciples do that which is not lawful to do upon the Sabbath day" (since "plucking" (הַתּוֹלֵשׁ) a minor act under the head of work "harvesting", is prohibited (J. Shab. 9c)).

The reply is based on syllogism [Matt. 12. 3-7]: a) Since David in time of hunger ate the shewbread which is unlawful for a non-priest to eat [see I Sam. 21. 7, the Haftarah] surely in this case the minor act of plucking is permitted in time of hunger. b) Since the priests may prepare the sacrifices on the Sabbath (Num. 28. 9, see Sifre Num. § 143 (54a), the reading on the New Moon (Meg. 21b)) a major violation, surely this minor act is permitted. The association with the day's reading is noted by Abrahams, op. cit., I p. 11. An added interpretation is recorded in Luke and Mark based on Ex. 31. 14, "Ye shall keep the Sabbath for it is holy unto you", since the Sabbath was sanctified for the people, therefore Jesus concludes: "The Sabbath was made for man and not man for the Sabbath" [compare Mech., Ki Tissa, (p. 109b)].

Case B: Healing a man who had a withered hand on the Sabbath in the synagogue. [Matt. 12. 9-13, Mk. 3. 1-6, Luk. 6. 6-11].

The question posed by the scribes and the Pharisees: "Is it lawful to heal on the Sabbath day?"

The reply is based on syllogism (as found in Matt.): Since it is permissible to rescue a domestic animal which falls into a pit on the Sabbath (the Pharisaic teachers permitted assisting at the birth of a calf on the Sabbath [M. Shab. 18. 3], and assisting the animal to rescue herself [b. Shab. 128b], although the Essene teachers prohibited the rescue of a domestic animal [C.D. 11. 13]) surely a man is better than a domestic animal.

The reading in Luke and Mark is based on an accepted ruling arising from the school of Shemayah and Abtalion [b. Yom. 35b]: "Is it lawful to save life or to let it die on the Sabbath day?". The question would be answered that in case of life or death work is permitted on the Sabbath according to the Pharisaic ruling. Jesus cites here as proof the accepted Halachah, the normal procedure of a Yelammedenu Homily.

Case C: Curing a woman [Luk. 13. 10-17] or a man [John 5. 1-16, which also mentions the violation of carrying on the Sabbath (v. 8, 12 see M. Shab. 6. 8. The question, "if the lamed can carry his wooden stump on the Sabbath", was debated by the disciples of R. Aqiba)] of a prolonged sickness of paralysis on the Sabbath.

The head of the congregation presented the following argument (similarly presented by the school of Hillel in a different case; see T. Shab. 1. 21 (111.13)): It is written, Ex. 31.15, "There are six days in which men ought to do work", therefore, only on these days may one heal, a form of work, but not on the Sabbath. Ex. 31. 1 ff is a pericope.

The reply is based on a simile: As on the Sabbath it is permitted to untie the ox or the ass to lead him to water (that is, one may not lead the animal by rope to drink on Sabbath, but he is permitted to untie her so she can pursue water herself; see M. Shab. 5. 4) so the manner of healing is similar to untying the bonds of the sick, but not a form of work. The reply in John 7. 22, 23 is based on syllogism: "Moses gave unto you circumcision [Lev. 12. 3] and ye on the Sabbath day circumcise a man [see M. Shab. 19. 2], an operation made but on one limb, surely an operation to save a whole human being is permissible" (compare the yelammedenu homily, Tanhuma (regular edition) Jethro. 8, and ed. Buber, p. 91a, based on Mech. on 31. 13 (109b)). Lev. 12. 1 ff is a pericope.

Case D [Luk. 14. 1-6]: Healing a man suffering from dropsy on the
   Sabbath. The reply is identical with the explanation in case B
   recorded in Matt.
Case E [John 9. 13 ff]: Healing a blind man which occurs on the
   Sabbath. No explanation is given.
   Another Yelammedenu homily recorded in Mk. 10. 1-15 and Matt.
19. 1-12 was delivered in connection with the law of divorce [Deut.
24. 1]. In this manner "he taught them" [Mk. 10. 1] at the coasts of
Judea on the way to Jerusalem.
   The question posed by the Pharisees, which was debated in the
academies [M. Git. 9. 10], is: "Is it lawful for a man to put away his
wife?"
   The reply is based on the analogy of two verses: Gen. 1. 27,"(God)
created them male and female", and Gen. 2. 24,"Therefore a man leaves
his father and mother and cleaves to his wife". As demonstrated above,
pp. 161, 164, the reply was:"What God hath joined together, let no
man put asunder".
   In all the four Gospels there is a frequent mention of synagogue
preaching [Matt. 4. 23, 9. 35, Mk. 1. 21, 39, Luk. 4. 15, 44, John 6. 59]
on the Sabbath [Mk. 1. 3 Luk. 4. 16, 31, 13. 10]. In some accounts
the teaching in the synagogue on the Sabbath is presented [Mk.
3. 1-5, a yelammedenu-homily; Luk. 4. 16-21, a proem-homily and
John 6. 32-59, a pericope-homily]. Thus, it can be assumed that Jesus
preached in the manner of the Pharisees, that is with the homiletic
tools of pesher and hermeneutics in the form of proem-homily,
pericope-homily and yelammedenu-homily.

SOME OF JESUS' TEACHINGS BASED ON HERMENEUTICS [1])

   Jesus taught: "O ye of little faith? worry not ye what ye shall eat or
what ye shall drink . . . Be therefore not worried for tomorrow" [Matt.
6. 30c, 31, 34, Luk. 12. 28c, 29]—a teaching demonstrated also by the
Pharisaic R. Eleazer of Modin (c. 70-135 A.D.). "Ex. 16. 4 states:
'Yahweh spoke to Moses: Behold I will cause bread to rain from
heaven for you: and the people shall go out and gather a day's portion
every day'. This teaches us that anyone who has what to eat to day
and says what shall I eat tomorrow, that one is lacking faith; as it also
states [passim]: "that I may. prove them whether they will walk in
My law or not'" (see Mech. ad loc.). Jesus illustrates the teaching

---
[1]) See Doeve, J. Hermeneutics.

with a syllogism [Matt. 6. 30, Luk. 12. 28] "*If* God so clothed the grass of the field which today is and tomorrow is cast unto the oven, *how much more* (He shall clothe) you?" The rabbinic formula for Aggadic syllogism is: *If* × *how much more* (עַל אַחַת כַּמָּה וְכַמָּה ... אִם) [1]). So do the Rabbis (Pesiqta 14 (p. 122b)), in reference to the death of Zecharia (see p. 142) and the revenge taken by Nebuzaradan, explain: "(God) said: '*If* this one (Nebuzaradan) who is of flesh and blood ... who to day is here and tomorrow he is not, was filled with pity for My son (Zechariah), I of whom it is written, Deut. 4. 31, 'For Yahweh thy God is a merciful God '*how much more*' ". Similar formulation is attributed to R. Jochanan ben Zakkai [b. Ber. 28b].

Jesus taught [Matt. 7. 7, Luk. 11. 9] [2]): "Ask and it shall be given you, seek and ye shall find, knock and it shall be opened unto you". The Rabbis [Lev. R. 5 on 4. 15 (p. 74)] compare the one who prays and obtains favour from his Creator to those who are clever at obtaining alms, or to a woman who knocks on her neighbour's door to borrow, or to a tenant who asks for a loan. Jesus illustrates the teaching with a syllogism [Matt. 7. 11, Luk. 11. 13]: "*If* ye then being evil know how to give good gifts unto your children, *how much more* shall your Father which is in heaven give good [3]) (things) to them that ask Him?" Similarly R. Simeon in the name of R. Eliezer (c. 250 A.D.) [Lev. R. 34 on 25. 25 (p. 432)] states in reference to Abraham who received the angels [Gen. 18. 8]: "Now does not this afford a deduction a minori ad maius? *If* in the case of one who showed kindness (Abraham) to those who did not need kindness (the angels) the Holy One blessed be He rewarded his children (they inherited the land of Canaan), *how much more* in the case of one who shows kindness to one who needs it?"—surely God will enrich him.

Comparison of two subjects is applied to aggadic material as in the question of Messiahship. R. Berechia states in the name of R. Levi (c. 280 A.D.) [Num. R. on XI. 2 (p. 413)] a premise: "As it was with the first redeemer (Moses) so it will be with the last redeemer (Messiah), as the first redeemer appeared to them and then he was concealed from them — R. Tunḥuma in the name of R. Ḥama (c. 300 A.D.) clarifies — for the duration of six months" [see Ex. R. 5 on 5.10 (p. 99). After Moses had appeared in Egypt to free the Israelites and failed,

---

[1]) On the formula see Billerbeck, Kommentar, III p. 225.
[2]) In Luk. the teaching follows a demonstration of prayer.
[3]) Lk. reads כְּדֵי רוּחָא for Matt. טִיבוּתָא.

he then left for Midian for six months]. So it will be with the last redeemer, i.e., the Messiah will be concealed for a duration of time and then he shall reappear. In the same manner, the Rabbis [Gen. R. 56 on 22. 4 (p. 595 cf. p. 1129)] explain Hos. 6. 2, "After two days will He revive us; on the third day He will raise us up", to denote that redemption will arrive after the passing of three days as it was on the third day in the time of Jonah [Jon. 2. 1]: "and Jonah was in the belly of the fish three days and three nights". Thus Matthew [12. 40] attributed to Jesus a comparison of subjects, comparing the event in the days of Jonah and at the time of the "son of man" [see Dan. 7. 13, the designated redeemer]. "For as 'Jonas was three days and three nights in the whale's belly' so shall the son of man be three days and three nights in the heart of the earth", i.e., concealed from the people and then "on the third day he shall arise" [see Matt. 20. 19]. Luke 11. 30, on the other hand, reads: "For as Jonah was a sign unto the Ninevites so shall the son of man be to his generation", which is further illustrated in Luke 11. 32 [so Matt. 12. 41]: "The men of Nineveh shall rise up in the Judgement with this generation and shall condemn it: for they repented at the preaching of Jonah [Jon. 3. 5] and *greater is this* (situation) than Jonah's".

Analogy of words is applied by the Rabbis [Sifra, Kedoshim (p. 91a), on 19. 34] to "And thou shalt love him (the stranger or proselyte) as thyself" and to 19. 18, "Thou shalt love thy neighbour as thyself". Since in both cases the expression is "thou shalt love", therefore, respect the feelings of a stranger or a proselyte because you (the Israelites) were also strangers in Egypt. In the same manner Jesus' reply to the question [Matt. 22. 34-30, Mk. 12. 28-34, Luk. 10.25-37]: "Teacher, which is the first [1]) commandment in the Law?" is based on analogy of words. It is written in Deut. 6. 5: "Thou shalt love thy God with all thy heart and with all thy soul and with all thy mind" [Massora: מְאֹדֶךָ (might), Gospels read: מַדָּעֲךָ (mind)]. This is the first and great commandment, and it is also written Lev. 19. 18: "Thou shalt love thy neighbour as thyself". The exact application of the words "thou shalt love" is found in both commandments and as love to God is a principle so is love to man, therefore: "On these two commandments rest all the Law and Prophets".

Luke 17. 3 reads: "If thy brother trespass against thee rebuke him and if he repent, forgive him". The rule of rebuke and forgiveness

---

[1]) Luk. reads רֵישָׁא, Matt. רַבָּא.

is stated in Lev. 19. 17 as follows: "Thou shalt not hate thy brother in thy heart: thou shalt surely rebuke (הוֹכֵחַ תּוֹכִיחַ) thy neighbour, and not bear sin because of him". The presentation of the verb יכח in two forms, the infinitive absolutus הוֹכֵחַ and the Hiph'il (causative) imperfect, indicates emphasis or as the Rabbis maintained [1]) it points to extra instruction. "If you have rebuked him even four or five times (and he did not listen) rebuke him again". In the same manner Jesus teaches [Luk. 17. 4, Matt. 18. 22]: "And if he trespass against thee seven times in a day, and seven times in a day turn again to thee (i.e. upon rebuke) saying I repent, thou shalt forgive him". Thus, Jesus applies the same rule to rebuking as well as to forgiving.

With the application of hermeneutics to the Scriptures Jesus, as well as the Rabbis, arrived at certain conclusions. These conclusions in form of teachings became the inherited precepts of the Christians and the Jews; the Jews drawing their religious knowledge from the Tannaitic Writings and the Christians from the Gospels.

---

[1]) Sifra on 19. 17 (89a) and b. B.M. 31a.

BIBLIOGRAPHY

I. Sources (including translations)

a) *Old and New Testaments*

Authorized (King James) version of the New Testament.
Biblia Hebraica, ed. R. Kittel and P. Kahle, 7 ed. Stuttgart, 1961.
Biblia Sacra Juxta Versionem Simplicem quae dictur Pschitta, Mosul, 1887.
Habrith Hachadashah (The Hebrew New Testament), translated by F. Deilitzch, rep. London, 1954.
The Holy Scriptures According to the Masoretic text, A New Translation, Jewish Publication Society, Philadelphia, 1945.
Novum Testamentum Graece cum apparatu critico, Eberhard et Erwin Nestle, 20 ed., Stuttgart, 1950.
Prophetae Chaldaice, ed. Paulus De Lagarde, Leipzig, 1872.
Pseudo-Jonathan (Thargum Jonathan ben Usiel zum Pentateuch) nach der Londoner Handschrift, ed. M. Ginsburger, Berlin, 1903.
Septuaginta, ed. A. Rahlfs, Stuttgart, 1935.
Targum Onkelos, ed. A. Berliner, Berlin, 1884.

b) *Apocrypha and Pseudepigrapha*

The Apocrypha and Pseudepigrapha of the Old Testament, ed. R. H. Charles. Oxford, 1913.
Hasepharim Haḥiṣonim, ed. A. Kahana, 2ed. Israel, 1956.
M. Z. Segal, Sepher Ben-Sira Hashalem, Jerusalem, 1953.
S. Zeitlin and S. Tedesche, The First Book of Maccabees, Dropsie College, 1950.

c) *Philo, Josephus and Eusebius*

Eusebius, Kirchengeschichte, ed. E. Schwartz, 5ed. Berlin/Leipzig, 1952.
Josephus, with an English Translation by H.St.J. Thackeray, The Loeb Classical Library:
    Vol. I: The Life, Against Apion, 2ed. London/Cambridge, Mass., 1956.
    Vol. II-III: The Jewish War, 2ed. London/Cambridge, Mass., 1956/57.
    Vol. IV-VII: Jewish Antiquities (Book I-XIV), 2ed. London/Cambridge, Mass., 1957.
Des Flavius Josephus Jüdische Altertümer, übersetzt ... v. Heinrich Clementz, 2 vol., Berlin/Vienna, 1923.
Philo, with an English Translation by F. H. Colson and G. H. Whitaker, The Loeb Classical Library, London, 1956.
J. N. Simchoni, Toledoth Milḥemeth Hayehudim 'im Haroma' im, Tel-Aviv, 1956.
A. Shalit, Kadmoniyoth Hayehudim, 2 vol., 2ed. Israel, 1955.

d) *Qumran and other texts*

J. M. Allegro, The Treasure of the Copper Scroll, 1960.
U. Cassuto, The Goddess Anath: Canaanite Epics of the Patriarchal Age. Texts, Hebrew Translation, Commentary and Introduction, Jerusalem, 1951.
A. E. Cowley, Aramaic Papyri of the Fifth Century B. C., Oxford, 1923.
The Dead Sea Scrolls of St. Mark's Monastery, vol. I: The Isaiah Manuscript and the Habakkuk Commentary, ed. M. Burrows, New Haven, 1950.

Discoveries in the Judean Desert I, ed. D. Barthélemy and J. T. Milik, Oxford, 1955; II, ed. P. Benoit, J. T. Milik and R. de Vaux, 1961.
G. R. Driver, Aramaic Documents of the Fifth Century B.C., Oxford, 1956.
A Genesis Apocryphon, A Scroll from the Wilderness of Judea, ed. N. Avigad and Y. Yadin, Jerusalem, 1956.
A. M. Haberman, Megilloth Midbar Yehudah (The Scrolls from the Judean Desert), Israel, 1959.
J. Licht, The Thanksgiving Scroll, Jerusalem, 1957.
J. B. Pritchard, Ancient Near Eastern Texts Relating to the Old Testament, 2ed., Princeton, N. J., 1955.
Ch. Rabin, The Zadokite Documents, Oxford, 1954.
A. Ungnad, Aramäische Papyrus aus Elephantine, Leipzig, 1911.
Y. Yadin, Megillath Milchemeth Bney Choshekh bibney 'Or (The Scroll of War of the Sons of Light against the Sons of Darkness), Jerusalem, 1957.

e) *Rabbinic Texts*

Abudirahim, D. Sefer Abudraham (Commentary to the Prayer Book and Rituals), pr. Sdilikow, 1818.
Abodath Israel, ed. S. Baer, Rödelheim, 1901. A German translation of the Eighteen Benedictions in P. Riessler, Altjüdisches Schrifttum ausserhalb der Bibel, Ausgburg, 1928.
Aboth de Rabbi Nathan (2 recensions), ed. S. Schechter Vienna, 1886; English Translation by J. Goldin, New-Haven, 1955.
Bereschit Rabba mit kritischem Apparat und Kommentar v. J. Theodor, vol. I, Berlin, 1912 and Ch. Albeck, vol. II (1927), III (1929).
Beth Hamidrash, Sammlung kleiner Midrashim und vermischter Abhandlungen aus der älteren jüdischen Literatur, ed. A. Jellenik, 4 vol. Leipzig, 1853 ff; Parts are translated in German by A. Wünsche, Aus Israels Lehrhallen, Leipzig, 1907.
Cosri of R. Jehudah Halevi, ed. J. Ruxtorfius, with Latin Translation, Basileae.
Genizah Studies, ed. L. Ginzberg, 2 Vol., New York, 1928, 1929.
Mechilta . . . according to R. Ishmael, ed. I. H. Weiss, Vienna, 1865, English Translation by J. Z. Lauterbach, 3 vol. Philadelphia, 1949.
Mechilta de Rabbi Simeon b. Yochai, ed. D. Hoffmann, Frankfurt a. M., 1905.
Megillath Ta'anith, ed. A. Neubauer in Medieval Jewish Chronicles II, Oxford, 1895. German Translation in P. Riessler, Altjüdisches Schrifttum ausserhalb der Bibel, Augsburg, 1928.
Midrash Hagadol to Genesis and Exodus, ed. M. Margolioth, Jerusalem, 1947-56.
Midrash Psalms (Midrash Tehillim or Shoḥar Tob), ed. S. Buber, Vilna, 1891.
Midrash Rabbah, 2 vol. Vilna, 1887. English Translation with notes, glossary and indices under the editorship of H. Freedman and M. Simon, 10 vol., London, Soncino Press, 2ed. 1951.
Midrash Samuel ed. S. Buber, Cracow. 1893.
Midrash Tanḥuma (ordinary edition), pr. New York-Berlin, 1927.
Midrash Tanḥuma, ein agadischer Kommentar zum Pentateuch, ed. S. Buber, Vilna, 1885.
Midrash Tannaim, ed. D. Hoffmann, Berlin, 1908.
Mishnayoth, repr. Berlin, 1925.
Mishneh Torah or Yad Haḥazaqah of Maimonides. A Photocopy of Roman Ms. (5240), pr. Israel, 5715 (1955).
Oṣar Hage'onim, ed. B. M. Levin, Israel, 5688 (1928-)
Oṣar Midrashim: a Library of 200 Minor Midrashim, ed. J. D. Eisenstein, New York, 1928.

Pesiqta Rabbati, ed. M. Friedmann, Vienna, 1880.
Pesiqta de Rabbi Kahana, ed. S. Buber, Lyck, 1868. German Translation by
    A. Wünsche, Leipzig, 1885.
Pirqe Rabbi Eliezer with commentary by D. Luria, pr. New York, 1946.
Seder Eliyahu Rabba and Seder Eliyahu Zuṭa, ed. M. Friedmann, 2ed. Jerusalem,
    1960.
Seder Olam Rabba, ed. A. Neubauer in Medieval Jewish Chronicles II, Oxford,
    1895.
Sifra debe Rab to Leviticus with a commentary by Abraham ben David, ed. I. H.
    Weiss, Vienna, 1862.
Sifre debe Rab, der älteste halachische und hagadische Midrasch zu Numeri und
    Deuteronomium, ed. M. Friedmann, Vienna, 1864. German Translation to
    Sifre Numeri ed. K. G. Kuhn, Stuttgart, 1954 and to Sifre Deuteronomium
    by G. Kittel, Stuttgart, 1922.
Sifre Zuṭa to Numeri, ed. S. Horovitz, Breslau, 1917.
Talmud Babli pr. Vilna, 1927. English Translation, with notes, glossary and indi-
    ces under the editorship of I. Epstein, London, 1928-1952; (in this work
    the text is compared with Rabbinovicz, Variae Lectiones).
Talmud Yerushalmi, ed. princeps Venice, 5282 (1522), rep. 1925.
Tosefta nach den Erfurter und Wiener Handschriften, ed. M.S. Zuckermandel I,
    Pasewalk, 1881, II, Trier, 1882.
Yam shel Shlomo, Baba Kamma—of S. Luria, 1st pr. 1615.
Yalqut Shim'oni, 2 vol., pr. Jerusalem, 5712 (1952).
Yosippon ed. princeps Venice 1543, ed. Hominer, Jerusalem, 1956.

II. Aids

(Dictionaries, Concordances, Commentaries and Grammers)

W. Bacher, Die exegetische Terminologie der jüdischen Traditionsliteratur II:
    Der Bibel und traditionsexegetische Terminologie der Amoräer, Leipzig,
    1905.
P. Billerbeck, Kommentar zum neuen Testament aus Talmud und Midrash,
    2ed., 5 vol., Munich, 1956.
A Concordance to the Greek Testament ed. W. F. Moulton and A. S. Geden,
    Edinburgh, 1957.
A Concordance to the Septuagint ed. E. Hatch and H. A. Redpath, Oxford, 1897.
G. Dalman, Grammatik des jüdisch-palästinischen Aramäisch, rep. Darmstadt,
    1960.
Eliezer ben Yehudah, A Complete Dictionary of Ancient and Modern Hebrew,
    Jerusalem.
Gesenius' Hebrew Grammer as edited E. Kautzsch, 2. Eng. ed. by A. E. Cowley.
    Oxford, rep. 1960.
J. Hastings' A Dictionary of the Bible, 5 vol., Edinburgh, 1898-1904.
A Greek-English Lexicon compiled by H. G. Liddell and R. Scott, A new edition
    revised by H. S. Jones, Oxford, rep. 1953.
The International Critical Commentary to the Old and New Testaments.
M. Jastrow, A Dictionary of the Targumim, the Talmud Babli and Yerushalmi
    and the Midrashic Literature, 2 vol. New York, 1950.
Ch. J. Kassowsky, Concordantiae Totius Mishnae, 2 vol. Frankfurt a.M., 1927,
idem, Thesaurus Tosephthae, Jerusalem 1932 ff.
idem, Thesaurus Talmudus, Jerusalem 1954 ff.
A. Kohut, Arukh ha-shalem . . . Arukh Completum, 8 vol. and supplement, Vienna,
    1878-1892.

S. Krauß, Griechische und lateinische Lehnwörter in Talmud, Midrash und Targum, 2 vol., Berlin, 1898, 99.

J. Lichtenstein, Kommentar zum Matthäus Evangelium, Leipzig, 1913.

Maimonides, Commentary to the Mishnah, printed in Vilna, 1927 edition.

S. Mandelkern, Veteris Testamenti Concordantiae Hebraicae atque Chalidaicae, 2 vol., Graz, 1955.

C. C. Montefiore, The Synoptic Gospels, 2 vol., 2 ed., London, 1927.

Rashi (R. Solomon Iṣḥaqi), Commentary to the Talmud printed in Vilna, 1927 edition.

M. H. Segal, A Grammer of Mishnaic Hebrew, Oxford, 1927.

Theologisches Wörterbuch zum Neuen Testament, ed. G. Kittel and G. Friedrich, 6 vol., Stuttgart, rep. 1957.

III. Secondary Literature

Abrahams, I., Studies in Pharisaism and the Gospels, 1st series, Cambridge, 1917, 2nd series, Cambridge, 1924.

Albeck, Ch., Das Buch der Jubilaeen und die Halachah, in 47. Bericht der Hochschule für die Wissenschaft des Judentums in Berlin, Berlin, 1930.

——, Mabo Lamishnah (Introduction to the Mishnah), Jerusalem/Tel-Aviv, 1959.

——, Untersuchungen über die Redaktion der Mischna, Berlin, 1923.

Allon, G., Toledoth Hayehudim Be'eretz Yisra'el Bitqufath Hamishnah vehatalmud, 3ed. Israel, 1958.

——, Meḥqarim Betoledoth Yisrael, 2 vol., Israel, 1957.

Bacher, W. Die Agada der babylonischer Amoräer, Strassburg, 1878.

——, Die Agada der Tannaiten I, 2 ed., Strassburg, 1903.

——, Die Agada der palästinischen Amoräer I, Strassburg, 1892, II 1896, III 1899.

——, Die Proömien der alten jüdischen Homilie, Leipzig, 1913.

——, Tradition und Tradenten in den Schulen Palästinas und Babyloniens, Leipzig, 1914.

Baeck, L., Die Pharisäer, Schocken Verlag/6, Berlin 1934.

Baer, S., Über den Geist des Jeruschalmi (Pseudo-Jonathan), M.G.W.J., 1851-52.

Bahrdt, K. F., Ausführung des Plans und Zwecks Jesu, 12 vol., 1784-92.

Baron, S. W., A Social and Religious History of the Jews I: Ancient Times, 2 ed,. New York, 1952.

Bassfreund, J., Der Bann gegen R. Elieser und die veränderte Haltung gegenüber den Schammaiten, M.G.W.J., 42 (1898).

Bickermann, E., Viri Magnae Congregationis, Revue Biblique, 55 (1948).

Bischoff, E., Jesus und die Rabbiner, Leipzig, 1905.

Black, M., An Aramaic Approach to the Gospels and Acts, 2ed., Oxford, 1954.

Blau, L., Bible Canon, J. Enc. III.

Bloch, J. S., Einblicke in die Geschichte der Entwicklung der talmudischen Literatur, Vienna, 1884.

Bousset, W., Die Religion des Judentums im neutestamentlichen Zeitalter, 2 ed., Berlin, 1906.

——, Jesus Predigt in ihrem Gegensatz zum Judentum, Göttingen, 1892.

Buechler, A., Der Galiläische 'Am Ha'ares des zweiten Jahrhunderts, Vienna, 1906.

——, The Reading of the Law and Prophets in a Triennial Cycle, Part I: The Law, J.Q.R.V (1893), Part II: The Prophets, J.Q.R. VI (1894).

——, Studies in Jewish History, ed. I. Brodie and J. Rabbinowitz, Oxford University Press, 1956.

——, Die Tobiaden und die Oniaden im 2. Makkabäerbuch und in der verwandten jüdisch-hellenistischen Literatur, Vienna, 1899.

Burkitt, F. C., Jesus and the Pharisees, Journal of Theological Studies XXVIII, 1927.

Burney, C. F., The Aramaic Origin of the Fourth Gospel, Oxford, 1922.

Burrows, M., More Light on the Dead Sea Scrolls, London, 1958.

Chajes, Z. H., The Student's Guide through the Talmud, English Translation by J. Shachter, London, 1952.

Chwolson, D., Das letzte Passamahl Christi und der Tag seines Todes, 2 ed., Leipzig, 1908.

Dalman, G., Jesu-Jeschua. Die drei Sprachen Jesu: Jesu in der Synagoge, auf dem Berge, beim Passahmahl, am Kreuz, Leipzig, 1922.

——, Orte und Wege Jesu, 3 ed., Gütersloh, 1924.

——, Die Worte Jesu, Leipzig, 1898.

Daube,D,. The New Testament and Rabbinic Judaism, University of London, 1956.

Doeve, J. W., Jewish Hermeneutics in the Synoptic Gospels and Acts, Aasen, 1954.

Drews, A., Die Christusmythe, Jena, 1924.

Elbogen, I., Einige neuere Theorien über den Ursprung der Pharisäer und Sadduzäer, in Jewish Studies in Memory of I. Abrahams, New York, 1927, pp. 135-148.

——, Geschichte des Achtzehngebets, M.G.W.J., 46 (1902).

——, Der jüdische Gottesdienst in seiner geschichtlichen Entwicklung, 2 ed. Frankfort, 1924.

Elbogen, J., Die Religionsanschauungen der Pharisäer, in 220. Bericht über die Lehranstalt für Wissenschaft des Judentums in Berlin, Berlin, 1904.

Englander, M., The Men of the Great Synagogue, H.U.C. Jub. Volume.

Epstein, J. N., Mebu'oth Lasiphruth Hatana'ith (Introduction to Tannaitic Literature, Mishnah, Tosephta and Halachic Midrashim) ed. E.Z. Melamed, Jerusalem/Tel-Aviv, 1957.

Fiebig, P., Die Gleichnisreden Jesu im Lichte der rabbinischen Gleichnisse des neutestamentlichen Zeitalters, Tübingen, 1912.

——, Jesu Bergpredigt: rabbinische Texte zum Verständnis der Bergpredigt, Göttingen, 1924.

——, Jüdische Wundergeschichten des neutestamentlichen Zeitalters, Tübingen 1911.

——, Das Vaterunser, Ursprung, Sinn und Bedeutung des christlichen Hauptgebets, in Beiträge zur Förderung christlicher Theologie, Bd. 30 Heft 3, 1927.

Finch, R. G., The Synagogue Lectionary and New Testament, London, 1939.

Finkelstein, L., The Pharisees: The Sociological Background of Their Faith, 2 vol., Philadelphia, 1946.

——, Haperushim Ve-Anshey Keneseth Hagedolah, New York, 1950.

Frankel, Z., Darkey Hamishnah (Hodegetica in Mischnam) Leipzig, 1859, reprinted Israel, 1959.

——, Die Essäer nach talmudischen Quellen, M.G.W.J. 2 (1853).

——, Mabo Hayerushalmi (Einleitung in den jeruschalmischen Talmud), Breslau, 1870.

——, Über den Lapidarstyl der talmudischen Historik, M.G.W.J. 1851-52.

——, Über den Einfluß der palästinischen Exegese auf die alexandrinische Hermeneutik, Leipzig 1851.

Friedländer, M., Die religiösen Bewegungen innerhalb des Judentums im Zeitalter Jesu, Berlin, 1905.

Fürst, J., Der Kanon des Alten Testaments nach den Überlieferungen in Talmud und Midrasch, Leipzig, 1868.

Gaster, M., Die Ketubbah bei den Samaritanern, M.G.W.J. 54 (1910).

Geiger, A., Das Judentum und seine Geschichte bis zum Zerstörung des zweiten Tempels, 2 ed. Breslau, 1865.

——, Urschrift und Übersetzungen der Bibel, 2 ed. Frankfurt a. M., 1928, Hebrew Translation, Jerusalem, 1949.

Gerhardsson, B., Memory and Manuscript, Uppsala, 1961.

Ginsburg, Ch. D., The Essenes, Their History and Doctrines, reprinted London, 1956.

——, Introduction to the Masoretico—Critical Edition of the Hebrew Bible, London, 1897.

Ginzberg, L., ʿAl Halachah ve-ʾAggadah, Tel-Aviv 1960, English Edition, On Jewish Law and Lore, Philadelphia, 1955.

——, Aquila in rabbinical Literature, J. Enc. II.

——, The Legends of the Jews, Vol. I: From the Creation to Jacob, II: From Joseph to Exodus, III: Moses in the Wilderness, IV: From Joshua to Esther, V: From the Creation to Exodus (Notes), VI: From Moses to Esther (Notes), VII: Index, Philadelphia, 1954.

——, Pirushim Vechidushim Biyerushalmi I, New York, 1941.

Goudoever, J., Biblical Calendars, Leiden, 1959.

Grätz, H., Geschichte der Juden von den ältesten Zeiten bis auf die Gegenwart Leipzig, 1853-1870.

——, Die Große Versammlung (Kenneset-Hagedolah) ihre Geschichtlichkeit, Zahl, Bedeutung, Zeit und Leistung, M.G.W.J. 6 (1857).

——, Sinai et Golgatha, ou les origines du Judaisme et du Christianisme suivi d'un examen critique des Evangiles anciens et modernes, translated by M. Hess, Paris 1867.

——, Über Entwicklung der Pentateuch-Perikopen-Verlesung, M.G.W.J. 18 (1869).

Grant, F. C., The Gospels: Their Origin and Their Growth, London, 1957.

Guilding, A., The Fourth Gospel and Jewish Worship, Oxford, 1960.

Guignebert, Ch., The Jewish World in the Time of Jesus, New York, 1959.

Guttmann, A., Das redaktionelle und sachliche Verhältnis zwischen Mišna und Tosephta, Breslau 1928.

——, Akiba, "Rescurer of the Torah", H.U.C.A. XVII (1942-43).

Haeckel, E., Die Welträthsel, Bonn, 1903.

Haupt. P., The Aryan Ancestry of Jesus, The Open Court vol. XXIII no. 635, 1909.

Heinemann, I., Die Lehre vom Heiligen Geist im Judentum und in den Evangelien, M.G.W.J. 66 (1922), 67 (1923).

Herford, R. T., The Pharisees, London, 1924. German Translation by W. Fischel Leipzig, 1928.

Herr, M. D., The Problem of War on the Sabbath in the Days of the Second Temple (in Hebrew), Tarbiz, 30, 1960/61.

Hirsch, E. G., Sacrifice, J. Enc. X.

Hoenig, S. B., The Great Sanhedrin: A study of the Origin, Development, Composition and Functions of the Bet-Din Ha-gadol during the Second Jewish Commonwealth, Philadelphia, 1953.

Hoffmann, D., Die erste Mishnah und die Controversen der Tannaim, Berlin, 1882.

——, Zur Einleitung in die halachischen Midraschim, in Beiträge zum Jahresbericht des Rabbiner-Seminars zu Berlin, 5647 (1886-87).

Hoschander, J., The Book of Esther in the Light of History, Philadelphia, 1923.

Husband, R. W., The Prosecution of Jesus, Princeton, 1916.

Hyman, A., Toledoth Tannaʾim Veʾamoraʾim, 3 vol., London, 1910.

Jackson, F. J. Foakes, Josephus and the Jews. The Religion and History of the Jews as Explained by Flavius Josephus, London, 1930.

Jacobs, L., The Concept of Hasid in the Biblical and Rabbinic Literature, in Journal of Jewish Studies, vol. VIII (1957).

Jeremias, J., Jerusalem zur Zeit Jesu: Kulturgeschichtliche Untersuchung zur N.T. Zeitgeschichte, 2 ed. Teil I und II, Göttingen, 1958.

Jaubert, A., Le Calendrier des Jubilees, Vetus Testamentum III (1953).

Judaism and Christianity, vol. I: The Age of Transition, ed. W. O. E. Oesterley, London, 1937,
vol. II: The Contact of Pharisaism with Other Cultures, ed. H. Loewe, 1937,
vol. III: Law and Religion, ed. E. I. J. Rosenthal, 1938.

Kahle, P., The Cairo Geniza (Schweich Lectures 1941), London, 1947.

——, Masoreten des Ostens, Leipzig, 1913.

——, Masoreten des Westens I, Stuttgart, 1927, II 1930.

Kalthoff, A., Die Entstehung des Christentums, Leipzig, 1904.

Kaminka, A., Studien zur Geschichte Galiläas, Berlin 1889.

Kanowitz, I., Rabbi Akiba (in Hebrew), Jerusalem, 1956.

Katz, B. Z., The Pharisees, Sadducees, Zealots and Christians (in Hebrew), Tel-Aviv, 1947.

Klausner, J., From Jesus to Paul, English Translation, London, 1946.

——, Historiah Shel Habayit Hasheni, 5 vol., Jerusalem, 1954.

——, Jesus of Nazareth, His Life, Times and Teachings, English Translation, New York, 1926.

——, The Messianic Idea in Israel from its Beginning to the Completion of the Mishna, English Translation, London, 1956.

Kohler, K., Pharisees, J. Enc., IX.

——, Sadducees, J. Enc., X.

——, The Origin and Composition of the Eighteen Benedictions, H.U.C.A., I.

Krauß, S., Synagogale Altertümer, Berlin/Vienna, 1922.

——, Talmudische Archäologie, 3 vol., Leipzig, 1910-12.

Krochmal, N., More Neboche Haseman, ed. L. Zunz, Lemberg, 1863.

Kuhn, K. G., Phylacterien aus Höhle 4 von Qumran, Heidelberg, 1957.

Kuenen, A., Over de Mannen der Groote Synagoge, German translation in Gesammelte Abhandlungen zur biblischen Wissenschaft, 1894.

Lagrange, M. J., Le Judaisme avant Jésus-Christ, 3 ed. Paris, 1931.

Landau, W., Shemaja und Abtalion, M.G.W.J., 7 (1858).

Lauterbach, J. Z., The Sadducees and the Pharisees, in Studies in Jewish Literature in Honour of K. Kohler, Berlin, 1913.

——, Three Books Found in the Temple-Court, J.Q.R.N.S. 8.

Leszynsky, R., Die Sadduzäer, Berlin, 1912.

Levy, J., Die Präsidenten im Synhedrium, M.G.W.J., 4 (1855).

Lewy, J. and H., The Origin of the Week and the Oldest West Asiatic Calendar, H.U.C.A. XVII (1942-43).

Lichtenstein, H., Die Fastenrolle, eine Untersuchung zur jüdisch-hellenistischen Geschichte, H.U.C.A., VIII-IX (1931-32).

Lieberman, S., Hellenism in Jewish Palestine, Texts and Studies of the Jewish Theological Seminary of America, vol. XVIII, New York, 1950.

——, Tosefta Kipshutah: A Comprehensive Commentary on the Tosefta I, New York, 1955.

Loew, L., Gesammelte Schriften, Szegedin, 1881, reprinted from Ben-Chananja I, 1858.

Mann, J., Rabbinic Studies in the Synoptic Gospels, H.U.C.A., I, 1924.

——, The Bible as Read and Preached in the Old Synagogue, Cincinnati, 1940.

Marmorstein, A., Studies in Jewish Theology, ed. J. Rabbinowitz and H. S. Lew, Oxford, 1950.
——, The Old Rabbinic Doctrine of God, London, I: 1927, II: 1937.
Mc Curdy, J. F., Prophets and Prophecy, J. Enc. X.
Meyer, Ed., Ursprung und Anfänge des Christentums, 3 vol. Stuttgart, 1921/23.
Michel, O., Paulus und seine Bibel, Gütersloh, 1929.
Mielziner, M., Introduction to the Talmud, 2 ed. New York, 1925.
Milik, J. T., Dix Ans de Découvertes dans le Désert de Juda, Paris, 1957.
Mirsky, S. K., Haderashah Bitqufath Hamishnah Vehatalmud, Horeb, 1943.
Moore, G. F., Christian Writers on Judaism, Harvard Theological Review XIV, 1921.
——, Judaism in the First Centuries of the Christian Era, 3 vol. (Cambridge Mass.), 1927-1930.
——, Simon the Righteous, in I. Abrahams Memorial Volume, 1927.
Montefiore, C. G., Rabbinic Literature and the Gospels. Teachings, London, 1930.
Morgenstern, J., The Calendar of the Book of Jubilees, Vetus Testamentum V (1955).
Mowinckel, S., He That Cometh, English translation, Oxford, 1956.
Muss-Arnolt, W., Urim and Thummim, J. Enc. XII.
Nicolas, N., Des doctrines religieuses des Juifs pendants les deux siecles antérieurs a l'ère chrétienne, Paris, 1860.
Oesterley, W. O. E., and Th. H. Robinson, Hebrew Religion, Its Origin and Development, London, 1931.
——, An Introduction to the Books of the Old Testament, London, 1934.
Oesterley, W. O. E., A History of Israel II From the Fall of Jerusalem 586 B.C. to the Bar-Kochba Revolt A.D. 135, Oxford, 1957.
Parkes, J., Jesus, Paul and the Jews, London, 1936.
Perles, F., Boussets Religion des Judendums . . . kritisch untersucht, Berlin 1903.
Pfeiffer, R. H., History of New Testament Times with an Introduction to the Apocrypha, New York, 1949.
——, Introduction to the Old Testament repr. London 1953.
Rabin, Ch., Qumran Studies, Scripta Judaica II, Oxford 1957.
Rabinowitz, L., The Synagogue and Its Worship, in A Companion to the Bible, ed. T. W. Manson, Edinburgh, 1945.
Reimarus, H. S. Vom Zwecke Jesu und seiner Jünger, published by G. E. Lessing, Braunschweig, 1778.
Renan, E., La Vie de Jésu, 7 ed., Paris, 1863, German translation, 4 ed. Leipzig 1880.
Réville, A., Jésus de Nazareth, Paris, 1897.
Roth, C., The Historical Background of the Dead Sea Scrolls, Oxford, 1958.
Rowley, H. H., Jewish Proselyte Baptism, H.U.C.A., 15 (1940).
Schachter, M., The Babylonian and Jerusalemian Mishna Textually Compared, Jerusalem, 1959.
Schechter, S., Studies in Judaism, 3 series, Philadelphia, 1945.
Schoenfelder, J. M., Onkelos und Peschitto, Munich, 1869.
Schoeps, H. J., Die jüdische Prophetenmorde, Uppsala, 1943.
Schuerer, E., Geschichte des jüdischen Volkes im Zeitalter Jesu Christi, 4 ed. Leipzig, 1901-11.
Schwarz, A., Die Controversen der Schammaiten und der Hilleliten, Karlsruhe, 1893;
——, Die hermeneutische Antinomie in der talmud. Literatur, Vienna, 1913.
——, Die hermeneutische Induktion in der talmud. Literatur, Vienna, 1909;
——, Die hermeneutische Quantitätsrelation in der talmud. Literatur, Vienna, 1916.
——, Der hermeneutische Kontext in der talmud. Literatur, Vienna, 1921.

——, Der hermeneutische Syllogismus in der talmud. Literatur, Vienna, 1901.

Schweitzer, A., Von der Geschichte der Leben-Jesu-Forschung, 6 ed. Tübingen, 1951.

Segal, J. B., Intercalation and the Hebrew Calendar, Vetus Testamentum VII (1957).

Sperber, A., Problems of the Masora, H.U.C.A. XVII (1942-43).

Strack, H. L., Große Synagoge in "Real-encyklopädie für Protestantische Theologie und Kirche", 3 ed., XIX Leipzig, 1901.

——, Introduction to the Talmud and Midrash, English Translation, Meridian Books, Inc. and the Jewish Publication Society of America, 1959.

——, Kanon des Alten Testaments in "Real-encyklopädie für Protestantische Theologie und Kirche", 3 ed. IX Leipzig 1901.

Swete, H. B., Introduction to the Old Testament in Greek, 2 ed. Cambridge, 1914.

Talmon, S., The Calendar Reckoning of the Sect from the Judaean Desert, Scripta Hierosolymitana IV, 1958.

Tchernowitz, Ch., Toledoth Hahalachah, 3 vol. New York, 1934-43.

Thackeray, J., The Septuagint and the Jewish Worship (Schweich Lectures for 1920), London 1921.

Theodor, J., Die Midraschim zum Pentateuch und der dreijährige palästinische Cyclus, M. G.W.J., 34-36 (1885-87).

——, Midrash Haggadah, J. Enc. VIII.

Torrey, Ch. C., Our Translated Gospels, New York, 1936.

Turner, C. H., Chronology, in Hasting's Dictionary of the Bible I, 1888.

Venturini, K. H., Natürliche Geschichte des großen Propheten von Nazareth, 4 vol., 1800-02.

Vogt, E., Kalendarfragments aus Qumran, Biblica 39 (1958).

Waxman, M., A History of Jewish Literature I: From close of the Canon to the end of 12th cent. New York, 1930.

Weiss, A., Leḥeqer Hatalmud, New York, 1956.

Weiss, I. H., Dor Dor Wedorshaw (Zur Geschichte der jüdischen Tradition) 4 vol. 4 ed. Vilna, 1904.

Welch, A. C., The Works of the Chronicler, Its Purpose and Its Date, Oxford, 1939.

Wellhausen, J., Einleitung in die drei ersten Evangelien, Berlin, 1905.

——, Israelitische und jüdische Geschichte, 5 ed. Berlin, 1904.

——, Die Pharisäer und die Sadducäer, 2 ed. Hannover, 1924.

Wilnai, Z., Jerusalem-Birath Yisrael, Jerusalem 1960.

Wrede, W., Das Messiasgeheimnis in den Evangelien zugleich ein Beitrag zum Verständnis des Markusevangeliums, Göttingen, 1901.

Yadin, Y., Hamegilloth Hagenuzoth Memidbar Yehudah, 2 ed. Tel-Aviv, 1958, English ed. "The Message of the Scrolls", London, 1957.

Zeitlin, S., The Halaka in the Gospels and its Relation to the Jewish Law at the Time of Jesus, H.U.C.A. I 1924.

——, Who Crucified Jesus, 2 ed. N.Y. and London 1947.

——, The Propoganda of the Hebrew Scrolls and the Falsification of History, J.Q.R.N.S. XLVI (1955).

——, On the Phrase "yitleh ʾanašim ḥayim", in Journal of Jewish Studies, vol. VIII. 1957.

——, Passover and the Last Supper, in The Passover Anthology ed. P. Goodman, Philadelphia, 1961.

——, The Semikah Controversy between the Zugoth, J.Q.R. VII, 1917.

——, Shimeon Haṣadiq Ukeneseth Hagedolah, Ner Maʿaravi, New York, 1924.

Zobel, M., Der Sabbat, Schocken Verlag/25, Berlin, 1935.

Zuckermann, B., Materialien zur Entwickelung der altjüdischen Zeitrechnung im Talmud, Breslau, 1882.

Zunz, L., Gottesdienstliche Vorträge der Juden historisch entwickelt, 2 ed. Frankfurt a. M. 1892.

INDEX

A. AUTHORS

B. NAMES

C. TERMS

D. TEXTS

E. TOPICS